P9-DZN-491

Teach Yourself Visually
Knitting & Crocheting

Teach Yourself VISUALLY™

Knitting & Crocheting

Visual™

From
maranGraphics®

&

Wiley Publishing, Inc.

Teach Yourself VISUALLY™ Knitting & Crocheting

Published by
Wiley Publishing, Inc.
111 River Street
Hoboken, NJ 07030-5774
www.wiley.com

Published simultaneously in Canada

Copyright © 2004 by maranGraphics Inc.
5755 Coopers Avenue
Mississauga, Ontario, Canada
L4Z 1R9

Library of Congress Control Number:

ISBN: 0-7645-6914-7

Manufactured in the United States of America

10 9 8 7 6 5 4 3 2 1

1K/QR/QY/QU/MG

No part of this publication may be reproduced, stored in a retrieval system or transmitted in any form or by any means, electronic, mechanical, photocopying, recording, scanning or otherwise, except as permitted under Sections 107 or 108 or the 1976 United States Copyright Act, without the prior written permission of maranGraphics Inc., 5755 Coopers Avenue, Mississauga, Ontario L4Z 1R9.

Trademark Acknowledgments

maranGraphics Inc. has attempted to include trademark information for products, services and companies referred to in this guide. Although maranGraphics Inc. has made reasonable efforts in gathering this information, it cannot guarantee its accuracy.

The maranGraphics logo is a trademark or registered trademark of maranGraphics, Inc.. Wiley, the Wiley Publishing logo, Visual, the Visual logo, Teach Yourself VISUALLY, Read Less - Learn More and all related trademarks, logos, and trade dress are trademarks or registered trademarks of John Wiley & Sons, Inc. and/or its affiliates. All other trademarks are the property of their respective owners. maranGraphics, Inc. and Wiley Publishing, Inc. are not associated with any product or vendor mentioned in this book.

Important Numbers

For U.S. corporate orders, please call maranGraphics at 800-469-6616 or fax 905-890-9434.

For general information on our products and services, please contact our Customer Care Department within the U.S. at 800-762-2974, outside the U.S. at 317-572-3993 or fax 317-572-4002.

DISCLAIMER: THE PUBLISHER AND THE AUTHOR MAKE NO REPRESENTATIONS OR WARRANTIES WITH RESPECT TO THE ACCURACY OR COMPLETENESS OF THE CONTENTS OF THIS WORK AND SPECIFICALLY DISCLAIM ALL WARRANTIES, INCLUDING WITHOUT LIMITATION WARRANTIES OF FITNESS FOR A PARTICULAR PURPOSE. NO WARRANTY MAY BE CREATED OR EXTENDED BY SALES OR PROMOTIONAL MATERIALS. THE ADVICE AND STRATEGIES CONTAINED HEREIN MAY NOT BE SUITABLE FOR EVERY SITUATION. THIS WORK IS SOLD WITH THE UNDERSTANDING THAT THE PUBLISHER IS NOT ENGAGED IN RENDERING LEGAL, ACCOUNTING, OR OTHER PROFESSIONAL SERVICES. IF PROFESSIONAL ASSISTANCE IS REQUIRED, THE SERVICES OF A COMPETENT PROFESSIONAL PERSON SHOULD BE SOUGHT. NEITHER THE PUBLISHER NOR THE AUTHOR SHALL BE LIABLE FOR DAMAGES ARISING HEREFROM. THE FACT THAT AN ORGANIZATION OR WEBSITE IS REFERRED TO IN THIS WORK AS A CITATION AND/OR A POTENTIAL SOURCE OF FURTHER INFORMATION DOES NOT MEAN THAT THE AUTHOR OR THE PUBLISHER ENDORSES THE INFORMATION THE ORGANIZATION OR WEBSITE MAY PROVIDE OR RECOMMENDATIONS IT MAY MAKE. FURTHER, READERS SHOULD BE AWARE THAT INTERNET WEBSITES LISTED IN THIS WORK MAY HAVE CHANGED OR DISAPPEARED BETWEEN WHEN THIS WORK WAS WRITTEN AND WHEN IT IS READ.

© 2004 maranGraphics, Inc.
The front cover image and the photographs and diagrams contained within this book are the copyright of maranGraphics, Inc.

Wiley Publishing, Inc.   is a trademark of
                           Wiley Publishing, Inc.

U.S. Corporate Sales	U.S. Trade Sales
Contact maranGraphics at (800) 469-6616 or fax (905) 890-9434.	Contact Wiley at (800) 762-2974 or fax (317) 572-4002.

VISUAL TESTIMONIALS

"I write to extend my
thanks and appreciation
for your books.
They are clear, easy to follow,
and straight to the point.
Keep up the good work!
I bought several of your books
and they are just right!
No regrets! I will always
buy your books because
they are the best."

**Seward Kollie
Dakar, Senegal**

"I just had to let you and
your company know how
great I think your books are.
I just purchased my third
Visual book (my first two
are dog-eared now!) and,
once again, your product has
surpassed my expectations.
The expertise, thought, and
effort that go into each book
are obvious, and I sincerely
appreciate your efforts.
Keep up the wonderful work!"

**Tracey Moore
Memphis, TN**

"I am an avid fan of
your Visual books.
If I need to learn anything,
I just buy one of your books and
learn the topic in no time.
Wonders! I have even trained
my friends to give me
Visual books as gifts."

**Illona Bergstrom
Aventura, FL**

"I have quite a few of your
Visual books and have been
very pleased with all of them.
I love the way the
lessons are presented!"

**Mary Jane Newman
Yorba Linda, CA**

"Like a lot of other people,
I understand things best
when I see them visually.
Your books really make
learning easy and
life more fun."

**John T. Frey
Cadillac, MI**

maranGraphics is a family-run business.

At **maranGraphics**, we believe in producing great consumer books– one book at a time.

Each maranGraphics book uses the award-winning communication process that we have been developing over the last 28 years. Using this process, we organize photographs and text in a way that makes it easy for you to learn new concepts and tasks.

We spend hours deciding the best way to perform each task, so you don't have to! Our clear, easy-to-follow photographs and instructions walk you through each task from beginning to end.

We want to thank you for purchasing what we feel are the best books money can buy. We hope you enjoy using this book as much as we enjoyed creating it!

Sincerely,

The Maran Family

Please visit us on the Web at:
www.maran.com

CREDITS

Author:
maranGraphics Development Group

Content Architects:
Kelleigh Johnson
Wanda Lawrie
Ruth Maran

Technical Consultant/ Pattern Designer:
Joanne Yordanou

Project Manager:
Judy Maran

Copy Development Director:
Jill Maran-Dutfield

Copy Developers:
Raquel Scott
Adam Giles
Roderick Anatalio

Editor:
Adam Giles

Layout Designer:
Richard Hung

Front Cover Image, Photographic Backgrounds and Overviews:
Designed by Russ Marini

Photographic Retouching:
Russ Marini
Richard Hung
Steven Schaerer

Indexer:
Raquel Scott

Knitters:
Dolly D'Costa
Kelleigh Johnson
Joan Kass
Joyce Murray
Joyce Samuel
Kamla Sharma
Lilias Wontas
Joanne Yordanou

Pattern Editing:
Joyce Murray

Crochet Technical Advisor:
Svetlana Avrakh

Wiley Vice President and Executive Publisher:
Kathy Nebenhaus

Wiley Staff:
Dawn Barnes
Roxane Cerda
Cindy Kitchel
Lisa Murphy
Susan Olinsky

Models:
Fiona Addison
Kade Dutfield
Deidra Jones
Alexis Kelly
Brooke Lavery
Judy Maran
Jill Maran-Dutfield
Emily Strohl
Nicholas Strohl

Photography and Post Production:
Robert Maran

ACKNOWLEDGMENTS

Thanks to the dedicated staff of maranGraphics, including Adam Giles, Richard Hung, Kelleigh Johnson, Wanda Lawrie, Jill Maran-Dutfield, Judy Maran, Robert Maran, Ruth Maran, Russ Marini, Raquel Scott and Roxanne Van Damme.

Finally, to Richard Maran who originated the easy-to-use graphic format of this guide. Thank you for your inspiration and guidance.

ABOUT THE TECHNICAL CONSULTANT...

Joanne Yordanou

Joanne Yordanou has been knitting since she was 14, crocheting for the past 5 years and designing for major yarn companies and magazines for the past 8 years. She has had her designs published in magazines including Vogue Knitting, Family Circle Knitting, Better Homes and Gardens' Knit It, Self, Interweave Knits and Knitter's Digest. She has also freelance designed for Patons, Bernat, Classic Elite Yarns and others. While working with the Patons Design Studio, Joanne learned a lot under the expert guidance there. Before that, she spent 17 years in the retail industry, while at the same time, knitting her own designs and selling them at craft shows and boutiques. Her Web store, www.baabaaknits.com, opened in 2001, selling her original knitting and needlepoint designs.

A few words from Joanne...

I would like to thank Rob, Ruth, Judy and Jill at maranGraphics for extending this opportunity to me and express my gratitude to their team of very talented writers, editors and artists. It has been a pleasure and an honor to be a part of this book and to work with such wonderful writers as Kelleigh and Wanda. Thanks to all of the knitters and editors who have contributed to the integrity of the patterns and produced such fine work. To my family and friends who have been my cheerleaders, thank you. Your support and enthusiasm will stay with me always. Above all, I would like to thank my husband Louis and our children, Lucy and Elizabeth, whose love and support have allowed me to spend lots of time on the computer, reviewing, designing and editing.

YARN RESOURCES

Thank you to these (**) companies for contributing yarn to our book:

Spinrite
Patons and Lily Yarns
P.O. Box 40
Listowel, ON
N4W 3H3
www.patonsyarns.com
www.sugarncream.com

Classic Elite Yarns
300 Jackson St.
Bldg #5
Lowell, MA
01852
classicelite@aol.com

The Cable Cardigan
pictured on pages 3 and
291 was made using
yarn provided by Classic
Elite. The pattern is
available through
www.baabaaknits.com

Needful Yarns, Inc.
4476 Chesswood Drive
Ste. 10 & 11
Toronto, ON
M3J 2B9
866-800-4700
www.needfulyarnsinc.com

Dale of Norway
N16 W23390
Stoneridge Drive, Ste. A
Waukesha, WI
53188
www.daleofnorway.com

Distributed in Canada by:
**Estelle Designs and Sales Ltd.
Units 65/67
2220 Midland Avenue
Scarborough, ON
M1P 3E6
800-387-5167

S.R. Kertzer Ltd.,
105A Winges Road
Woodbridge, ON
L4L 6C2
800-263-2354
www.kertzer.com

Stahl
Distributed in USA by:
Skacel Collection
PO Box 88110
Seattle, WA
98138-2110

Distributed in Canada
by: S.R. Kertzer Ltd.

Sirdar
Distributed in USA by:
Knitting Fever Inc.
35 Debevois Avenue
Roosevelt, New York
11575
www.knittingfever.com
www.sirdar.co.uk

Yarn Stores
Thank you to these stores for lending or contributing yarn:

Baa Baa Knits & Needleworks
www.baabaaknits.com

Romni Wools
658 Queen St., W.,
Toronto, ON
M6J 1E5
www.romniwools.com

Table of Contents

Table of Contents

Chapter 1

Knitting is a long-standing craft that people have been practicing for thousands of years. Knitting is easy to learn and requires only a few tools. This chapter will introduce you to these essential tools. Here you will learn about the different types of yarn and knitting needles as well as how to read a yarn label and purchase yarn.

Getting Started

In this Chapter...

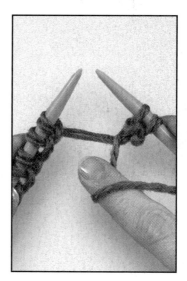

introduction to knitting

Knitting is an activity that is easy to learn and requires very few tools to practice. You can create a vast array of knitted items with just a ball of yarn and two needles. Your knitted projects can range from decorative items, such as a lace edging for a shelf, to more practical items, such as a scarf, sweater or blanket.

History of Knitting

Historical evidence, such as an Egyptian sock dated between 1200 and 1500 AD and 15th century European paintings that depict knitting, shows that knitting is a long-standing tradition that dates back thousands of years. It is believed that the craft of knitting was spread around the world by early traders and sailors during their travels.

Early knitters practiced out of necessity to produce garments for themselves and their families, but the practice was not limited to creating items for personal use. Some families knit socks and other items to sell or trade as a way to supplement income. During wars, women and children at home knit socks and bandages for soldiers. Today, many knitters knit simply for the joy of the craft.

Why Knit?

Knitting is a creative and rewarding hobby from which anyone can benefit. Knitting has been likened to meditation in the way the repetitive movements of needles and yarn relieves stress and helps a knitter relax. The sense of satisfaction a knitter gets from completing a knitted project also adds to the emotional benefits of the craft. Creating a finished product that you can use or share is an accomplishment to take pleasure in.

Knitting is also convenient for a busy lifestyle, as you can complete a project over time, laying it aside as often as you like. Since knitting is portable and requires very few tools, you can work on your knitted project while on the bus or train or during your lunch break at work.

Knitting: The New Generation

Once the domain of grandmothers, knitting has, in recent years, become a trendy pastime for people of all ages. Thousands of new people are learning to knit each year and many celebrities such as actors and models are also avid knitters.

The growing popularity of knitting as a hobby in the United States can be seen in the large number of knitting clubs and designer yarn shops now found in cities such as Washington DC, Chicago and New York.

Knitting and the Internet

The Internet is a valuable resource for new and experienced knitters alike who want information about knitting and the opportunity to interact and share ideas with other knitters around the world. The following are some popular Web sites devoted to sharing information about knitting.

Popular Knitting Web Sites	
Interweave Knits Magazine	www.interweave.com/knit
Knit 'N Style Magazine Online	www.knitnstyle.com
Vogue Knitting International	www.vogueknitting.com
The Red Sweater	www.theredsweater.com
Knitting Now	www.knittingnow.com
Craft Yarn Council of America	www.craftyarncouncil.com
ChicKnits	www.chicknits.com
The KnitList	www.knitlist.com
Baa Baa Knits & Needleworks	www.baabaaknits.com

types of yarn

Yarn can be produced from natural or synthetic fibers. There are two types of natural fibers—plant fibers and animal fibers. Plant fibers are made from plants, including cotton and hemp plants. Animal fibers are derived from animals such as sheep and rabbits. Synthetic fibers are produced from chemical sources.

Understanding the properties of different fibers can help you choose which yarn to use for your knitting project. The properties of a fiber determine the method of care for the knitted fabric and the degree of warmth or absorbency the fabric will provide.

Yarn Colors

Natural colors of yarn include off-white, brown, beige and black. To create other colors, yarn is dyed either one solid color or multiple colors. There are many techniques used to create multicolored yarn. For example, space-dyed yarn has been dyed by soaking equal lengths of the yarn in different colors. Yarn can be space-dyed by machine or by hand. Yarn can also be hand painted. Hand-painted yarn is dyed manually, often by using brushes or squirt bottles. This type of dyed yarn is increasing in popularity due to the vibrant colors that are produced.

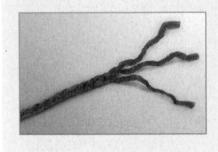

Spinning and Ply

The process of producing yarn involves spinning fibers together to form a single strand of yarn. Twisting two or more strands together forms a plied yarn. For example, twisting two strands together forms a two-ply yarn, while twisting three strands together forms a three-ply yarn.

Plied yarn is stronger, smoother and has a more uniform appearance than a single strand of yarn, but is not necessarily thicker.

Skein

Ball

Hank

Balls, Skeins and Hanks

Yarn is commonly packaged in balls, skeins or hanks. Balls are made up of yarn wound into a round shape, while skeins are made up of yarn wound into an oblong shape. It is best to use yarn that has been packaged as a center-pull ball or skein, which allows you to pull the yarn from the center of one end of the ball or skein as you work. This makes the ball or skein less likely to bounce or roll around. Balls and skeins are available in various sizes.

Hanks are loosely, but neatly, twisted coils of yarn. Before using a hank, the yarn must be wound into balls. You can have the yarn wound into balls at the store where you purchased the yarn or you can wind the yarn yourself.

PLANT FIBERS

Plant fibers are made from cellulose, which is the main component of plant tissue. Plant fibers produce garments that are durable, breathable and absorb moisture extremely well. Plant fibers are also hypo-allergenic, which makes them an excellent choice for people who are allergic to animal fibers such as wool.

When choosing yarn for a project, you should keep in mind that yarn produced from plant fibers does not provide as much insulation as yarn derived from animal fibers.

Cotton

Cotton is a very absorbent and quick-drying fiber, making cotton garments comfortable to wear in hot weather. Since cotton is stronger wet than dry, no special care is required when washing. This makes cotton an ideal fiber for knitting items that are frequently washed, such as dish cloths, tea towels and baby items.

Compared to wool, cotton is a more difficult fiber to work with, as it is not as elastic and shows imperfections in your knitting more easily.

The highest-quality and most expensive types of cotton include Egyptian, Sea Island and Pima. Egyptian cotton is known for its soft, luxurious texture. Sea Island cotton is prized for its silky feel and lustrous appearance. Pima cotton is valued for its strength.

Linen

Linen is made from the fibers of the flax plant. Like cotton, linen garments are durable, easy to care for and comfortable to wear in hot weather. Since linen fabric tends to be stiff and wrinkles easily, linen fiber is often blended with cotton to add softness. Linen is commonly used for knitting garments such as lightweight sweaters and cardigans.

Hemp

Hemp is derived from the hemp plant. Hemp yarn is increasing in popularity among knitters and is often used to make tops, tunics and other clothing items. Hemp can also be used to knit decorative items.

types of yarn

ANIMAL FIBERS

Animal fibers are protein-based and come from the coat of animals such as sheep, goats and rabbits. Animal fibers provide good insulation, which helps keep you warm in cold weather and cool in warm weather. Animal fibers are also soft, lightweight, absorbent and stretch resistant.

Animal fibers are vulnerable to moth larvae, as the larvae eat the protein-based fiber.

Wool

Wool is spun from fleece that has been sheared from sheep and is the most popular yarn choice for knitters. Wool is warm, durable, elastic and resists wrinkling. Wool is also very absorbent, which makes it dye-friendly.

There are several different types of wool available, with each type having its own special properties. For example, Merino Wool from the Merino sheep is very fine and soft, while Pure New Wool is rougher but is more water resistant due to increased amounts of lanolin.

Wool is often used for knitting items such as sweaters, hats, mittens and scarves. Wool garments may not be suitable for people who have allergies or sensitive skin.

Mohair

Mohair fiber comes from the Angora goat and produces a warm, lightweight yarn. Mohair tends to shed and can feel scratchy against the skin so it is often blended with wool or Nylon to create a less itchy yarn. Mohair can be used for knitting items such as sweaters, hats and mittens.

Alpaca

Alpaca fiber comes from the coat of a llama-like animal of the same name that lives in South America. Alpaca yarn is soft, silky, lightweight and very warm. Since the natural color of alpaca ranges from beige to brown, alpaca fibers must be bleached before being dyed another color. Alpaca is not as expensive as cashmere, but is more costly than wool. Alpaca is commonly used to knit sweaters, scarves and gloves.

Angora

Angora, which is derived from the fur of the Angora rabbit, is soft, delicate, warm and downy, but it tends to shed. Angora is expensive, so it is often blended with other fibers to lower the cost and increase the strength of the resulting yarn. Angora is commonly used for knitting items such as hats and sweaters.

Silk

Silk yarn is produced from silkworm cocoons that have been unraveled to form long, lustrous fibers. Silk garments have a wonderful drape and feel. Silk is strong, but not very resilient. As a result, silk garments tend to stretch with wear. Because silk is expensive, it is often blended with other fibers to lower the cost. Due to the special care required to clean silk, knitters often use silk just for special projects.

Cashmere

Cashmere, which is made from the hair of the Cashmere goat, is one of the softest and most luxurious yarns available. Like wool, cashmere dyes easily and makes a resilient fabric that resists stretching and wrinkling. Cashmere is very expensive, so it is often blended with wool to create a stronger yarn at a lower price. Cashmere is often used to knit sweaters and accessory items, such as scarves.

types of yarn

MAN-MADE FIBERS

Man-made fibers are derived from chemical sources and are usually inexpensive. Yarn produced from man-made fibers is generally easy to care for, which makes it ideal for knitting items that are frequently washed, such as blankets, afghans and sweaters. You should be careful when ironing an item made from man-made fiber, as these types of fibers can lose their shape and even melt if excess heat is applied.

Man-made fibers do not offer the warmth, absorbency or elasticity of natural fibers. Man-made fibers are often blended with natural fibers to obtain some of these properties and produce a higher-quality yarn.

Acrylic

Yarn made from acrylic is lightweight and strong. Although acrylic lacks insulating properties and tends to pill, this fiber remains very popular with knitters because of its low price, availability and washability. When blended with wool, acrylic is more enjoyable to work with and wear. Acrylic is used for knitting sweaters, hats, mittens, blankets and many other items.

Nylon

Nylon, or polyamide, is the strongest man-made fiber and is often added to other fibers to provide durability and prevent pilling. When blended with other fibers, Nylon is useful for knitting frequently used items, such as mittens. Fabrics made predominantly from Nylon do not breathe well and are prone to static cling, but are water resistant.

Rayon

Rayon is considered a man-made fiber but it is not derived from chemical sources. Instead, rayon is made from wood sources. This fiber creates a soft, lustrous and absorbent yarn that is popular with knitters.

Polyester

Polyester is strong and wrinkle resistant, so it is often blended with other fibers to increase their strength and durability. Polyester is also commonly found in novelty yarns.

Polypropylene

Polypropylene is a lightweight and very inexpensive fiber. Unlike most other man-made fibers, polypropylene provides good insulation and is less prone to static cling. Polypropylene can be found in novelty and blended yarns.

Metallic Fibers

Metallic fibers incorporate small amounts of metal to create yarn that sparkles and glitters. Metallic fibers are not very strong and so are often blended with other fibers to increase their strength. Metallic fibers are increasing in popularity and are commonly used to knit evening wear and holiday items.

NOVELTY YARNS

Novelty yarn has an interesting texture and appearance, making it fun to work with. You can use novelty yarn to knit many items, including scarves, purses and cuffs or collars for sweaters. Novelty yarn can be made from natural, man-made or blended fibers and is often produced by twisting different yarns together or twisting multiple strands of the same yarn together at different tensions. Popular examples of novelty yarn include bouclé, chenille and eyelash.

yarn weights

Yarn is categorized by weight, which is simply the thickness of the yarn. The weight of the yarn you use affects the appearance of the garment you knit as well as how long the project will take to complete. For example, a thicker yarn not only produces a warmer, bulkier item, but it knits quicker than a thinner yarn as it requires fewer stitches to make the same size garment.

Determining a yarn weight can be confusing as different manufacturers and different countries use their own names for each weight.

Here are some of the most common weights (from thinnest to thickest). For the purposes of illustration, the yarn weights pictured below are displayed in proportion to each other, but are not actual size.

Fingering Weight

Fingering weight, also known as Baby Weight, is a fine yarn ideal for knitting baby garments and socks.

Sport Weight

Sport Weight is a light yarn suitable for knitting non-bulky items such as gloves, mittens and light sweaters.

Double Knitting Weight

Double Knitting Weight, also referred to as DK Weight, is a light-to-medium weight yarn that produces slightly heavier items than Sport Weight.

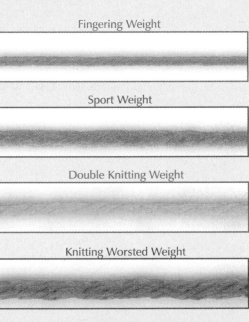

Fingering Weight

Sport Weight

Double Knitting Weight

Knitting Worsted Weight

Bulky Weight

Extra Bulky Weight

Knitting Worsted Weight

Knitting Worsted Weight, also called Worsted Weight and Aran Weight, is the most common yarn weight. Not only is it easy for beginners to work with, but its medium-to-heavy weight makes it perfect for knitting garments, accessories and afghans.

Bulky Weight

Bulky Weight, also called Chunky Weight, as its name implies, is a thick yarn which is growing in popularity. You can use Bulky Weight yarn and larger needles to knit blankets and scarves quickly.

Extra-bulky Weight

Extra-bulky Weight, also called Super-bulky, Very Bulky and Gigantic, is the thickest yarn of all. Like Bulky Weight, its heavy weight makes it easy to knit blankets, coats and hats very quickly.

purchase yarn

When purchasing yarn, there are several things you should consider. First, you should purchase the best yarn you can afford. Higher quality yarn is not only nicer to work with, but you will appreciate the look and feel of better-quality yarn when your project is complete. You should also make sure the yarn you choose will be comfortable to wear. For example, if you are knitting a wool scarf, hold the yarn to your neck to see how it feels.

Before you buy yarn, it is important to know that manufacturers dye yarn in specific lots, with each lot assigned a number. Although some colors of yarn may look alike, always check the dye lot number on each package of yarn you buy for a project to make sure they are all the same.

Lastly, your pattern may provide instructions for knitting the project in several different sizes. Before going to the store, decide which size you are going to knit. The size you choose will determine how much yarn you need to purchase.

Where to Buy Yarn

You can purchase yarn from several types of stores. Large department stores stock affordable yarns that appeal to most knitters. Craft stores offer middle of the road yarns. Specialty yarn shops and boutiques carry a wider variety of yarns, including high-end, fancy and novelty yarns. Specialty shops often have experienced staff that can offer advice and help you choose yarn.

You can even buy yarn on the Internet, such as on eBay or online stores. When shopping on the Internet, you should buy yarn you are familiar with so you are not disappointed by the texture or color when the yarn arrives.

Substituting Yarn

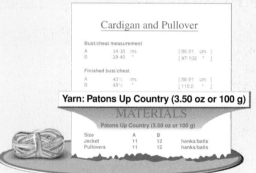

A pattern will suggest the yarn you should use for your knitting project, but you can replace the yarn depending on the yarn's cost, availability or your own preference. If you decide to use another yarn, look for a yarn with the same weight, length and recommended needle size as the suggested yarn.

Remember that choosing a different fiber type or color than the pattern suggested will affect the feel and look of the garment you are knitting.

reading a
yarn label

ABC Yarn
123 Lane Street
New York, NY
10258

ABC YARN
Knitter's Delight
100% Acrylic
4 ply Worsted Weight
Net wt. 3½ oz./100g
190 yds./175m

Suggested Gauge
Needles US 7 (4.5 mm)
20 sts & 20 rows =
4" (10 cm)

CARE INSTRUCTIONS

Colorfast

Col 222
Sage

Lot 83754

When purchasing yarn, you should carefully read the label wrapped around the ball of yarn. The label includes valuable information and can help you determine if the yarn is suitable for your project. You may find the following information on a yarn label.

Manufacturer's Name and Address

The name and address of the yarn manufacturer.

Brand Name

The manufacturer's name for the line of yarn.

Fiber Content

The fiber the yarn is made of. For example, 100% Acrylic.

Ply

The number of strands that have been twisted together to make up the yarn.

Yarn Thickness

The thickness classification of the yarn, also called yarn weight. For example, Worsted Weight yarn is of medium thickness and is perfect for knitting clothing and blankets. For more information on yarn weights, see page 24.

Weight

Refers to how much the package of yarn actually weighs. Common weights include 1.75 ounces (50 g) and 3.5 ounces (100 g).

Yarn Length

The total length of the yarn in the ball measured in yards or meters. Some fibers are heavier than others, so focus on yarn length (not weight) to determine how much yarn the ball contains.

Suggested Needle Size and Gauge

The recommended needle size to use with the yarn. Gauge refers to the number of stitches and rows you should have when you knit a square of fabric with the suggested needle size. For more information on gauge, see page 62.

Care Instructions

Words or symbols that indicate how to care for the fabric. For information on caring for knitwear, see page 28.

Special Processing

The special treatments the yarn has been subjected to, such as Colorfast (prevents colors from fading or running) and Superwash (allows wool to be machine washed and dried without shrinkage).

Color Name and Number

The name and/or number of the yarn color.

Dye Lot Number

Yarn is dyed in specific lots. Each lot is assigned a number, called a dye lot number. When you buy a specific color of yarn, the color may vary slightly between different dye lots. To ensure the color remains consistent in your project, always buy the yarn from the same dye lot number. To prevent running out, it is a good idea to buy more than you think you will need.

caring for knitwear

Your knitwear projects take a lot of time and money to create. If not washed properly, handmade knitwear is more likely to shrink than store-bought knitwear. To help preserve your knitted garments, pay close attention to the care symbols found on the yarn labels and follow the recommended cleaning instructions carefully. Depending on the type of yarn used, the garment will need to be either washed or dry-cleaned. See the chart below for a list of common care symbols.

When you hand wash knitwear, use a gentle detergent and never let the garment soak in the water for an extended period of time. You should squeeze the garment to remove dirt and then empty the water from the wash basin. Rinse the knitwear one or two times, carefully removing as much water as possible. After taking the garment out of the wash basin, position it on a colorfast towel and loosely roll up the towel. You can then reshape the garment to its proper dimensions and let it air dry.

When using a washing machine to clean knitwear, make sure to use the correct water temperature. To help keep your knitted garments looking great, you should machine wash knitwear by itself to avoid pilling, which refers to the formation of little balls of fiber on the surface of the garment. You can also try washing the garment in a pillowcase to keep it from stretching. To prevent creasing, you should remove the garment from the washing machine as soon as the cycle is finished.

COMMON CARE SYMBOLS

⊠	Do not wash
🤚	Hand wash
40°c	Machine wash at displayed temperature
⊻	Machine wash, cold water
⊻	Machine wash, warm water
⊻	Machine wash, hot water
⊻	Machine wash, cold water, gentle cycle
⊻	Machine wash, warm water, gentle cycle
⊻	Machine wash, hot water, gentle cycle
▲	Do not use chlorine bleach

COMMON CARE SYMBOLS (CONTINUED)

△	Chlorine bleach can be used
⚠	Non-chlorine bleach can be used
⊟	Dry flat
⊠	Do not tumble dry
⬤	Tumble dry, no heat
⊙	Tumble dry, low heat
⊙⊙	Tumble dry, medium heat
⊙⊙⊙	Tumble dry, high heat
⬤	Tumble dry, no heat, gentle cycle
⊙	Tumble dry, low heat, gentle cycle
⊙⊙	Tumble dry, medium heat, gentle cycle
⊠	Do not press
🡣	Do not press with steam
⊡	Press with a cool iron
⊡	Press with a warm iron
⊡	Press with a hot iron
⊗	Do not dry clean
○	Dry clean

all about knitting needles

Needles are an essential part of your knitting toolkit, so you should choose your needles with care. In general, the needles you select should enable you to knit with speed and comfort.

Needles are available in various materials, including aluminum, plastic, steel, wood and bamboo.

Aluminum needles are widely used because they are inexpensive, as well as smooth and light, helping you knit faster.

Plastic needles are also commonly used. They are similar to aluminum in smoothness, but are lighter and quieter than aluminum. Larger needles are often made of plastic to make them light enough to work with.

Bamboo and wooden needles are becoming popular choices. Wooden needles are often made of birch, ebony or rosewood and are usually expensive. Both wood and bamboo needles are lightweight, with a polished surface. Beginners may find bamboo needles easier to work with, since the surface of the needle is not as slippery as aluminum, allowing the stitches to remain in place better. However, after repeated use, bamboo needles tend to split at the tips and get caught on the yarn.

KNITTING NEEDLE SIZES

The diameter of a knitting needle determines its size. Needle sizes are usually shown in US, metric or UK measurements.

You would usually choose your needle size based on the needle size suggested on the pattern.

US	Metric	UK
0	2mm	14
1	2¼mm	13
	2½mm	
2	2¾mm	12
	3mm	
3	3¼mm	10
4	3½mm	
5	3¾mm	9
	4mm	8
6		
7	4½mm	7
8	5mm	6

US	Metric	UK
9	5½mm	5
10	6mm	4
10½	6½mm	3
	7mm	2
	7½mm	1
11	8mm	0
13	9mm	00
15	10mm	000
17	12mm	
19	15mm	
35	19mm	
36	20mm	

TYPES OF KNITTING NEEDLES

There are three main types of knitting needles. Although each needle type is useful for a different style of project, you may need several types of needles for a single project.

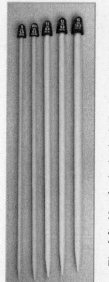

Single-pointed Knitting Needles

This is the type of knitting needle that is familiar to most people. Single-pointed needles are straight with a point at one end for knitting and a knob at the other end to keep the stitches from falling off the needle. These needles are ideal for flat knitting, which involves working on the right side of the fabric, then turning the work over and knitting on the wrong side.

Single-pointed needles are sold in pairs and are available in a variety of lengths. The most common lengths are 10 inches (25cm) and 14 inches (36cm).

Double-pointed Knitting Needles

Double-pointed needles are straight needles that have a working point at each end and are useful for knitting small, seamless tubular items, such as socks. Knitting that involves circular objects is referred to as knitting "in the round."

Double-pointed needles are usually available in shorter lengths than single-pointed needles, such as 7-inch (18cm) and 10-inch (25cm) lengths. They are often sold in sets of 4 or 5.

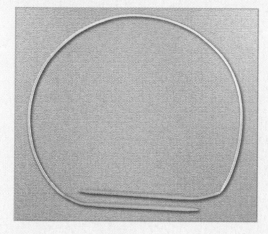

Circular Knitting Needles

Circular knitting needles consist of a pair of short, straight needles attached by a flexible plastic or nylon cord. Not only are these needles excellent for knitting large tubular items, such as sweaters, but they are also useful for knitting large flat items, such as an afghan. When knitting large, heavy pieces, circular needles allow you to hold a large number of stitches on your needle and to balance the bulk of the material on your lap rather than on the needles.

Circular needles are commonly available in 16, 24, 29 and 36 inch (40, 60, 80 and 90cm) lengths.

items you will need

There are several items you should have on hand while knitting. You can find the following inexpensive tools at most craft and knitting stores.

Scissors

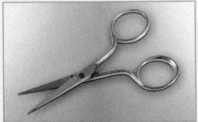

Knitting patterns may direct you to "break" yarn, which simply means to cut. To cut yarn, use small, sharp scissors, preferably ones that you can fold up or put in a case to avoid damaging your project.

Tape Measure

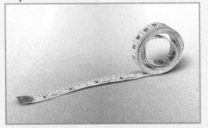

Use a tape measure to determine the measurements of various parts of your project, such as the sleeve length of a sweater you are knitting. A good tape measure is flexible, but it should not stretch.

Stitch Holders

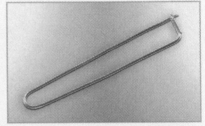

Use stitch holders to temporarily hold stitches you are not working with to prevent them from unraveling. They are available in varying sizes, but the smaller sizes are used most often.

Needle Gauge

Needle gauges make it easy to determine the size of needles that are not labeled. Simply slide your needle into each hole, starting with the smallest. The size corresponding to the first hole your needle passes through is your needle size. Needle gauges commonly feature a stitch gauge, which is an L-shaped window you use to count the number of stitches and rows.

Safety Pins

Safety pins can be used in a variety of situations when knitting, such as marking the right side of your garment or to temporarily hold a small number of stitches. You can purchase coil-less safety pins, which will not tangle in yarn, from specialty knitting shops.

Stitch Markers

Stitch markers are commonly used to leave a visual reminder where pattern changes occur and to maintain your place in circular knitting. For information on circular knitting, see page 160. Stitch markers are available in various colors and can be either a solid or split ring. Split ring markers are advantageous as you can attach them mid-row.

Crochet Hook

A crochet hook is used to correct errors in your knitting, such as picking up a dropped stitch. Crochet hooks come in a variety of sizes. Try to keep a few different sizes on hand—bigger hooks for thicker yarn and smaller hooks for thinner yarn.

Cable Needles

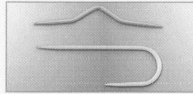

Cable needles are pointed at both ends and are used to hold stitches when working with cables. For information on creating cables, see page 124.

Bobbins

When knitting with multiple colors, you can avoid tangles by wrapping small lengths of yarn around plastic bobbins and working from the bobbin instead of a whole ball of yarn.

Row Counter

You can place a row counter on the end of your needles to keep track of how many rows you have completed. Row counters are not automatic so remember to turn the dial or push the button to advance the counter after each row.

Point Protectors

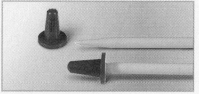

Point protectors are small rubber caps you put on the pointed ends of your needles when they are not in use. They help keep stitches from coming off needles when you put away or transport your work.

Project Bag

You should store each of your knitting projects, including a copy of the pattern and the tools you are working with, in a separate canvas or cotton bag. The ideal project bag is large enough to hold everything you need for your current project.

Tapestry Needles

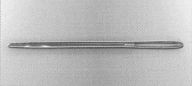

Tapestry needles, also known as sewing, darning and yarn needles, look like large sewing needles and have a dull tip. These needles are often used to sew pieces of knitted fabric and weave in yarn ends. Considering that tapestry needles come in many different sizes, make sure the eye of the needle is large enough for the yarn you are using to pass through.

Straight Pins

Straight pins are used to hold knitted pieces together as you complete your project. The best straight pins have large heads so you do not lose sight of them in your project. Straight pins are also vital for blocking. For more information on blocking, see page 196.

Chapter 2

This chapter will introduce you to the fundamental concepts and techniques involved in knitting. Once you become familiar with these basics, you will be able to complete many simple knitted projects. Here you will learn how to hold the yarn and needles, make a slip knot, cast on the first row of stitches and knit and purl stitches. This chapter also explains how to read knitting patterns and charts.

Knitting Basics

In this Chapter...

knitting terms you should know

When creating knitted pieces, there are several terms that you should be familiar with. Knowing these terms will help you during the process of learning how to knit. Since these terms are repeated often throughout the book, understanding what these terms mean will help you more easily follow the tasks covered. You may want to mark this page so you can quickly refer to it at a later time.

Stitch

When you knit, you connect a series of loops, called stitches, that hold together to form a piece of fabric. One horizontal line of stitches is known as a "row" of stitches.

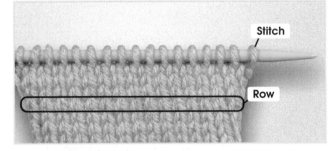

Stitch

Row

Tail of Yarn

The tail of yarn is a strand of yarn that is left over when you cast on (add) stitches, bind off (finish) stitches or start a new ball of yarn. You can weave in a tail of yarn to incorporate the yarn seamlessly into your knitted fabric. For information on weaving in tails of yarn, see page 208.

Tail

Right Side and Wrong Side of Fabric

Each knitted piece has a right side and a wrong side. The right side, abbreviated as RS in patterns, is the side of the fabric that will show, such as the outside of a sweater. The wrong side, abbreviated as WS in patterns, is the side of the fabric that will not show, such as the inside of a sweater. Many knitted items, such as sweaters, have a definite right side and wrong side. For some knitted items, such as scarves, you cannot tell the difference between the right side and the wrong side.

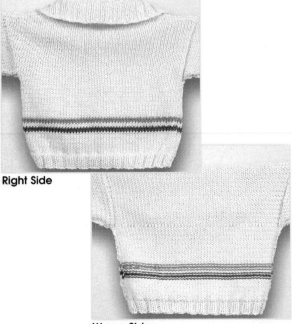

Right Side

Wrong Side

How to Insert the Needle

When creating and working with stitches, you will need to insert a needle into the front or the back of a stitch. You will most commonly insert a needle into the front of a stitch.

Front of stitch (left to right)

Inserting a needle into the front of a stitch from left to right is referred to as inserting the needle into the stitch "knitwise" because this is the same way you insert the needle when you perform the knit stitch—a basic stitch in knitting. For more information on the knit stitch, see pages 46 to 49.

Front of stitch (right to left)

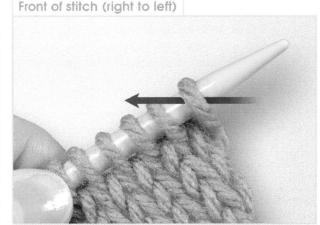

Inserting a needle into the front of a stitch from right to left is referred to as inserting the needle into the stitch "purlwise" because this is the same way you insert the needle when you perform the purl stitch—a basic stitch in knitting. For more information on the purl stitch, see pages 50 to 53.

Back of stitch (left to right)

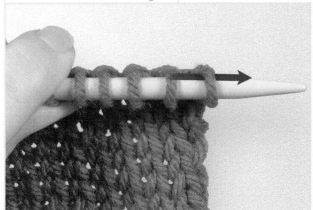

You can insert a needle into the back of a stitch, from left to right.

Back of stitch (right to left)

You can insert a needle into the back of a stitch, from right to left.

hold the yarn and needles

There are two styles of knitting—English, in which you hold the yarn in your right hand, and Continental, in which you hold the yarn in your left hand.

Knitters adapt these styles to their own needs and preferences so there is no right or wrong way to hold the yarn and needles. You should try both the English and Continental styles to see which feels most comfortable to you and allows you to control the tension on the yarn most effectively. Applying a slight tension to the yarn will not only produce neater

stitches, it will help you knit more efficiently. When experimenting with different styles, you should also pay attention to your grip on the yarn. The method you use should allow the yarn to flow smoothly through your fingers.

The methods of holding the yarn and needles shown below for the English and Continental styles are the most popular.

ENGLISH STYLE

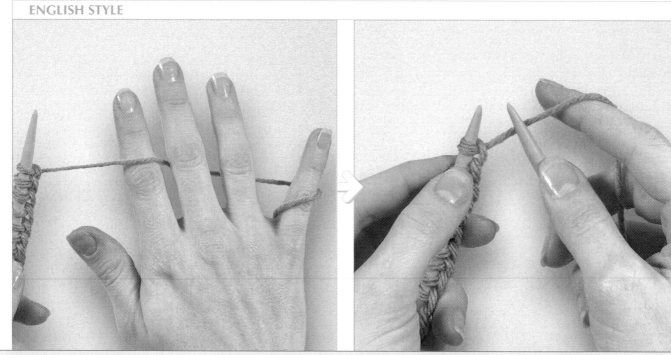

1 With the yarn in your right hand, wrap the yarn counterclockwise around your pinky finger.

2 Weave the yarn under your ring and middle fingers and then over your index finger.

- The yarn should lie between the first and second knuckles on your index finger.

- Use your pinky, ring and middle fingers to hold the yarn loosely in your hand.

3 Hold the needle with the stitches in your left hand. Your thumb and index finger hold the needle just behind the first stitch.

- Use your other fingers to help support the needle.

4 Hold the empty needle in your right hand. Position your thumb approximately an inch from the tip of the needle and use your middle, ring and pinky fingers to help support the needle.

Is there a variation of the English style that I can try?

With the yarn in your right hand, weave the yarn under your pinky finger, over your ring finger, under your middle finger and over your index finger. The yarn should lie between your fingernail and first knuckle on your index finger. Use your pinky, ring and middle fingers to hold the yarn loosely in your hand.

Is there a variation of the Continental style that I can try?

With the yarn in your left hand, wrap the yarn one and a half times around your index finger clockwise. The yarn should lie between the first and second knuckles on your index finger. Use your pinky, ring and middle fingers to hold the yarn loosely in your hand.

CONTINENTAL STYLE

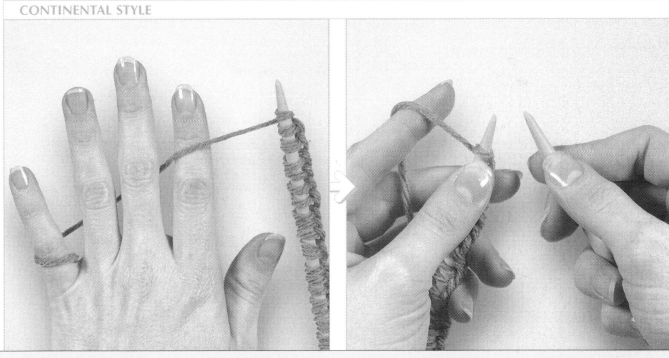

1 With the yarn in your left hand, wrap the yarn clockwise around your pinky finger.

2 Weave the yarn under your ring and middle fingers and then over your index finger.

● The yarn should lie between the first and second knuckles on your index finger.

● Use your pinky, ring and middle fingers to hold the yarn loosely in your hand.

3 Hold the needle with the stitches in your left hand. Position your thumb just behind the first stitch and use your middle, ring and pinky fingers to help support the needle.

4 Hold the empty needle in your right hand. Your thumb and index finger hold the needle approximately an inch from the tip.

● Use your other fingers to help support the needle.

make a slip knot

Before you begin knitting, you need to add a slip knot to a knitting needle. This slip knot will become your first stitch. Once the slip knot is on your needle, tighten it up gently. The slip knot should be tied snugly around the needle, but still be loose enough to slide along the needle.

The length of the strand between the slip knot and the end of the yarn, known as the "tail," depends on the cast on method you will use. Casting on, abbreviated as **CO** in patterns and instructions,

creates the first row of stitches following the slip knot. You will need to leave approximately 4 to 6 inches of yarn for the tail if you will use the single cast on method. If you will use a double cast on method, leave a long enough tail to allow you to cast on all the stitches you need. For more information on casting on, see pages 41 to 45. After you cast on your stitches, you can begin knitting your project.

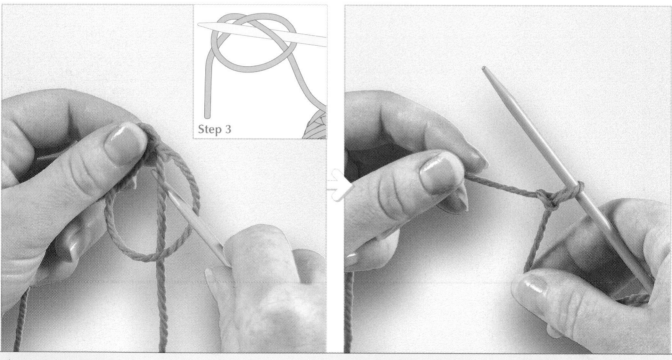

Step 3

1 Make a loop with your yarn, allowing the strand of yarn connected to the ball to hang down behind the loop.

2 Insert the tip of a needle through the loop, from front to back.

3 Move the tip of the needle behind the strand of yarn connected to the ball and then bring the tip through the front of the loop.

4 Gently pull both ends of the yarn in opposite directions to tighten the slip knot around the needle.

• The slip knot becomes the first stitch on the needle.

single cast on

To learn how to cast on, start with the single cast on method. While this easy method does not produce the neatest row of stitches, it is ideal for first-time, beginner projects. If you want a more polished appearance, try one of the double cast on methods instead, as shown on pages 42 to 45.

Casting on is an integral part of knitting as it adds the first row of stitches to a needle and impacts all the rows after the first row. For example, if your first row is too snug, it will be difficult for you to knit the next row. If your first row is too loose, your garment may be stretched out. The goal is to form neat stitches with consistent tension.

Unlike the double cast on methods, the length of the yarn's tail does not matter when using the single cast on method. Leave the tail about 4 to 6 inches long, which is enough to easily weave into the finished project later.

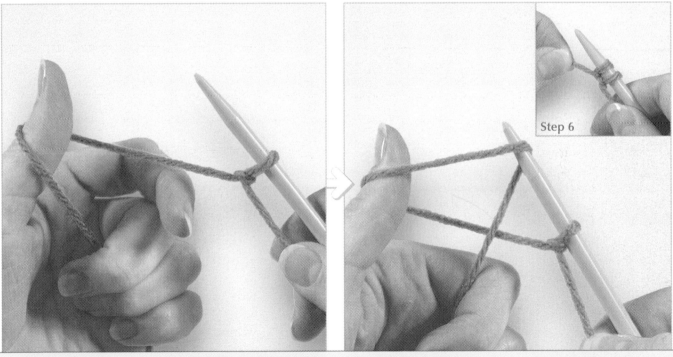

Step 6

1 Make a slip knot on one needle. To make a slip knot, see page 40.

2 Hold the needle containing the slip knot in your right hand.

3 Wrap the strand of yarn connected to the ball around your left thumb, clockwise from front to back.

• Use the fingers of your left hand to hold the strand of yarn connected to the ball loosely in your palm.

4 Insert the tip of the needle between your thumb and the strand of yarn, from bottom to top.

5 Remove your thumb from the loop of yarn.

6 Gently pull on the strand of yarn connected to the ball to tighten the stitch.

7 Repeat steps 3 to 6 for each stitch you want to cast on.

double cast on

Method One

Casting on is an important part of knitting, as it adds the first row of stitches to a needle. There are many different ways to cast on the first row of stitches, each way leaving a unique edge at the bottom of your work. The double cast on method is neater in appearance than the single cast on method. While the single cast on method produces stitches from the ball of yarn, the double cast on method uses both ends of the yarn—the tail and the strand attached to the ball. Doubling-up on the yarn in this way creates both flexible stitches and a firm edge.

Since the double cast on method incorporates the tail into the first row of stitches, you must ensure that the tail will be long enough for you to complete the row. From the slip knot to the end of the tail, you should measure approximately 1 inch of yarn for each stitch that you plan to cast on. Then add 3 to 4 extra inches, which will remain as the tail after you finish casting on.

There are two main methods of the double cast on. The method described below is often referred to as the thumb method.

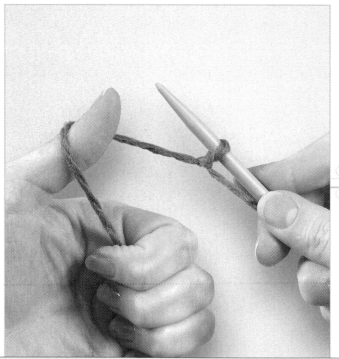 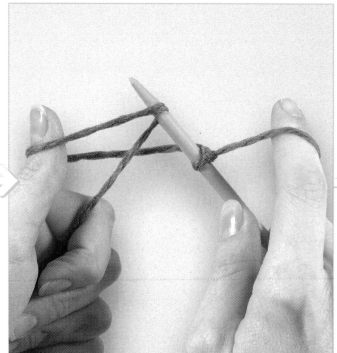

1 Make a slip knot on one needle. To make a slip knot, see page 40.

2 Hold the needle containing the slip knot and the strand of yarn connected to the ball in your right hand.

3 Wrap the tail of yarn around your left thumb, clockwise from front to back.

• Use the fingers of your left hand to hold the tail of yarn loosely in your palm.

4 Insert the tip of the needle between your thumb and the strand of yarn, from bottom to top.

How can I become more comfortable with casting on?

When you begin casting on, you may not feel comfortable right away. To practice, try casting on over and over. Cast on stitches until you run out of yarn, then take all the stitches off the needle, unravel the yarn, make another slip knot and start again. When the yarn starts to fray, cut off the yarn and start over with new yarn. Keep practicing until you feel comfortable.

Are there any cast on methods that use two needles?

Yes. The cable cast on method requires you to use two needles to cast on your stitches. The cable cast on method is usually used for adding stitches within a piece of work, but can also be used to cast on your starting edge. For more information on the cable cast on method, see page 86.

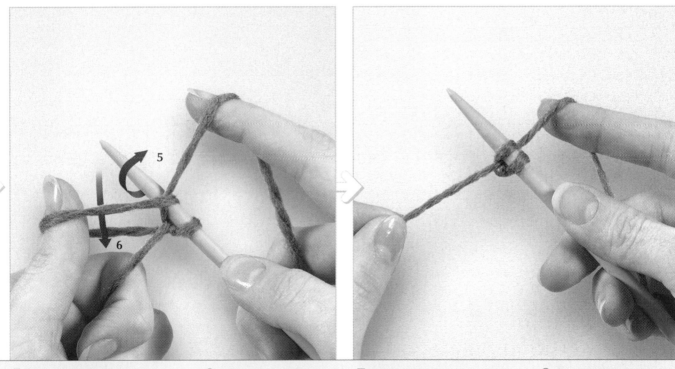

5 Wrap the strand of yarn connected to the ball around the tip of the needle, counterclockwise from back to front.

6 Bring the needle through the loop of yarn on your thumb.

7 Remove your thumb from the loop of yarn.

8 Gently pull on both ends of yarn to tighten the stitch.

9 Repeat steps 3 to 8 for each stitch you want to cast on.

CONTINUED...

double cast on

(continued)

Method Two

The second of the two main double cast on methods involves wrapping the yarn around the index finger and thumb of your left hand to place the stitches on the needle. This differs from the thumb method described on page 42 in that the fingers of your right hand are not used to hold the yarn while casting stitches onto the needle. This method is popular with people who hold the yarn in their left hand, knitting in the Continental style. For information on knitting in the Continental style, see page 48.

While both approaches produce identical stitches on the needle, every knitter has their own preference for how they cast on their first row of stitches. You should try both of the double cast on methods to see which method feels more natural for you.

As with the thumb method, make sure the tail of yarn you leave is long enough for you to complete the row of stitches. Use 1 inch of yarn for each stitch you are going to cast on plus 3 to 4 extra inches for the tail that will remain.

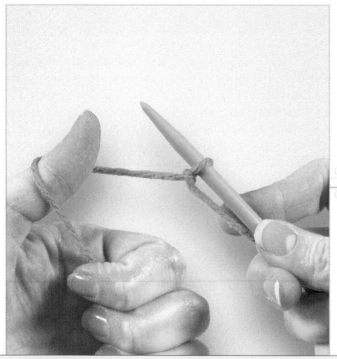

1 Make a slip knot on one needle. To make a slip knot, see page 40.

2 Hold the needle containing the slip knot in your right hand.

3 Wrap the tail of yarn around your left thumb, clockwise from front to back.

● Use the fingers of your left hand to hold the tail of yarn loosely in your palm.

4 Wrap the strand of yarn connected to the ball over your left index finger, clockwise from front to back.

● Use the other fingers of your left hand to hold the strand of yarn loosely in your palm.

5 Insert the tip of the needle between your thumb and the strand of yarn, from bottom to top.

How do I tighten a cast-on stitch that is too loose?

Stitches should be snug on the needle, but should still be able to slide up and down easily. If you discover that a stitch you just cast on is a little loose, gently pull the strand of yarn attached to the ball.

How do I prevent casting on stitches too tightly?

When you finish casting on and begin knitting your first row, cast-on stitches should be loose enough that the right needle slides between the left needle and the stitches smoothly. If you find you are casting on too tightly, try casting the stitches onto a needle one size larger than you will use to knit the piece. Then switch to the correct needle size for knitting the first row.

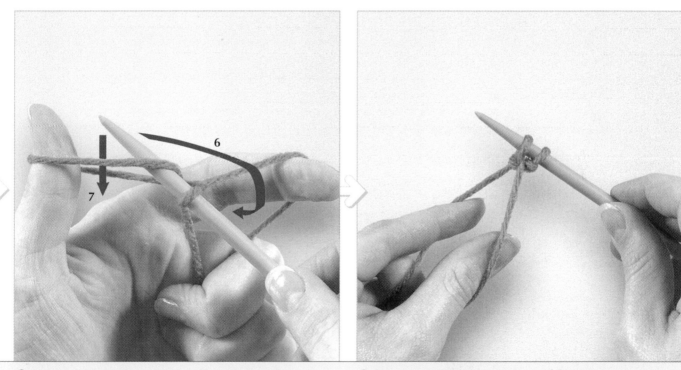

6 Insert the tip of the needle between your index finger and the strand of yarn, from top to bottom.

7 Bring the needle through the loop of yarn on your thumb.

8 Remove your thumb from the loop of yarn.

9 Gently pull on both ends of the yarn to tighten the stitch.

10 Repeat steps 3 to 9 for each stitch you want to cast on.

the knit stitch

English style

The knit stitch is the most basic stitch in knitting. In patterns, the knit stitch is represented by a **K**. For example, **K12** indicates to knit twelve stitches.

There are two styles of performing the knit stitch—the English style (holding the yarn in the right hand) and the Continental style (holding the yarn in the left hand). The English style is the most popular.

A stitch is shaped like an upside down droplet (♡). When you knit a stitch, the bottom part of the droplet (the V shape) is on the front of your work.

The top part of the droplet (the bump) is on the back of your work.

Once you have cast stitches onto your needle, you can start knitting. You continue to knit a row until there are no stitches remaining on the left needle. To begin a new row, you move the needle with the stitches to your left hand, hold the empty needle in your right hand and continue knitting. Remember to always keep the yarn at the back of your work for the knit stitch.

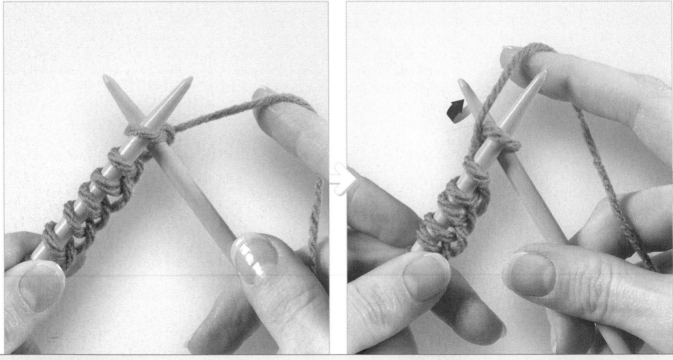

1 Hold the needle containing the stitches in your left hand.

2 Hold the empty needle and yarn in your right hand, with the yarn resting behind the needle.

3 Insert the tip of the right needle into the front of the first stitch on the left needle, from left to right.

• The right needle is behind the left needle and the tips of the needles form an "X."

4 Wrap the yarn around the tip of the right needle once, counterclockwise from back to front.

Why is there an extra stitch on my needle when I finish knitting a row?

The yarn may be lying overtop of your needle, making it seem as if there is an extra stitch. This is a common mistake. Once you finish a row of knit stitches and are ready to begin a new row, make sure the yarn is hanging straight down from your needle and all the stitches are below the needle.

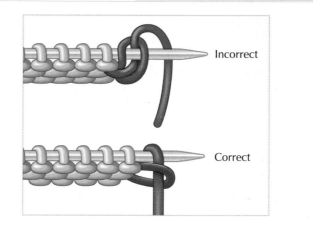

Incorrect

Correct

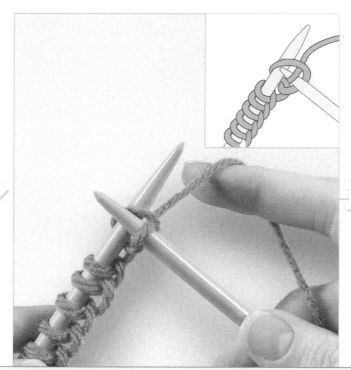

5 Slide the tip of the right needle and the wrapped yarn back through the stitch toward you.

Note: You can position the tip of your left forefinger on the point of the right needle as you perform step 5 to help prevent the wrapped yarn from slipping off the needle.

- The right needle will end up in front of the left needle and will hold a new stitch.

6 Slide the original stitch off the left needle.

- You have now completed one knit stitch.

7 Repeat steps 3 to 6 for each stitch on the left needle, ensuring the yarn rests behind the needles before you knit each stitch.

Note: To view an example of completed rows of knit stitches, see page 54.

the knit stitch

Continental style

You can perform the knit stitch using the English style or the Continental style. In the Continental style, you hold both the needle with the stitches and the yarn in your left hand. Your right hand holds the empty needle. You should remember to always keep the yarn behind your work when performing the knit stitch.

Once you have cast stitches onto your needle, you can start knitting. You can continue to knit a row until there are no stitches remaining on the left needle.

To begin a new row, you move the needle with the stitches to your left hand, hold the empty needle in your right hand and continue knitting.

In patterns, the knit stitch is represented by a **K**. For example, **K12** indicates to knit 12 stitches.

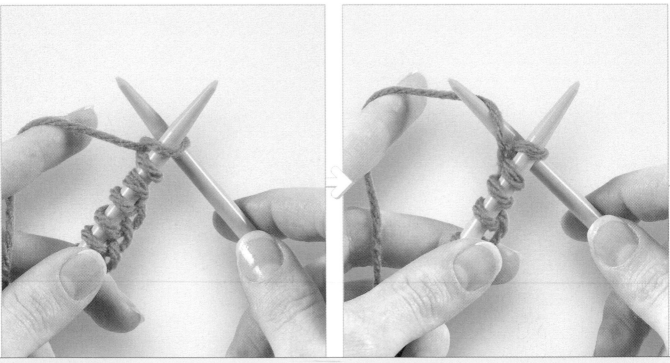

1 Hold the yarn and the needle containing the stitches in your left hand, with the yarn resting behind the needle.

2 Hold the empty needle in your right hand.

3 Insert the tip of the right needle into the front of the first stitch on the left needle, from left to right.

• The right needle is behind the left needle and the tips of the needles form an "X."

4 Place the yarn over the tip of the right needle, from front to back.

How can I get more comfortable performing the knit stitch?

If you are having trouble getting your knit stitches to flow comfortably, you can try changing the way you hold the yarn or the way you hold the needles until you find a position that works best for you.

I am a left-handed knitter. Which style of knit stitch should I use?

You can try both the English and Continental styles to determine which style works best for you. However, if you find both styles too awkward, you can try the styles in reverse, substituting right for left and left for right throughout the steps. Hold the needle containing the stitches in your right hand and the empty needle in your left hand. As you knit, move the stitches from the right needle to the left needle.

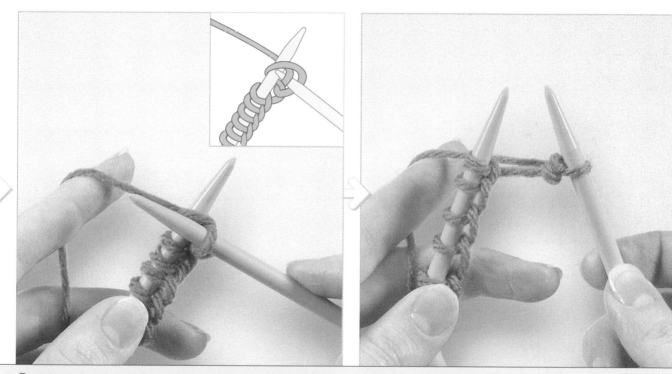

5 Slide the tip of the right needle and the wrapped yarn back through the stitch toward you.

• The right needle will end up in front of the left needle and will hold a new stitch.

6 Slide the original stitch off the left needle.

• You have completed one knit stitch.

7 Repeat steps **3** to **6** for each stitch on the left needle, ensuring the yarn rests behind the needles before you knit each stitch.

Note: To view an example of completed rows of knit stitches, see page 54.

the purl stitch

English style

The purl stitch is the reverse of the knit stitch. When making a purl stitch, you put your needle into the stitch from right to left, instead of left to right. You also hold the yarn in front of your work for a purl stitch, instead of behind your work.

There are two styles of purling—the English style (holding the yarn in the right hand) and the Continental style (holding the yarn in the left hand). If you knit in the English style, you should also purl in the English style.

Each stitch you make is shaped like an upside down droplet (♡). When you purl a stitch, the top part of the droplet (the bump) is on the front of your work. The bottom part of the droplet (the V shape) is on the back of your work.

In patterns, the purl stitch is represented by a **P**. For example, **P15** indicates to purl 15 stitches.

When purling or knitting, you continue to purl or knit a row until there are no stitches remaining on the left needle. To begin a new row, you move the needle with the stitches to your left hand and hold the empty needle in your right hand.

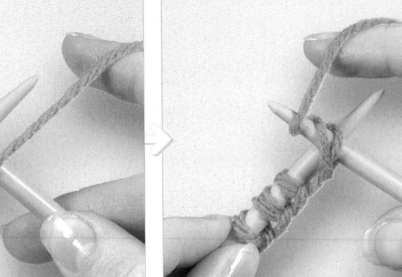

1 Hold the needle containing the stitches in your left hand.

2 Hold the empty needle and yarn in your right hand, with the yarn resting in front of the needle.

3 Insert the tip of the right needle into the front of the first stitch on the left needle, from right to left.

• The right needle is in front of the left needle and the tips of the needles form an "X."

4 Wrap the yarn around the tip of the right needle once, counterclockwise from back to front.

I put my work down in the middle of a row. How can I tell which is the left needle and which is the right?

When you pick up your knitting needles, make sure the yarn is hanging down from the first stitch at the tip of the needle in your right hand. This will ensure that your hands are holding the correct needles. To avoid this type of confusion in the future, you should always try to complete an entire row before putting down your work.

After I am comfortable with the purl stitch, what should I work on next?

You can start working on the tension of your stitches next. Try to aim for equal tension on every stitch in every row of your knitting project to create a consistent look in your project. This will ensure you do not have some stitches that are too loose and some that are too tight.

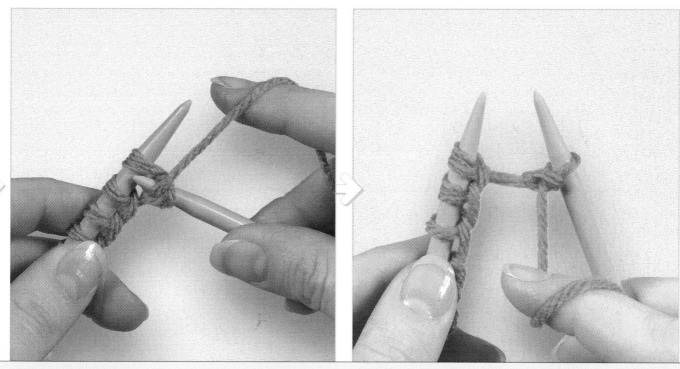

5 Slide the tip of the right needle and the wrapped yarn back through the stitch away from you.

• The right needle will end up behind the left needle and will hold a new stitch.

6 Slide the original stitch off the left needle.

• You have now completed one purl stitch.

7 Repeat steps 3 to 6 for each stitch on the left needle, ensuring the yarn rests in front of the needles before you purl each stitch.

the purl stitch

Continental style

You can perform the purl stitch in either the Continental style (holding the yarn in your left hand) or the English style (holding the yarn in your right hand). If you knit in the Continental style, you should also purl in the Continental style.

Like the English style, the Continental style also requires you to hold the yarn in front of your work when making a purl stitch.

No matter which purl style you use, each stitch you make is shaped like an upside down droplet (♡). When you purl a stitch, the top part of the droplet

(the bump) is on the front of your work. The bottom part of the droplet (the V shape) is on the back of your work.

In patterns, the purl stitch is represented by a **P**. For example, **P15** indicates to purl 15 stitches.

When purling or knitting, you continue to purl or knit a row until there are no stitches remaining on the left needle. To begin a new row, you move the needle with the stitches to your left hand and hold the empty needle in your right hand.

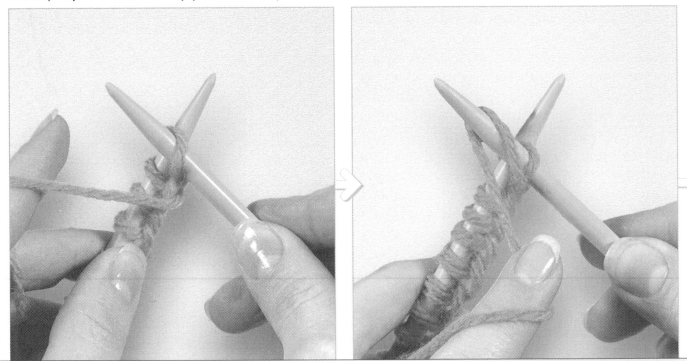

1 Hold the yarn and the needle containing the stitches in your left hand, with the yarn resting in front of the needle.

2 Hold the empty needle in your right hand.

3 Insert the tip of the right needle into the front of the first stitch on the left needle, from right to left.

• The right needle is in front of the left needle and the tips of the needles form an "X."

4 Place the yarn over the tip of the right needle from front to back and then position the yarn between the needles.

How can I increase my knitting speed?

To increase your speed, try knitting to music that has a steady beat. The faster the music, the faster you will tend to knit. Remember to hold your knitting needles gently and minimize your movements as much as possible. Knitting to music may also help improve your rhythm, which will give your stitches a more uniform appearance.

Why should I learn both the purl stitch and the knit stitch?

You can use the purl and knit stitches together, in different combinations, to create interesting textures. For examples of stitch patterns that you can create by combining the knit and purl stitches, see pages 54 to 57.

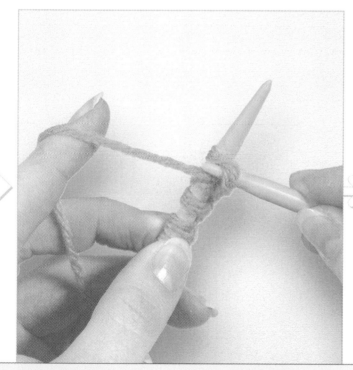

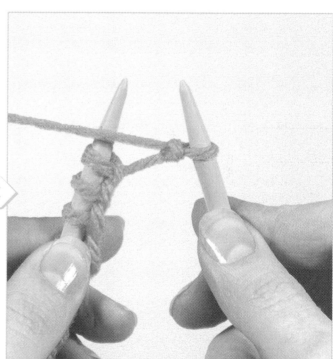

5 Slide the tip of the right needle and the wrapped yarn back through the stitch away from you.

• The right needle will end up behind the left needle and will hold a new stitch.

6 Slide the original stitch off the left needle.

• You have now completed one purl stitch.

7 Repeat steps 3 to 6 for each stitch on the left needle, ensuring the yarn rests in front of the needles before you purl each stitch.

basic patterns you can knit

Once you have learned to knit and purl, you can create different patterns. While working in entire rows of either the knit or purl stitch, you can create two of the most common patterns—garter stitch and stockinette stitch.

Garter stitch is formed when stitches are either knit on every row or purled on every row. A knitted piece created in garter stitch looks exactly the same on the front and back, which makes garter stitch a popular fabric for items such as scarves and blankets. Garter stitch is easy to identify by its rows of bumps on both sides.

Stockinette, or stocking, stitch is formed by alternating between a row of knit stitches and a row of purl stitches. This pattern creates a knitted fabric that is smooth on one side (the right side) and bumpy on the other (the wrong side). Stockinette stitch is commonly used to create the main fabric for many types of garments. In patterns and instructions, the abbreviation for stockinette stitch is **St st**.

Fabric knitted in stockinette stitch tends to curl at the edges. The top and bottom edges curl toward the right side of the fabric, while the side edges curl toward the wrong side of the fabric.

GARTER STITCH

1 Knit all the stitches in the row.

Note: To knit a stitch, see page 46.

2 Repeat step **1** until your work is the length you want.

- Your work will have the same appearance on both sides.

- You can also create garter stitch by purling all the stitches in every row.

What is reverse stockinette stitch?

Reverse stockinette stitch is similar to stockinette stitch, except it starts with a row of purl stitches instead of knit stitches. Reverse stockinette stitch creates a knitted fabric that is opposite to stockinette stitch—the bumpy side is on the right side and the smooth side is on the wrong side. In patterns and instructions, the abbreviation for reverse stockinette stitch is **rev St st**.

- To create reverse stockinette stitch, repeat steps **1** to **3** below, except purl the stitches in step **1** and knit the stitches in step **2**.

STOCKINETTE STITCH

Wrong Side

1 Knit all the stitches in the row.

Note: To knit a stitch, see page 46.

2 Purl all the stitches in the next row.

Note: To purl a stitch, see page 50.

3 Repeat steps **1** and **2** until your work is the length you want.

- Your work will appear smooth on the right side and bumpy on the wrong side.

basic knit and
purl designs

Seed Stitch

Cast on a multiple of 2 stitches (2, 4, 6, etc.).

Row 1: *K1. P1; Repeat from * to end of row.

Row 2: *P1. K1; Rep from * to end of row.

Rep Rows 1 and 2.

EASY

Double Seed Stitch

Cast on a multiple of 4 stitches (4, 8, 12, etc.).

Row 1: *K2. P2; Repeat from * to end of row.

Row 2: As Row 1.

Row 3: *P2. K2; Rep from * to end of row.

Row 4: As Row 3.

Rep Rows 1 to 4.

EASY

Moss Stitch

Cast on a multiple of 2 stitches (2, 4, 6, etc.).

Row 1: *K1. P1; Repeat from * to end of row.

Row 2: As Row 1.

Row 3: *P1. K1; Rep from * to end of row.

Row 4: As Row 3.

Rep Rows 1 to 4.

EASY

Simple Seed Stitch

Cast on a multiple of 4 stitches (4, 8, 12, etc.), plus 1 stitch.

Row 1 (RS): P1. *K3. P1; Repeat from * to end of row.

Row 2 and all wrong-side (WS) rows: Purl.

Row 3: Knit.

Row 5: K2. P1. *K3. P1; Rep from * to last 2 sts, K2.

Row 7: Knit.

Row 8: Purl.

Rep Rows 1 to 8.

Horizontal Dash

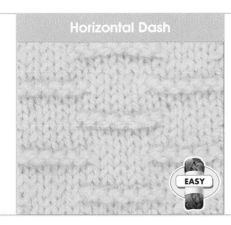

Cast on a multiple of 10 stitches (10, 20, 30, etc.), plus 6 stitches.

Row 1 (RS): P6. *K4. P6; Repeat from * to end of row.

Row 2 and all wrong-side (WS) rows: Purl.

Row 3: Knit.

Row 5: P1. *K4. P6; Rep from * to last 5 sts, K4. P1.

Row 7: Knit.

Row 8: Purl.

Rep Rows 1 to 8.

Ripple Stitch

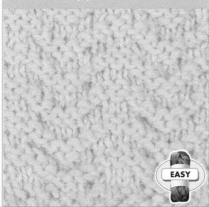

Cast on a multiple of 8 stitches (8, 16, 24, etc.), plus 6 stitches.

Row 1 (RS): K6. *P2. K6; Repeat from * to end of row.

Row 2: K1. *P4. K4; Rep from * to last 5 sts, P4. K1.

Row 3: P2. *K2. P2; Rep from * to end of row.

Row 4: P1. *K4. P4; Rep from * to last 5 sts, K4. P1.

Row 5: K2. *P2. K6; Rep from * to last 4 sts, P2. K2.

Row 6: P6. *K2. P6; Rep from * to end of row.

Row 7: P1. *K4. P4; Rep from * to last 5 sts, K4. P1.

Row 8: K2. *P2. K2; Rep from * to end of row.

Row 9: K1. *P4. K4; Rep from * to last 5 sts, P4. K1.

Row 10: P2. *K2. P6; Rep from * to last 4 sts, K2. P2.

Rep Rows 1 to 10.

basic knit and purl designs

Parallelogram Check

Cast on a multiple of 10 stitches (10, 20, 30, etc.).

Row 1 (RS): *K5. P5; Repeat from * to end of row.

Row 2: K4. *P5. K5; Rep from * to last 6 sts, P5. K1.

Row 3: P2. *K5. P5; Rep from * to last 8 sts, K5. P3.

Row 4: K2. *P5. K5; Rep from * to last 8 sts, P5. K3.

Row 5: P4. *K5. P5; Rep from * to last 6 sts, K5. P1.

Row 6: *P5. K5; Rep from * to end of row.

Rep Rows 1 to 6.

EASY

Basketweave

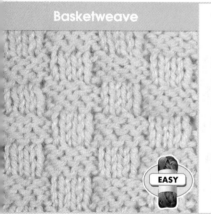

Cast on a multiple of 8 stitches (8, 16, 24, etc.), plus 5 stitches.

Row 1 (RS): Knit.

Row 2: K5. *P3. K5; Repeat from * to end of row.

Row 3: P5. *K3. P5; Rep from * to end of row.

Row 4: As Row 2.

Row 5: Knit.

Row 6: K1. *P3. K5; Rep from * to last 4 sts, P3. K1.

Row 7: P1. *K3. P5; Rep from * to last 4 sts, K3. P1.

Row 8: As Row 6.

Rep Rows 1 to 8.

EASY

Lattice Stitch

Cast on a multiple of 6 stitches (6, 12, 18, etc.), plus 1 stitch.

Row 1 (RS): K3. *P1. K5; Repeat from * to last 4 sts, P1. K3.

Row 2: P2. *K1. P1. K1. P3; Rep from * to last 5 sts, K1. P1. K1. P2.

Row 3: K1. *P1. K3. P1. K1; Rep from * to end of row.

Row 4: K1. *P5. K1; Rep from * to end of row.

Row 5: As Row 3.

Row 6: As Row 2.

Rep Rows 1 to 6.

EASY

Diamond Panels

Cast on a multiple of 8 stitches (8, 16, 24, etc.), plus 1 stitch.

Row 1 (RS): Knit.

Row 2: K1. *P7. K1; Repeat from * to end of row.

Row 3: K4. *P1. K7; Rep from * to last 5 sts, P1. K4.

Row 4: K1. *P2. K1. P1. K1. P2. K1; Rep from * to end of row.

Row 5: K2 *P1. (K1. P1) twice. K3; Rep from * to last 7 sts, P1. (K1. P1) twice. K2.

Row 6: As Row 4.

Row 7: As Row 3.

Row 8: As Row 2.

Rep Rows 1 to 8.

EASY

King Charles Brocade

Cast on a multiple of 12 stitches (12, 24, 36, etc.), plus 1 stitch.

Row 1 (RS): K1. *P1. K9. P1. K1; Repeat from * to end of row.

Row 2: K1. *P1. K1. P7. K1. P1. K1; Rep from * to end of row.

Row 3: K1. *P1. K1. P1. K5. (P1. K1.) twice; Rep from * to end of row.

Row 4: P1. *(P1. K1) twice. P3. K1. P1. K1. P2; Rep from * to end of row.

Row 5: K1. *K2. (P1. K1) 3 times. P1. K3; Rep from * to end of row.

Row 6: P1. *P3. (K1. P1) twice. K1. P4; Rep from * to end of row.

Row 7: K1. *K4. P1. K1. P1. K5; Rep from * to end of row.

Row 8: As Row 6.

Row 9: As Row 5.

Row 10: As Row 4.

Row 11: As Row 3.

Row 12: As Row 2.

Rep Rows 1 to 12.

INTERMEDIATE

bind off

Binding off, also known as casting off, is a method of finishing the stitches on a completed knitted piece. Binding off removes stitches from your needles and secures the stitches to keep them from unravelling. A piece of knitting that has been bound off can remain on its own or be joined to other knitted pieces, such as joining a sleeve to the body of a sweater.

The knit bind off is the easiest bind off method to learn and the most commonly used. The knit bind off produces a firm, clean edge. Unless a project specifies a particular bind off method, you should use the bind off method that matches the stitch pattern used in your knitted piece. For example, if you are working on a knit 2 purl 2 ribbing, you should do a knit bind off for the knit stitches and a purl bind off for the purl stitches.

The abbreviation for binding off in patterns and instructions is **BO**.

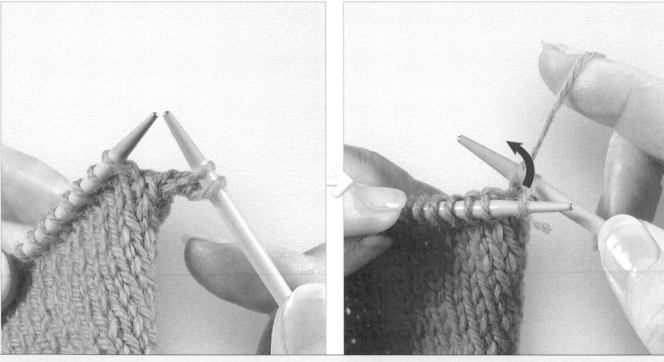

1 Knit the first two stitches on the left needle.

• The right needle now holds two stitches.

2 Insert the tip of the left needle into the front of the first stitch you knitted on the right needle, from left to right.

3 Using the left needle, lift the stitch over the second stitch you knitted and allow the lifted stitch to drop off both needles.

How do I bind off when working with purl stitches?

Perform steps **1** to **7** below, except purl the stitches instead of knitting them. Keep the yarn in front of your work as you bind off the stitches.

How can binding off be used to shape necks, shoulders and armholes?

To use binding off to shape necks, shoulders and armholes, you do not need to bind off the entire row of stitches. You can just bind off the stitches that allow you to shape your work. To bind off only some of the stitches, perform steps **1** to **5** below, repeating the steps only until you have bound off all the required stitches. When binding off a certain number of stitches for shaping, make sure to count each stitch you lift and drop off your needles.

● One stitch remains on the right needle and one stitch has been bound off.

4 Knit the next stitch on the left needle.

5 To bind off all the stitches, repeat steps **2** to **4** until there is only one stitch remaining on the right needle.

6 Cut the yarn, leaving a strand of yarn at least 3 inches long.

Note: When you bind off work that you will sew to another piece, leave a longer strand.

7 Slide the needle out of the last stitch. Then thread the strand of yarn through the stitch and gently pull until the loop is closed.

check your gauge

Before you begin any project, you should always knit a gauge swatch. A gauge swatch is a piece of knitted fabric that allows you to determine if you are producing the correct number of stitches and rows per inch, referred to as the "gauge." Stitches that are too big or too small will change the size and feel of your project. When knitting a gauge swatch, you must use the same yarn and needles you will use for the project.

Pattern instructions usually indicate the gauge, or "tension," for a project by stating the width and

length of a one-inch square. For example, a pattern may specify that the stitch gauge (width) is seven stitches per inch and the row gauge (length) is nine rows per inch. A one-inch square, however, is not an adequate sample to accurately measure the gauge. You should create at least a four-inch square gauge swatch.

If you have too many stitches or rows for the required gauge, try knitting another swatch using larger needles. If you have too few stitches or rows, try using smaller needles.

MAKE AND MEASURE A GAUGE SWATCH

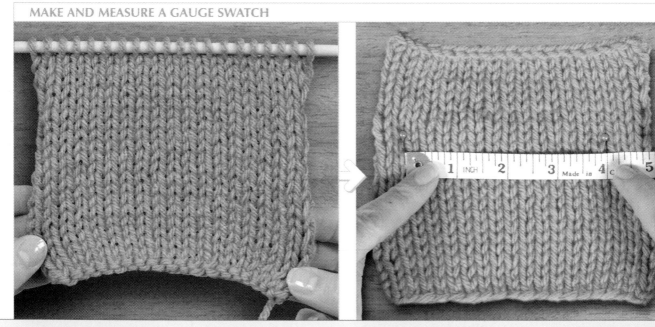

1 Cast on stitches until the stitches measure more than four inches across. To cast on stitches, see pages 41 to 45.

2 Knit one row and then purl one row until your knitted piece measures more than four inches long.

Note: Your pattern may indicate a different stitch pattern to use for the gauge swatch. In step 2, knit that pattern instead.

3 Bind off the stitches to remove the stitches from the needle. To bind off stitches, see page 60.

4 Smooth out the knitted piece on a flat surface.

5 Place a ruler horizontally on the knitted piece and mark four inches with pins.

6 Count the number of stitches between the pins.

What can affect the gauge ("tension") of my gauge swatch?

If you use a different yarn than is suggested by the pattern instructions, the gauge of your swatch may be incorrect. Different needle sizes and types, such as plastic and bamboo needles, may also produce different gauges. The gauge of your swatch also depends on the stitch pattern you use. For example, twisting cable patterns require more stitches per inch than simple knit and purl patterns.

How can I stop the edges of my gauge swatch from curling?

If the edges of your gauge swatch curl, you can make a border around your work to make the swatch lie flat. The stitches that form the border are called selvedge stitches. To make the top and bottom border, knit all the stitches in the first and last three rows of your swatch. To make the side borders, knit the first and last three stitches of each row. Do not include the selvedge stitch border when measuring the stitches and rows in your gauge swatch.

USING A STITCH GAUGE

7 Place a ruler on the knitted piece vertically and mark four inches with pins.

8 Count the number of rows between the pins.

9 Compare the number of stitches and rows you counted to the numbers given in your pattern instructions.

Note: Patterns usually provide the gauge for a one-inch square. You must multiply the numbers given by four to determine the number of stitches and rows for a four-inch square.

1 Create your gauge swatch by performing steps **1** to **3** on page 62.

2 Place a stitch gauge in the center of your knitted piece.

3 Count the stitches and rows within the opening of the stitch gauge.

4 Compare the number of stitches and rows you counted to the numbers given in your pattern instructions.

Note: Patterns usually provide the gauge for a one-inch square. Since most stitch gauges measure two inches, you must multiply the numbers given by two to determine the number of stitches and rows for a two-inch square.

make ribbing

Ribbing creates vertical ridges by alternating knit and purl stitches in the same row. Ribbing produces a stretchy fabric that is frequently used in neckbands, cuffs, edges and other borders. This elasticity allows neckbands and cuffs to expand over the head and hands and return to their original shape. Ribbing is usually worked on a smaller needle than the needle used for the rest of a project.

On each row, you purl the stitches that were knitted in the previous row and you knit the stitches that were purled in the previous row. In other words, if the flat side of the next stitch is facing you, you knit the stitch. If the bumpy side is facing you, you purl the stitch. You will notice that pattern instructions are often written as "knit the knit stitches and purl the purl stitches." As a result, the knits are aligned above the knit stitches and the purls are aligned above the purl stitches.

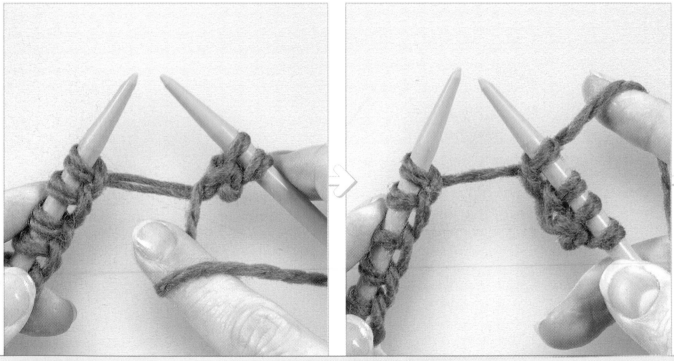

- In this example, we make a knit 2 purl 2 ribbing pattern.

1 Cast on the number of stitches you want your project to contain. To cast on stitches, see pages 41 to 45. In this example, we cast on 16 stitches.

2 Knit the first two stitches on the left needle.

3 Bring the yarn between the needles and place it in front of your work.

4 Purl two stitches on the left needle.

5 Bring the yarn between the needles and place it behind your work.

Are there other ribbing variations that I can create?

Yes. Although knit 2 purl 2 ribbing is very commonly used, there are many different ribbing variations you can use to produce the look you want. You can create a knit 1 purl 1 ribbing or a knit 3 purl 3 ribbing. You can also create ribbing in which the number of knit and purl stitches are different. For example, you can make a knit 4 purl 2 ribbing or a knit 2 purl 5 ribbing.

How can I make ribbing that is more elastic?

The number of stitches in the ribbing pattern determines the elasticity of the ribbed fabric. Fewer stitches will produce a more elastic ribbed fabric. For example, a knit 2 purl 2 ribbing is more elastic than a knit 5 purl 5 ribbing.

Is ribbing only used for cuffs and neckbands?

No. Ribbing can be used anywhere you want a stretchy fabric. You can even make an entire sweater in ribbing for a snugger or form-fitting style.

6 Repeat steps **2** to **5** until you complete all the stitches on the left needle.

7 Move the needle containing the stitches to your left hand and the empty needle to your right hand. Then repeat steps **2** to **6**.

8 Repeat steps **2** to **7** until your work is the desired length.

• Notice the ridged effect created by the alternated knit stitches and purl stitches.

ribbing designs

Knit 1 Purl 1 Rib

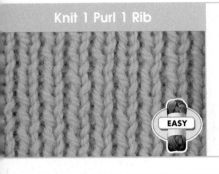

EASY

Cast on a multiple of 2 stitches (2, 4, 6, etc.).

Every Row: *K1. P1; Repeat from * to end of row.

Mistake Stitch Rib

EASY

Cast on a multiple of 4 stitches (4, 8, 12, etc.), plus 3 stitches.

Every Row: *K2. P2; Repeat from * to last 3 sts, K2. P1.

Broken 2 x 2 Rib

EASY

Cast on a multiple of 4 stitches (4, 8, 12, etc.).

Row 1 (RS): *K2. P2; Repeat from * to end of row.

Rows 2 to 6: Rep Row 1.

Row 7: *P2. K2; Rep from * to end of row.

Rows 8 to 12: Rep Row 7.

Rep Rows 1 to 12.

Knit 2 Purl 5 Rib

EASY

Cast on a multiple of 7 stitches (7, 14, 21, etc.), plus 2 stitches.

Row 1 (RS): K2. *P5. K2; Repeat from * to end of row.

Row 2: P2. *K5. P2; Rep from * to end of row.

Rep Rows 1 and 2.

Diagonal Ribbing

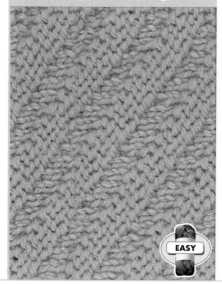

EASY

Cast on a multiple of 8 stitches (8, 16, 24, etc.), plus 6 stitches.

Row 1: K1. *P4. K4; Repeat from * to last 5 sts, P4. K1.

Row 2: K4. *P4. K4; Rep from * to last 2 sts, P2.

Row 3: K3. *P4. K4; Rep from * to last 3 sts, P3.

Row 4: K2. *P4. K4; Rep from * to last 4 sts, P4.

Row 5: P1. *K4. P4; Rep from * to last 5 sts, K4. P1.

Row 6: P4. *K4. P4; Rep from * to last 2 sts, K2.

Row 7: P3. *K4. P4; Rep from * to last 3 sts, K3.

Row 8: P2. *K4. P4; Rep from * to last 4 sts, K4.

Rep Rows 1 to 8.

Steps

EASY

Cast on a multiple of 8 stitches (8, 16, 24, etc.), plus 2 stitches.

Row 1 (RS): *K4. P4; Repeat from * to last 2 sts, K2.

Row 2: P2. *K4. P4; Rep from * to end of row.

Row 3: As Row 1.

Row 4: As Row 2.

Row 5: K2. *P4. K4; Rep from * to end of row.

Row 6: *P4. K4; Rep from * to last 2 sts, P2.

Row 7: As Row 5.

Row 8: As Row 6.

Row 9: *P4. K4; Rep from * to last 2 sts, P2.

Row 10: K2. *P4. K4; Rep from * to end of row.

Row 11: As Row 9.

Row 12: As Row 10.

Row 13: As Row 2.

Row 14: As Row 1.

Row 15: As Row 2.

Row 16: As Row 1.

Rep Rows 1 to 16.

read a knitting pattern

Knitting patterns provide you with all the information you need to create a knitted project, including detailed instructions that use common knitting abbreviations, terms and symbols. With practice, you will be able to read knitting pattern instructions quickly and easily. Before beginning a project, you should read all the instructions included in the pattern so you have a good understanding of how the entire project will be made.

Size

A knitting pattern usually specifies the approximate dimensions of the finished project. When a project can be made in multiple sizes, the pattern specifies the additional sizes in brackets, such as "Small (Medium, Large)." Throughout the pattern, you will find the instructions for the additional sizes in brackets. For example, a pattern may specify "knit 10 (15, 20) sts," which means you should knit 10 stitches for the small size, 15 stitches for the medium size or 20 stitches for the large size.

Each size will always be in the same position throughout the pattern. To help ensure you always refer to the instructions for the correct size, you may want to photocopy the pattern and highlight all the information for the size you want to make.

Materials

A pattern will tell you the type, color, weight and amount of yarn you will need. A pattern will also indicate the knitting needle size you should use and include information about any additional materials you will need, such as buttons or stitch holders.

Gauge

A pattern indicates the gauge, or "tension," required to ensure your finished project will be the correct size. Gauge is the number of stitches and rows you should have in a sample piece of knitted fabric when you use the same needles and yarn you will use for the project.

Stitch Glossary

If a pattern includes a stitch pattern that is repeated throughout the project, a stitch glossary may be included to provide row-by-row instructions for the stitch pattern. Stitch pattern instructions often include the number of stitches required to complete one repeat of the stitch pattern, such as "multiple of 8 stitches, plus 2 stitches." This means that the stitch pattern will be repeated evenly across a row as long as the total number of stitches on the needle is a multiple of eight, such as 16, 48 or 80, with an additional two stitches.

Abbreviations

Pattern instructions are written using abbreviations. A list of abbreviations used in the pattern you are following may be included in the pattern. The following is a list of some commonly used knitting abbreviations. For a more extensive list of abbreviations, see page 284.

st(s)	stitch(es)
K	knit
P	purl
inc	increase
dec	decrease
rep	repeat

Sl st	slip stitch
psso	pass slipped stitch over
K2tog	knit two stitches together
RS	right side
WS	wrong side

Common Knitting Symbols

*

An asterisk (*) marks the beginning of a set of instructions you will repeat. You work the instructions following the asterisk once and then repeat the instructions until you reach the specified location in the current row. For example, a pattern may specify *K2. P2; Rep from * to end of row.

Another common example of the asterisk is "*K2. P2; Rep to last 3 sts, K2, P1." This means you repeat the instructions until you have three stitches remaining on the left needle and then you follow the new instructions for those three stitches.

** **

Double asterisks (**) mark a long section of instructions that you will be asked to repeat later in the pattern. For example, if a section of the front of a sweater is worked the same as the back of a sweater, the instructions for the back are enclosed in double asterisks. The instructions for the front may state "Work from ** to ** as given for Back."

( ) or [ ]

You work the instructions enclosed in brackets as many times as indicated by the number immediately following the brackets. For example, if a pattern states "(K5. P5) 7 times," you work the instructions included in the brackets seven times.

Schematics

Some patterns include a schematic, which is a drawing of a finished piece of the project that shows the final measurements for all the sizes included in the pattern. Schematics are useful for determining which size is best for you and for ensuring that you block your project pieces to the correct size.

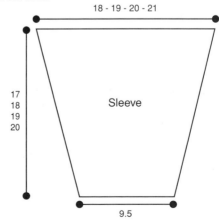

69

read a knitting chart

Knitting patterns are often presented as charts instead of as written instructions. These charts show how a pattern will appear on the right side of your knitted piece and can indicate specific stitches, colors and other elements of the piece.

A chart can represent the entire width of a knitted piece or just a single design that repeats across the entire fabric. Compared to written instructions, charts can help you more easily visualize and create a knitted piece.

How to Read a Chart

Every square in a chart symbolizes a stitch and every line of squares signifies a row of stitches. Row numbers are usually indicated on the sides of the chart.

To read a chart, unless otherwise directed, start from the bottom right corner, moving across to the bottom left corner and work up to the top of the chart. You read all odd-numbered rows, which are usually the right-side rows, from right to left. You read all even-numbered rows, which are usually the wrong-side rows, from left to right.

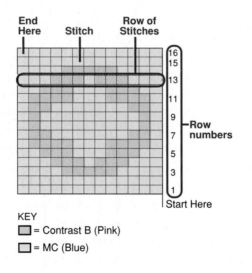

KEY
☐ = Contrast B (Pink)
☐ = MC (Blue)

When creating tube-shaped pieces using circular or double-pointed needles, you read all the rows in the chart from right to left.

To help you keep your place in a chart, you may want to place a ruler under the row you are working on and move the ruler up to the next row each time you complete a row.

Colors in Charts

Charts for knitting with different colors are presented in different ways. The squares on some charts may be colored or display the name of the color. Alternately, the squares can display a symbol to indicate a particular color. A key usually accompanies the chart to help you identify the color each symbol represents.

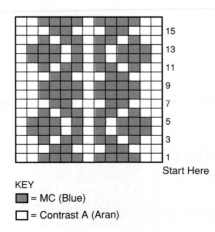

KEY
▨ = MC (Blue)
☐ = Contrast A (Aran)

If a square does not contain a symbol, color or name, you usually work the stitch using the main color for the knitted piece. When only two colors are used, the main color is often marked "MC" and the contrast color is often marked "CC."

Shaping in Charts

Some knitting patterns include charts that indicate how and when to increase or decrease stitches. These charts are typically used to show shaping for sweater sleeves or necklines.

When increasing or decreasing stitches at the beginning or end of rows, squares are often added or removed from the sides of a chart to indicate the increases or decreases.

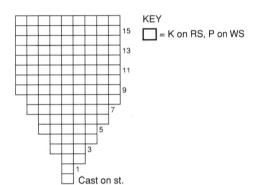

Alternately, symbols can appear in the squares of a chart to indicate when to increase or decrease stitches. For example, the ⊙ symbol can indicate when to increase a stitch and the ⊠ symbol can indicate when to decrease a stitch.

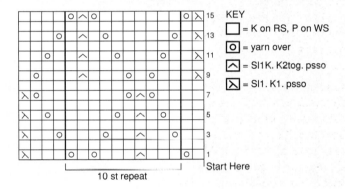

Common Chart Symbols

Charts typically include a legend, or key, to help you identify each symbol in the chart. Some common chart symbols include the following:

☐ or ⊺	knit on the right side, purl on the wrong side
⊟	purl on the right side, knit on the wrong side
⊙	yarn over
⊠	make one increase
⊼	knit two stitches together
⊠	slip slip knit
⊠	slip one, knit one, pass slipped stitch over
⬤	make a bobble
⤬	cable 4 stitches to the right
⤬	cable 4 stitches to the left

start a new ball of yarn

When you run out of yarn or want to introduce a new color into your project, you will have to start a new ball of yarn and join the yarn to your work. Ideally, you should start a new ball of yarn at the end of a row so you can hide the yarn ends in a seam. When you are unable to join yarn at the end of a row, try to join the yarn in a place where it will not stand out. For example, join the yarn where you have lots of knit and purl stitches that make up a design rather than joining the yarn in the middle of a plain stockinette stitch.

Every time you join yarn from a new ball, you will have strands of yarn to weave into your work. Remember to leave the strands long enough (approximately 4 to 6 inches) so they are easy to work with. If you take care when joining new balls of yarn, not only will your knitting be neat, but your work will hold together firmly.

1 Cut the original strand of yarn, leaving approximately 6 inches of yarn.

2 Tie the new yarn loosely around the original yarn near the first stitch, leaving approximately 6 inches of yarn.

3 Start knitting with the new yarn.

Note: When you finish your project, you can weave in the yarn ends. For information on weaving in yarn ends, see page 208.

child's winter scarf

Child's Winter Scarf

Size

Approx. 36 x 5.25 ins (91.5 x 13cm)

Materials

Sirdar Snuggly Baby Care 50g, #SH251 - white, 2 balls

Size 7 US (4.5mm) knitting needles or size needed to obtain gauge.

Gauge

20 stitches (sts) and 24 rows = 4 ins (10cm) in Stockinette St (knit 1 row, purl 1 row).

Instructions

Abbreviations: K = knit; P = purl; RS=right side.

Cast on 36 stitches.

Row 1 (RS): *K3. P3; Rep from * to end of row.

Row 2: *K1. P1; Rep from * to end of row.

Repeat Rows 1 and 2 until the scarf measures 36 ins (91.5cm), ending after a Row 2.

Bind off all stitches in pattern.

· Easy Project ·

• Easy Project •

Checkered Cloth

Size

Approx. 7.25 x 7.25 ins (18.5 x 18.5cm).

Materials

Lily Sugar'n Cream 2.5oz/70.9g, #10 Yellow, 1 ball.

Size 7 US (4.5mm) knitting needles or size needed to obtain gauge.

Gauge

20 stitches (sts) and 26 rows = 4 ins (10cm) in Stockinette St (knit 1 row, purl 1 row).

Instructions

Abbreviations: RS=right side; K = knit; P = purl.

Cast on 36 stitches.

Row 1 (RS): K4. *P4. K4; Rep from * to end of row.

Row 2: P4. *K4. P4; Rep from * to end of row.

Row 3: As Row 1.

Row 4: As Row 2.

Row 5: P4. *K4. P4; Rep from * to end of row.

Row 6: K4. *P4. K4; Rep from * to end of row.

Row 7: As Row 5.

Row 8: As Row 6.

Repeat these 8 rows five more times, ending after a Row 8.

Bind off all stitches.

good morning bathmat

• Easy Project •

Good Morning Bathmat

Size

Approx. 17 x 31 ins (43 x 78.5cm).

Materials

Approx. 24oz/480yds (680g/364m) of any Bulky Weight Craft Cotton to give gauge stated below.

Size 11 US (8mm) circular knitting needles (90cm long) or size needed to obtain gauge.

Gauge

10 stitches (sts) and 15 rows = 4 ins (10cm) in Stockinette St (knit 1 row, purl 1 row).

Instructions

Abbreviations: K = knit; P = purl.

Cast on 73 stitches.
Working back and forth on needles, work Rows 1 to 12 for King Charles Brocade.

Instructions (cont.)

King Charles Brocade:

Row 1 (RS): K1. *P1. K9. P1. K1; Rep from * to end of row.

Row 2: K1. *P1. K1. P7. K1. P1. K1; Rep from * to end of row.

Row 3: K1. *P1. K1. P1. K5. P1. K1. P1. K1; Rep from * to end of row.

Row 4: P1. *(P1. K1) twice. P3. K1. P1. K1. P2; Rep from * to end of row.

Row 5: K1. *K2. (P1. K1) 3 times. P1. K3; Rep from * to end of row.

Row 6: P1. *P3. (K1. P1) twice. K1. P4; Rep from * to end of row.

Row 7: K1. *K4. P1. K1. P1. K5; Rep from * to end of row.

Row 8: As Row 6.

Row 9: As Row 5.

Row 10: As Row 4.

Row 11: As Row 3.

Row 12: As Row 2.

Repeat Rows 1 to 12 four more times.

Bind off all stitches.

cotton candy scarf

• *Easy Project* •

Cotton Candy Scarf

Size

Approx. 50.5 x 8 ins (128.5 x 20.5cm).

Materials

Classic Elite La Gran 42g, #6519 Pink, 4 balls

Size 9 US (5.5mm) knitting needles or size needed to obtain gauge.

Gauge

16 stitches (sts) and 20 rows = 4 ins (10cm) in Stockinette St (knit 1 row, purl 1 row).

Instructions

Abbreviations: K = knit, RS = right side.

Cast on 32 stitches.

Work 7 rows in Garter St (knit every row).

Row 1 (RS): Knit.

Row 2: K3. Purl to last 3 sts, K3.

Row 3: As Row 1.

Row 4: As Row 2.

Row 5: As Row 1.

Row 6: As Row 2.

Row 7: As Row 1.

Row 8: Knit.

Repeat Rows 1 to 8 thirty-five more times.

Work 7 rows in Garter St (knit every row).

Bind off all stitches.

Chapter 3

O nce you are comfortable with knitting and purling stitches, you will be able to create a wide range of square or rectangular projects, such as cloths and scarves. However, you can shape your fabric in various ways by adding or removing stitches from your work. In this chapter, you will learn several different methods to increase and decrease stitches to help you shape your projects.

Increases and Decreases

In this Chapter...

increase one stitch

Make a Bar Increase

There are several popular methods of adding stitches in your knitted projects. Each method can be used in a particular situation and results in a specific look. In patterns, the standard abbreviation for an increase is **inc**.

A bar increase allows you to turn one stitch into two stitches and is the most common way to increase by one stitch. When you add a stitch using this method, a horizontal bar appears beneath the added stitch. These bars allow you to easily keep track of the number of increases you have made. Bar increases are often performed on the edge of a knitted piece that will be sewn to another knitted piece, so the horizontal bars may be hidden in the finished project.

If a pattern instructs you to increase a stitch but does not specify the method to use, you should use the bar increase method. You may also find instructions that indicate a bar increase by telling you to "knit into the front and back of the next stitch," abbreviated as **kfb**.

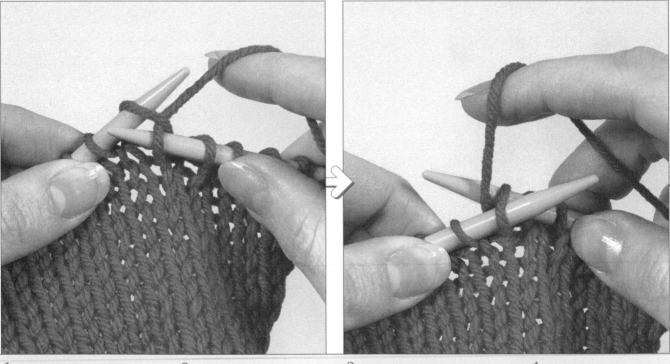

1 Work to where you want to increase by one stitch.

2 Knit the next stitch on the left needle, but do not slide the original stitch off the left needle.

3 Insert the tip of the right needle into the back of the original stitch, from right to left.

4 Wrap the yarn around the tip of the right needle once, counterclockwise from back to front.

How do I make a bar increase when working on the purl side?

To make a bar increase when working on the purl side of your work, purl one stitch on the left needle, but do not slide the original stitch off the left needle. Then insert the right needle into the back of the original stitch, moving the needle through the stitch from back to front. The tip of the right needle is now in front of the left needle. Wrap the yarn around the tip of the right needle once, counterclockwise from back to front. Bring the tip of the right needle and the wrapped yarn back through the stitch away from you and then slide the original stitch off the left needle.

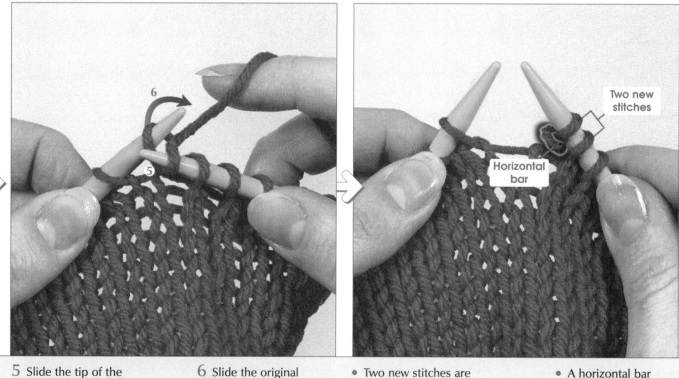

5 Slide the tip of the right needle and the wrapped yarn back through the stitch toward you.

6 Slide the original stitch off the left needle.

• Two new stitches are created on the right needle. You have increased the number of stitches by one.

• A horizontal bar appears below the added stitch.

CONTINUED...

increase one stitch
(continued)

Work a Make 1

To add a stitch to your work, you can use the make 1 increase method, also known as a "lifted increase." This method is typically used when increasing stitches in the center of your work or when increasing stitches at equal intervals across your work.

The make 1 increase method forms a new stitch between two existing stitches, so the increase must be made at least one stitch in from the beginning of a row. You can choose to make the new stitch either a right-twisting stitch or a left-twisting stitch, depending on the look you want to achieve.

When working a make 1, you create a new stitch by using the horizontal strand of yarn that connects the stitches on the left and right needles. You can clearly see this strand if you gently pull the needles away from each other.

In patterns, the standard abbreviation for a make 1 increase is **m1**.

WORK A MAKE 1 THAT TWISTS TO THE RIGHT

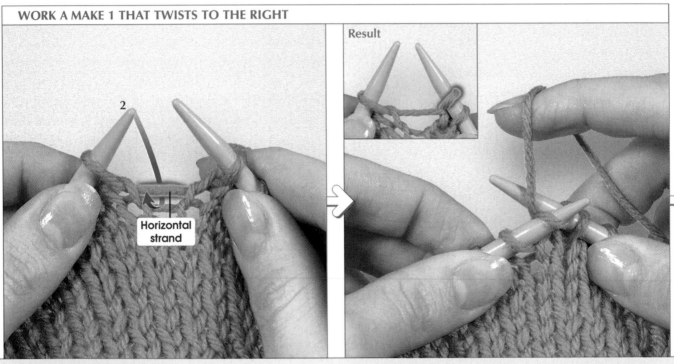

Result

Horizontal strand

1 Work to where you want to increase by one stitch.

2 Place the tip of the left needle under the horizontal strand of yarn that connects the stitches on both needles, from back to front.

- The strand of yarn creates a loop on the left needle.

3 Insert the tip of the right needle into the front of the loop, knitwise from left to right. Then knit the loop as you would knit a stitch.

- A new stitch is created on the right needle. You have increased the number of stitches by one.

How do I work a make 1 that twists to the right when working with purl stitches?

Place the tip of the left needle under the horizontal strand of yarn that connects the stitches on both needles, from back to front. The strand of yarn creates a loop on the left needle. Insert the tip of the right needle into the front of the loop, purlwise from right to left. Then purl the loop as you would purl a stitch.

How do I work a make 1 that twists to the left when working with purl stitches?

Place the tip of the left needle under the horizontal strand of yarn that connects the stitches on both needles, from front to back. The strand of yarn creates a loop on the left needle. Insert the tip of the right needle into the back of the loop, moving the needle through the loop from back to front. Then purl the loop as you would purl a stitch.

WORK A MAKE 1 THAT TWISTS TO THE LEFT

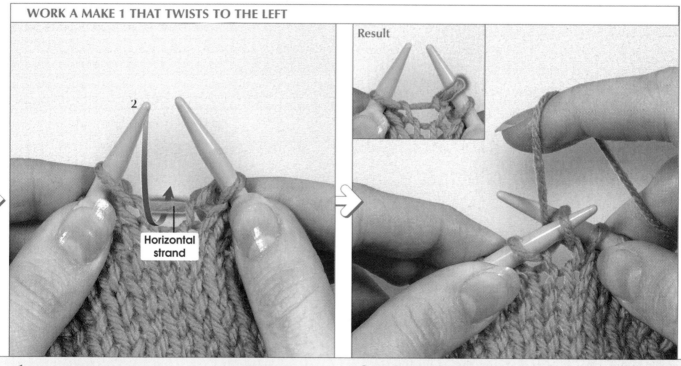

Horizontal strand

Result

1 Work to where you want to increase by one stitch.

2 Place the tip of the left needle under the horizontal strand of yarn that connects the stitches on both needles, from front to back.

• The strand of yarn creates a loop on the left needle.

3 Insert the tip of the right needle into the back of the loop, from right to left. Then knit the loop as you would knit a stitch.

• A new stitch is created on the right needle. You have increased the number of stitches by one.

CONTINUED...

Make a Yarn Over

A yarn over is a method of increasing one stitch that leaves a small, decorative hole, called an eyelet, in your work. The hole becomes more noticeable once you work the next row of stitches.

The yarn over method is often used for increasing stitches when working with lacy patterns to create delicate, decorative fabrics. You should not use the yarn over method for increasing stitches unless your project pattern specifies this method.

The yarn over method has several variations. The variation you should use depends on the type of stitch that is before and after the yarn over. For example, to increase one stitch between two knit stitches, you can use the standard yarn over (**yo**) variation, which is the most common variation, or the yarn forward (**yf** or **yfwd**) variation. If your pattern instructions specify that you should use a specific method to make a yarn over, you should follow the instructions provided in the pattern.

YARN OVER (YO)

- You make a yarn over between two knit stitches.

1 Work to where you want to increase by one stitch.

2 Wrap the yarn around the tip of the right needle once, counterclockwise from back to front.

3 Knit the next stitch on the left needle.

- You have increased the number of stitches on the right needle by one.

YARN FORWARD (YF or YFWD)

- You make a yarn forward between two knit stitches.

1 Work to where you want to increase by one stitch.

2 Bring the yarn between the needles to the front of your work.

3 Knit the next stitch on the left needle, keeping the yarn at the front of your work.

- You have increased the number of stitches on the right needle by one.

How do I make a yarn over at the beginning of a row?

Before a knit stitch, bring the yarn between your needles to the front of your work. Then knit the first stitch on the left needle, keeping the yarn at the front of your work.

Before a purl stitch, bring the yarn between your needles to the front of your work. Wrap the yarn around the right needle once, counterclockwise from front to back. Purl the first stitch on the left needle.

How can I make a larger hole in my knitted fabric?

You can make a larger hole in your fabric by wrapping the yarn around the right needle more than once. The more times you wrap the yarn around the needle, the larger the hole will be. When making a yarn over (**yo**) or a yarn round needle (**yfrn** or **yrn**), wrap the yarn around the right needle more than once. When making a yarn forward (**yf** or **yfwd**) or a yarn over needle (**yon**), wrap the yarn around the right needle more than once when knitting the next stitch on the left needle.

YARN ROUND NEEDLE (YFRN or YRN)

YARN OVER NEEDLE (YON)

- You make a yarn round needle between a knit and a purl stitch or two purl stitches.

1 Work to where you want to increase by one stitch.

2 Bring the yarn between the needles to the front of your work.

3 Wrap the yarn around the tip of the right needle once, counterclockwise from front to back.

4 Purl the next stitch on the left needle.

- You have increased the number of stitches on the right needle by one.

- You make a yarn over needle between a purl and a knit stitch.

1 Work to where you want to increase by one stitch.

2 Keep the yarn at the front of your work.

3 Knit the next stitch on the left needle, keeping the yarn at the front of your work.

- You have increased the number of stitches on the right needle by one.

increase
multiple stitches

When adding several stitches in one place in your work, you should use the cable cast on method for the best results. Using this method, you introduce new stitches to your work by knitting additional stitches onto your needle. Unlike the cast on methods learned in the Knitting Basics chapter, the cable cast on method requires the use of two needles.

You normally use the cable cast on method to increase stitches at the edge of your work.

For example, you can use the cable cast on method to increase stitches when working on a sleeve of a sweater.

The stitches you add may appear uneven at first, but the yarn should shift and equalize the stitches for you once you complete the following row of stitches. You can also gently stretch out the edges of your work once you are done knitting to make the stitches appear more even.

1 Work to where you want to increase the number of stitches in your project.

2 Insert the tip of the right needle between the first two stitches on the left needle, from front to back.

3 Wrap the yarn around the tip of the right needle, counterclockwise from back to front.

4 Slide the tip of the right needle and the strand of yarn back between the stitches toward you.

QUESTION & ANSWER

Can I use the cable cast on method to put stitches on my needle when starting a project?

Yes. In addition to using the cable cast on method to increase stitches while working on a project, you can also use the method to start your projects. To create the first stitch, make a slip knot on the needle in your left hand as shown on page 40. Knit the stitch as you normally would, but do not slide the original stitch off the left needle. Slip the loop of yarn from the right needle onto the tip of the left needle and remove the right needle from the loop. Then perform steps **2** to **5** below for each stitch you want to put on your needle.

Are there other cast on methods I can use to increase the number of stitches?

Yes. You can also use the single cast on method as shown in steps **3** to **6** on page 41 to increase the number of stitches on your left needle. However, the single cast on method does not create as neat an edge as the cable cast on method.

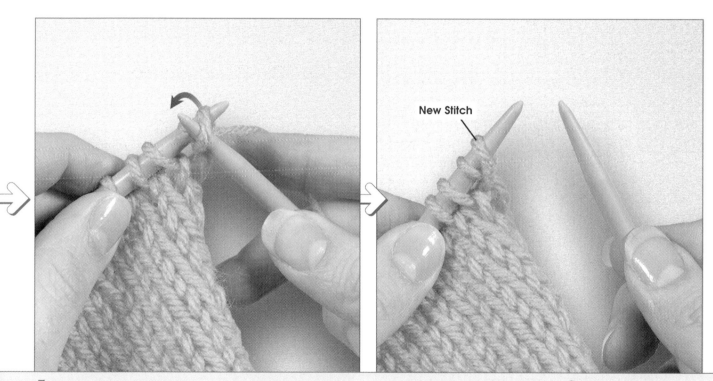

5 Slip the loop of yarn from the right needle onto the tip of the left needle and remove the right needle from the loop.

• You have now created a new stitch in front of the first stitch on the left needle.

6 Repeat steps **2** to **5** for each new stitch you want to add.

New Stitch

decrease one stitch

When you decrease one stitch, the number of stitches in the piece becomes fewer, making your work narrower. For example, when knitting a sweater, you create the curve of an armhole or neckline by decreasing stitches.

There are several popular techniques for decreasing one stitch in your knitting. Each technique has a particular use and creates a specific look in your knitted piece. In patterns, the standard abbreviation for a decrease is **dec**.

Knitting two stitches together (abbreviated as **k2tog**) produces stitches that slant to the right and is the easiest and most popular technique for decreasing

stitches. In most cases, when you knit two stitches together, you knit through the front loops of the stitches, as you would when knitting a single stitch. Knitting two stitches together is often done at the edge of a piece where it will be sewn to another piece.

You can also knit two stitches together through the back loop (abbreviated as **k2tog tbl**) to produce stitches that slant to the left. This method twists the stitches, creating an attractive design.

KNIT TWO STITCHES TOGETHER

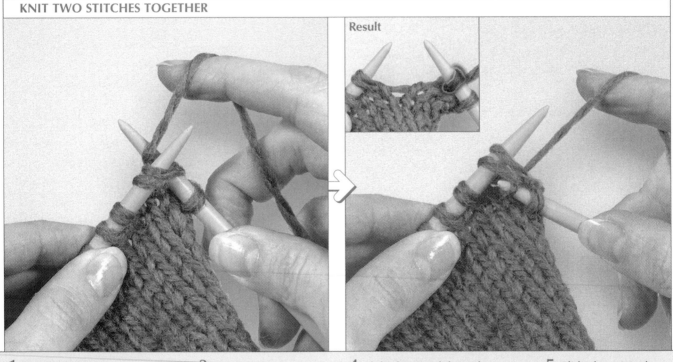

Result

1 Work to where you want to decrease by one stitch.

2 Insert the tip of the right needle into the front of the first two stitches on the left needle, knitwise from left to right.

3 Wrap the yarn around the tip of the right needle once, counterclockwise from back to front.

4 Slide the tip of the right needle and the wrapped yarn back through both stitches toward you.

5 Slide the original stitches off the left needle.

• The two stitches become one stitch on the right needle.

QUESTION & ANSWER

How do I purl two stitches together (p2tog)?

To purl stitches together, insert the right needle into the front of the first two stitches on the left needle, purlwise from right to left. Wrap the yarn around the right needle counterclockwise from back to front and then slide the tip of the right needle and the wrapped yarn back through both stitches away from you. Slide the original stitches off the left needle. This technique produces a decrease that slants to the right.

How do I purl two stitches together through the back loop (p2tog tbl)?

To make a left-slanting decrease when working with purl stitches, insert the right needle into the back of the first two stitches on the left needle, from left to right. Wrap the yarn around the right needle counterclockwise from back to front and then slide the tip of the right needle and the wrapped yarn back through both stitches away from you. Slide the original stitches off the left needle.

KNIT TWO STITCHES TOGETHER THROUGH BACK LOOP

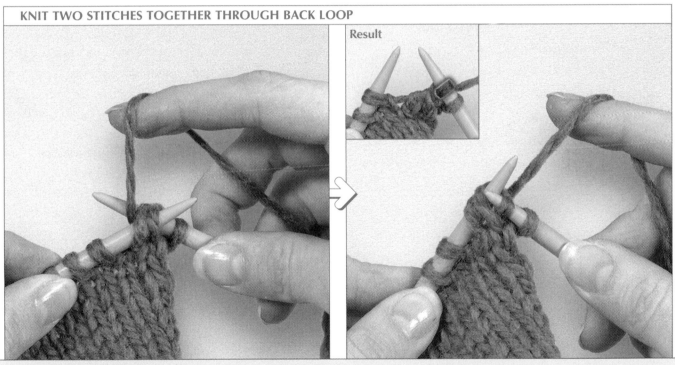

Result

1 Work to where you want to decrease by one stitch.

2 Insert the tip of the right needle into the back of the first two stitches on the left needle, from right to left.

3 Wrap the yarn around the tip of the right needle once, counterclockwise from back to front.

4 Slide the tip of the right needle and the wrapped yarn back through both stitches toward you.

5 Slide the original stitches off the left needle.

• The two stitches become one stitch on the right needle.

CONTINUED...

decrease one stitch

Slip Slip Knit

The slip slip knit technique (abbreviated as **ssk**) is another popular method for decreasing one stitch. The slip slip knit technique slants stitches to the left.

This method of decreasing involves slipping two stitches knitwise from the left needle to the right needle and then knitting the two slipped stitches together as a single stitch, which results in a decrease of one stitch.

Decreasing a stitch using the slip slip knit technique is normally performed on the knit side, or right side, of the work.

You can use the slip slip knit technique to add a decorative touch to your work. By placing the decreases in a visible location, such as two or three stitches from an edge of a sleeve where it will meet the body of a sweater, you will produce a decorative style referred to as "full-fashioning."

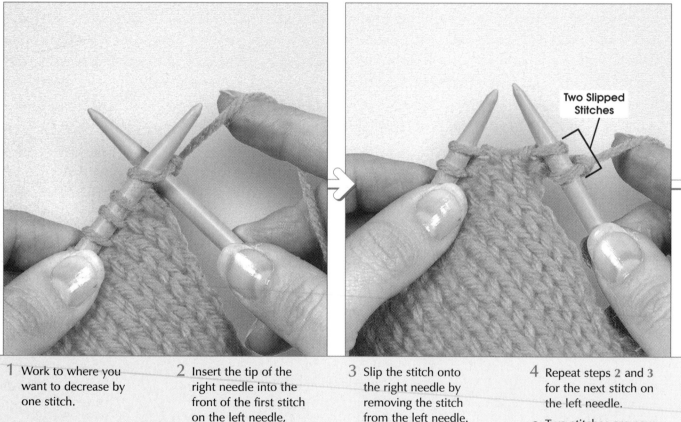

Two Slipped Stitches

1 Work to where you want to decrease by one stitch.

2 Insert the tip of the right needle into the front of the first stitch on the left needle, knitwise from left to right.

3 Slip the stitch onto the right needle by removing the stitch from the left needle.

4 Repeat steps **2** and **3** for the next stitch on the left needle.

• Two stitches are now slipped onto the right needle.

Would I use different decrease techniques in the same project?

Yes. Often you will need to use different decrease techniques in different locations in your work. For example, to decrease stitches at the right edge of a sweater, you can use the slip slip knit technique at the beginning of every knitted row. To decrease stitches at the left edge of a sweater, you can use the knit two stitches together technique at the end of every knitted row. For more information on the knit two stitches together technique, see page 88.

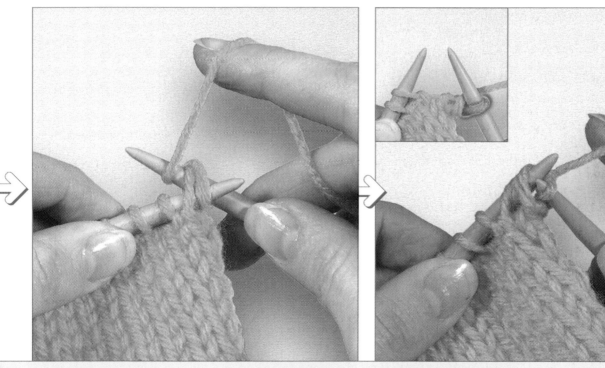

5 Insert the tip of the left needle into the front of both slipped stitches, from left to right.

6 Wrap the yarn around the tip of the right needle once, counterclockwise from back to front.

7 Slide the tip of the right needle and the wrapped yarn back through both stitches toward you.

• One stitch is created from the two slipped stitches.

CONTINUED...

decrease one stitch
(continued)

Slip One, Knit One, Pass Slipped Stitch Over

The slip one, knit one, pass slipped stitch over technique is a method of decreasing that slants stitches to the left. This technique involves slipping one stitch from the left needle to the right, then knitting the next stitch on the left needle. With both the slipped stitch and the knitted stitch on the right needle, the slipped stitch is then lifted over the knitted stitch and dropped off both needles. This causes the slipped stitch to bind around the knitted stitch, decreasing the row by one stitch.

The effect created by this technique is ideal for decorating the knit side of the work and is often used in lace patterns. For information on knitting lace, see page 128.

Decreasing a stitch using the slip one, knit one, pass slipped stitch over technique is normally performed on the knit side, or right side, of the work.

The slip one, knit one, pass slipped stitch over technique is usually abbreviated as **SKP** or **skpo**, but you may also see the technique abbreviated as **sl1, k1, psso**.

Knitted Stitch
Slipped Stitch

1 Work to where you want to decrease by one stitch.

2 Insert the tip of the right needle into the front of the first stitch on the left needle, knitwise from left to right.

3 Slip the stitch onto the right needle by removing the stitch from the left needle.

4 Knit the next stitch on the left needle.

I find the slip one, knit one, pass slipped stitch over technique difficult to perform. What can I do?

If a pattern instructs you to perform the slip one, knit one, pass slipped stitch over technique to decrease a stitch, you can use the slip slip knit technique as shown on page 90 instead. Both techniques produce the same effect, but many people find the slip slip knit technique easier.

Where should I decrease stitches in my work?

Where you should decrease stitches depends on the effect you want to create for your knitted piece. Decreasing stitches at the same end of every other row slants the edge of your work, while decreasing stitches in the middle of your work can produce subtle, decorative details in your projects. If you are following a pattern, the pattern instructions will tell you exactly where to decrease stitches in your project.

5 Insert the tip of the left needle into the front of the stitch you slipped onto the right needle, from left to right.

6 Lift the slipped stitch over the stitch you knitted and allow the slipped stitch to drop off both needles.

• One stitch is decreased.

decrease
two stitches

You can decrease two stitches at the same time using the double decrease technique. The double decrease technique creates slanting stitches that can give your work a certain look. This technique can also be used to shape parts of your work, such as the sleeves of a sweater.

There are two ways to make a double decrease. A left-slanting double decrease slants the stitches to the left on the knit side of your work. To perform a left-slanting double decrease, you will need to slip a

stitch as well as knit two stitches together. A right-slanting double decrease slants the stitches to the right on the knit side of your work. For a right-slanting double decrease, you knit three stitches together.

When needed, most patterns will give detailed instructions on how to make a double decrease. A left-slanting double decrease is sometimes shown in patterns as **sl1 k2tog psso**. A right-slanting double decrease is sometimes shown in patterns as **k3tog**.

MAKE A LEFT-SLANTING DOUBLE DECREASE

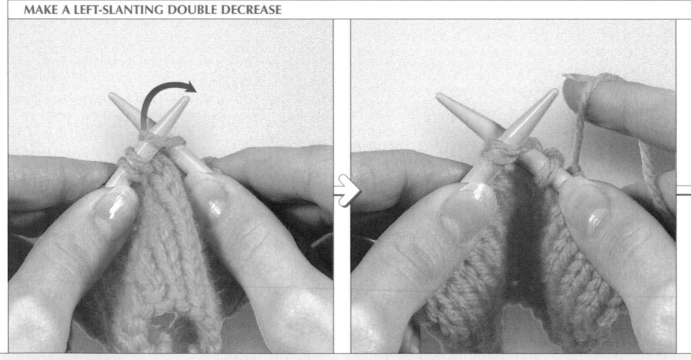

1 Work to where you want to decrease by two stitches.

2 Insert the tip of the right needle into the front of the first stitch on the left needle, knitwise from left to right.

3 Slip the stitch onto the right needle by removing the stitch from the left needle.

4 To knit the next two stitches together, insert the tip of the right needle into the front of the first two stitches on the left needle, knitwise from left to right. Then complete the knit stitch as you would any knit stitch.

● The two stitches become one stitch on the right needle.

Can I decrease two stitches without slanting stitches to the left or right?

Yes. You can make a vertical double decrease to create a vertical line in your fabric. Insert the right needle into the front of the first two stitches on the left needle, knitwise from left to right. Then slip the two stitches onto the right needle. Knit the next stitch on the left needle. Then use the left needle to lift the two slipped stitches over the knitted stitch and allow the slipped stitches to fall off both needles. This is sometimes shown in pattern instructions as **sl2tog k1 p2sso**.

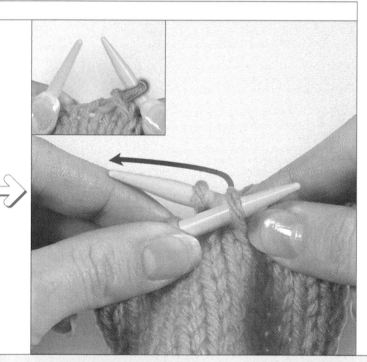

5 Insert the tip of the left needle into the front of the stitch you slipped onto the right needle in step 3, from left to right.

6 Lift the slipped stitch over the stitches you knitted together in step 4. Allow the slipped stitch to drop off both needles.

• The three stitches you worked with on the left needle become one stitch on the right needle. You have decreased the number of stitches by two.

MAKE A RIGHT-SLANTING DOUBLE DECREASE

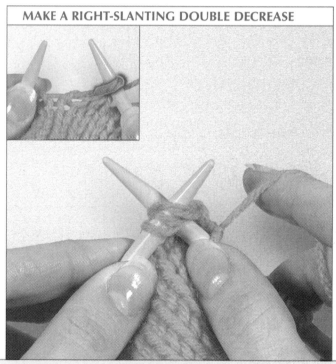

1 Work to where you want to decrease by two stitches.

2 To knit the next three stitches together, insert the tip of the right needle into the front of the first three stitches on the left needle, knitwise from left to right. Then complete the knit stitch as you would any knit stitch.

• The three stitches become one stitch on the right needle. You have decreased the number of stitches by two.

shape your work with short rows

Creating short rows allows you to curve or taper areas of your project without increasing or decreasing stitches. You can create a series of short rows to shape areas such as the collar of a sweater and the heel of a sock. Creating short rows is often referred to as partial knitting.

When creating short rows, you work across part of a row, then turn your work around and work back the way you came from. Before you turn your work, you wrap yarn around the base of a stitch to avoid leaving a hole in your work.

To create an even curve in your project, you need to create short rows at regular intervals. For example, if you started with 24 stitches, you might create the first short row at 18 stitches, the next short row at 12 stitches and the final short row at 6 stitches.

You normally work in short rows on the right side of your project. Most patterns provide detailed instructions for working short rows.

1 With the right side of your work facing you, knit to where you want to create a short row.

2 To slip the next stitch onto the right needle, insert the tip of the right needle into the front of the first stitch on the left needle, purlwise from right to left.

3 Slip the stitch onto the right needle by removing the stitch from the left needle.

4 Move the yarn between your needles to the front of your work.

5 Insert the tip of the left needle into the front of the stitch you slipped onto the right needle in step 3, from left to right.

6 Slip the stitch back onto the left needle by removing the stitch from the right needle.

After I finish creating short rows, is there anything else I need to do?

Yes. Each time you create a short row, the stitch where you started creating the short row will have yarn wrapped around it. You must hide all the wrapped yarn so the wraps do not show in your project. Perform the following steps in the first full row you work above your short rows.

Wrapped yarn

1 With the right side of your work facing you, knit to the first location where you created a short row. The next stitch on the left needle will have yarn wrapped around it.

2 Insert the right needle into the wrapped yarn from bottom to top. Then knit the next stitch and wrapped yarn together as a single stitch.

3 Continue knitting to the end of the row, repeating step 2 each time you reach the location where you created a short row.

7 Move the yarn between your needles to the back of your work.

8 Turn your work around so the wrong side of your work is facing you and then purl to the end of the row.

9 Repeat steps 1 to 8 for each short row you want to create.

Note: In this example, we create three short rows—the first short row at 12 stitches, the second short row at 8 stitches and the third short row at 4 stitches.

● After creating all the short rows, see the top of this page to work the next row.

striped hat

· *Easy Project* ·

Striped Hat

Sizes

Small	15 ins (38cm)
Medium	18.25 ins (46.5cm)
Large	21.5 ins (54.5cm)

Materials

Dale of Norway Free Style (50g)
Small:
MC (Main Color) = #2106 Yellow, 2 balls
Contrast A = #2427 Gold, 2 balls

Medium:
MC (Main Color) = #4114 Pink, 2 balls
Contrast A = #4417 Fushia, 2 balls

Large:
MC (Main Color) = #5444 Periwinkle, 2 balls
Contrast A = #5703 Light Blue, 2 balls

Size 8US (5mm) knitting needles or size needed
to obtain gauge.

Gauge

17 stitches (sts) and 24 rows = 4 ins (10cm) in
Stockinette St (knit 1 row, purl 1 row).

Instructions

Abbreviations: RS = right side; WS = wrong side;
K= knit; P = purl; K2tog = knit 2 stitches together.

Bracketed numbers are for sizes S (**M**-L).

With MC, cast on 64 (**78**-92) stitches.

Work 6 rows of Stockinette St (knit 1 row,
purl 1 row) in MC.
Work 6 rows of Stockinette St in A.
Repeat last 12 rows until work **from rolled edge**
measures 3 (**4**-4.5) ins [7.5 (**10**-11.5) cm], ending
with a RS facing for next row.

Dec row:

Row 1: K1. *K2tog. K7 (**9**-11); Rep from * to end
of row. 57 (**71**-85) sts.

Row 2: Purl.

Row 3: K1. *K2tog. K6 (**8**-10); Rep from * to end
of row. 50 (**64**-78) sts.

Row 4: Purl.

Row 5: K1. *K2tog. K5 (**7**-9); Rep from * to end
of row. 43 (**57**-71) sts.
Continue in this manner dec 7 sts evenly across
rows until there are 15 sts.

Next: Cut yarn leaving a long end.
Draw end through remaining sts,
tighten and secure. Sew
seam, reversing seam
at rolled edge.

simple summer
tank top

· *Intermediate Project* ·

Simple Summer Tank Top

Sizes

Bust measurement
Small   32 ins (81cm)
Medium   34 ins (86cm)
Large   36 ins (91.5cm)
X-Large   38 ins (97cm)

Finished bust
Small   33.5 ins (85cm)
Medium   35.5 ins (90cm)
Large   36.5 ins (92.5cm)
X-Large   39 ins (99cm)

Materials

Classic Elite Premiere 50g, #5268 Au Lait

Sizes	S	M	L	XL	
	5	5	6	6	hanks

Sizes 4 US (3.5mm) and 6 US (4mm) knitting needles and a set of four size 4 US (3.5mm) double-pointed needles (dpn) or size needed to obtain gauge.

Two stitch holders.

Gauge

21 stitches (sts) and 27 rows = 4 ins (10cm) in Stockinette St (knit 1 row, purl 1 row) using larger needles.

Stitch Glossary

Abbreviations: K = knit; P = purl; RS = right side; WS = wrong side; inc = increase; dec = decrease; Sl1P = slip one st purlwise; psso = pass slipped st over; K2tog = knit two sts together; P2tog = purl two sts together.

Instructions

Bracketed numbers are for sizes S (**M**-L-**XL**).

Back

With smaller needles, cast on 87 (93**-93-**99**) sts.

Row 1: K3. *P3. K3; Rep from * to end of row.

Row 2: P3. *K3. P3; Rep from * to end of row.

These two rows form (K3.P3) ribbing.

Continue in ribbing for 1.5 ins [4cm], ending with RS facing for next row, and inc 1 (**1**-3-**3**) sts evenly across last row. 88 (**94**-96-**102**) sts.

Change to larger needles and work in Stockinette St (knit 1 row, purl 1 row) until work from beginning measures 4.5 ins [11.5cm], ending with RS facing for next row.

Shaping:
Dec row: K1. Sl1P. K1. psso. K to last 3 sts, K2tog. K1.

Continue to dec 1 st at each side every alternate row 4 times more. 78 (**84**-86-**92**) sts. Work even in Stockinette St for 4.5 ins [11.5cm] or until work from beginning measures 9 ins [23cm], ending with RS facing for next row.

Note: You can adjust the number of rows you work in Stockinette St to suit your size.

Inc Row: Inc 1 st at each side every alternate row 5 times. 88 (**94**-96-**102**) sts.

Continue even in Stockinette St until work from beginning measures 14 (**15**-15.5-**16**) ins [35.5 (**38**-39.5-**40.5**) cm], ending with RS facing for next row.

simple summer
tank top

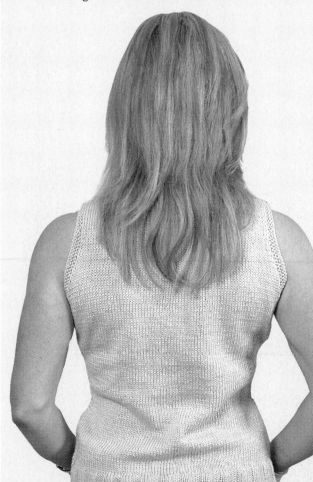

Back (cont.)

Armhole shaping:
Bind off 3 sts beginning next 2 rows and dec 1 st each end of needle on every following 9 (**12**-11-**14**) alternate rows. 64 (**64**-68-**68**) sts. **

Continue even in pattern until armhole measures 7 (**7.25**-7.5-**7.75**) ins [18 (**18.5**-19-**19.5**) cm], ending with RS facing for next row.

Shoulder shaping:
Bind off 5 (**5**-6-**6**) sts beginning next 4 rows. Place remaining 44 sts on a stitch holder.

Front

Work from ** to ** as given for Back.
Continue even in Stockinette St until armhole measures 4 (**4**-4.25-**4.5**) ins [10 (**10**-11-**11.5**) cm], ending with RS facing for next row.

Neck shaping:
Next row (RS): K25 (**25**-27-**27**). **Turn**. Leave remaining sts on a spare needle.

Next row: P2tog. Purl to end of row.

Next row: Knit to last 2 sts, K2tog.

Next row: P2tog. Purl to end of row.

Rep last 2 rows 6 times more. 10 (**10**-12-**12**) sts.

Continue even until armhole measures 7 (**7.25**-7.5-**7.75**) ins [18 (**18.5**-19-**19.5**) cm], ending with RS facing for next row.

Shoulder shaping:
Bind off 5 (**5**-6-**6**) sts beginning next row.
Work 1 row even.

Bind off remaining sts.

With RS facing, slip next 14 sts to a stitch holder. Join yarn to remaining sts and knit to end of row.

Next row: Purl to last 2 sts, P2tog.

Next row: K2tog. Knit to end of row.

Next row: Purl to last 2 sts, P2tog.

Rep last 2 rows 6 times. 10 (**10**-12-**12**) sts.

Continue even in pattern until armhole measures 7 (**7.25**-7.5-**7.75**) ins [18 (**18.5**-19-**19.5**) cm], ending with WS facing for next row.

Shoulder shaping:
Bind off 4 (**4**-5-**5**) sts beginning next row.
Work 1 row even.

Bind off remaining sts.

Finishing

Neckband:
Sew right shoulder seam. With RS facing and larger needles, pick up and knit 18 sts down left front neck edge. Knit across 14 sts on front neck stitch holder. Pick up and knit 18 sts up right front neck edge. Knit across 44 sts on back neck stitch holder, (dec 1 st at center back). 93 sts.

Work in (K3.P3) ribbing as given for Back starting on Row 2, for 2 ins [5cm], ending with RS facing for next row.

Bind off all sts loosely in ribbing.

Armbands:
With RS facing and double-pointed needles, pick up and knit 72 (**75-78-81**) sts evenly around armhole edge dividing sts evenly on 3 needles (24 (**25-26-27**) on each needle). Join in round and place a stitch marker on first st, proceed as follows:

Rnd 1: Purl.

Rnd 2: Knit.

Rep last 2 rnds once more.

Bind off all sts purlwise.

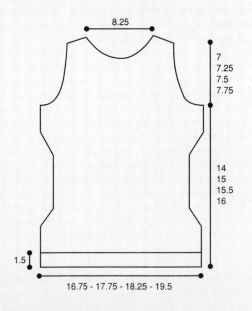

8.25

7
7.25
7.5
7.75

14
15
15.5
16

1.5

16.75 - 17.75 - 18.25 - 19.5

• Intermediate Project •

Baby Wonderful Outfit

Sizes

Chest measurements

6 mos 16 ins   (40.5cm)
12 mos 18 ins   (45.5cm)
18 mos 20 ins   (51cm)
2 yrs 22 ins   (56cm)

Finished chest

6 mos 21.5 ins   (54.5cm)
12 mos 25 ins   (63.5cm)
18 mos 26.5 ins   (67.5cm)
2 yrs 29.5 ins   (75cm)

Materials

Butterfly Super 10 by S. R. Kertzer (125g)

MC (Main Color) = Natural

Sizes	6mos	12mos	18mos	2yrs	
	1	2	2	3	hanks

Contrast A = #3728 Clover Green, 1 hank
Contrast B = #3606 Peridot, 1 hank

Sizes 6 US (4mm) and 7 US (4.5mm) knitting needles and two size 7 US (4.5mm) double-pointed needles (dpn) or size needed to obtain gauge.

8 buttons.

Stitch holder.

One yard (.95m) of 1 inch (2.5cm) wide elastic.

Gauge

20 stitches (sts) and 26 rows = 4 ins (10cm) in Stockinette St (knit 1 row, purl 1 row) using larger needles.

Stitch Glossary

Abbreviations:
K = knit; P = purl; RS = right side; WS = wrong side; dec = decrease; inc = increase; Sl1K = slip one st knitwise; Sl1P = slip one st purlwise; Sl1PB = slip slipped st back to left hand needle; yf = move yarn to front of work; yb = move yarn to back of work; K2tog = knit 2 sts together; P2tog = purl 2 sts together.

Instructions

Bracketed numbers are for sizes 6mos (**12mos**-18mos-**2yrs**).

Jacket: Back

With smaller needles and MC, cast on 54 (**62**-**66**-**74**) sts.

Row 1: P2. *K2. P2; Rep from * to end of row.

Row 2: K2. *P2. K2; Rep from * to end of row.

These 2 rows form (K2. P2) ribbing.

Continue in ribbing for .75 ins [2cm], ending with RS facing for next row.

Change to larger needles and work in Stockinette St (knit 1 row, purl 1 row) until work from beginning measures 2.5 (2.75**-3.25-**4.25**) ins [6 (**7**-8.5-**11**) cm], ending with RS facing for next row.

Next: Work 2 rows in A.

Next: Work 2 rows in MC.

Next: Work 2 rows in B.**

With MC, continue even in Stockinette St until work from beginning measures 10 (**10.5**-11.5-**13**) ins [25.5 (**26.5**-29-**33**) cm], ending with RS facing for next row.

Shoulder shaping: Bind off 6 (**8**-9-**10**) sts beginning next 2 rows, then bind off 7 (**8**-9-**11**) sts beginning following 2 rows. Leave remaining 28 (**30**-30-**32**) sts on a stitch holder.

Jacket: Left Front

*** With smaller needles and MC, cast on
26 (**30**-34-**38**) sts.

Row 1: P2. *K2. P2; Rep from * to end of row.

Row 2: K2. *P2. K2; Rep from * to end of row.

These 2 rows form (K2. P2) ribbing.

Continue in ribbing for .75 ins [2cm], ending with
RS facing for next row, and dec 0 (**2**-2-**2**) sts evenly
across last row. 26 (**28**-32-**36**) sts.

Work from ** to ** as given for Jacket: Back. ***

With MC, continue even in Stockinette St until
work from beginning measures 8.75 (**9**-9.75-**11**) ins
[22 (**23**-25-**28**) cm], ending with WS facing for
next row.

Neck shaping: Bind off 5 sts beginning next row.
Work to end of needle. Dec 1 st at neckline next
8 (**7**-9-**10**) rows. 13 (**16**-18-**21**) sts.

Continue in Stockinette St until work from beginning
measures 10 (**10.5**-11.5-**13**) ins [25.5 (**26.5**-29-**33**) cm]
ending with RS facing for next row.

Shoulder shaping: Bind off 6 (**8**-9-**10**) sts beginning
next row. Work 1 row even. Bind off remaining
7 (**8**-9-**11**) sts.

Jacket: Right Front

Work from *** to *** as given for Jacket: Left Front.

With MC, continue even in Stockinette St until
work from beginning measures 8.75 (**9**-9.75-**11**) ins
[22 (**23**-25-**28**) cm] ending with RS facing for next
row.

Neck shaping: Bind off 5 sts beginning next row.
Work to end of needle. Dec 1 st at neckline next
8 (**7**-9-**10**) rows. 13 (**16**-18-**21**) sts.

Continue in Stockinette St until work from beginning
measures 10 (**10.5**-11.5-**13**) ins [25.5 (**26.5**-29-**33**) cm]
ending with WS facing for next row.

Shoulder shaping: Bind off 6 (**8**-9-**10**) sts
beginning next row. Work 1 row even.
Bind off remaining 7 (**8**-9-**11**) sts.

Jacket: Sleeves

With smaller needles and MC, cast on 30 (**30**-34-**34**) sts.

Work .75 ins [2cm] in (K2. P2) ribbing as given for Jacket: Back. Change to larger needles.

Continue in Stockinette St and inc 1 st each end of needle on 3rd and every 4th (**alt**-alt-**alt**) row 5 (**6**-2-**6**) times to 42 (**44**-40-**48**) sts.

AT THE SAME TIME, work 2 rows of B on Left Sleeve and 2 rows of A on Right Sleeve, 2.5 ins [6cm] from beginning.

Sizes 12mos, 18mos and 2yrs only: Then inc 1 st each end of needle on every (**4th**-4th-**4th**) row to (**50**-52-**58**) sts.

All sizes: Continue in Stockinette St until work from beginning measures 5 (**5.5**-6.25-**7**) ins [12.5 (**14**-16-**18**) cm], ending with RS facing for next row. Bind off all sts.

Jacket: Finishing

Buttonhole Band:
With smaller needles, MC and RS of work facing, pick up and knit 58 (**62**-66-**70**) sts, along Left Front. Work 3 rows (K2. P2) ribbing as given for Jacket: Back.

Next row (RS): Work 4 (**4**-5-**4**) sts in ribbing. * Bind off 2 sts. Work 14 (**15**-16-**18**) sts in ribbing. Rep from * 2 more times. Bind off 2 sts. Work in ribbing to end of row.

Next row: Work in ribbing, casting on 2 sts over bound off sts.

Work 2 rows in ribbing.

Button Band:
On Right Front, work as Buttonhole Band, omitting all reference to buttonholes.

Sew shoulder seams.

Jacket: Finishing (cont.)

Collar:

With MC and smaller needles, pick up and knit 16 (**17**-**20**-**21**) sts up right front neck edge, 28 (**30**-**30**-**32**) sts from back neck stitch holder, inc 14 (**18**-**16**-**16**) sts evenly across back neck, and 16 (**17**-**20**-**21**) sts down left front neck edge. 74 (**82**-**86**-**90**) sts.

Work in (K2. P2) ribbing for 3 ins [7.5cm].

Bind off in ribbing.

Place markers 4.75 (**5**-**5.25**-**5.75**) ins [12 (**12.5**-**13**-**14.5**) cm] down from shoulders. Sew in sleeves between markers. Sew side and sleeve seams. Sew buttons to correspond to buttonholes.

Shorts: Right Leg

(Starting at the waist)

With smaller needles and A, cast on 58 (62**-**62**-**70**) sts.

Work 2.25 ins [5.5cm] in (K2. P2) ribbing as given for Jacket: Back, ending with WS facing for next row and dec 0 (**2**-**0**-**2**) sts evenly across row. 58 (**60**-**62**-**68**) sts.

Change to larger needles. **

Shape Back:

Next 2 rows: P30. Sl1P. yb. Sl1PB. yf. **Turn**. Knit to end of row.

Next 2 rows: P25. Sl1P. yb. Sl1PB. yf. **Turn**. Knit to end of row.

Next 2 rows: P20. Sl1P. yb. Sl1PB. yf. **Turn**. Knit to end of row.

Next 2 rows: P15. Sl1P. yb. Sl1PB. yf. **Turn**. Knit to end of row.

Next 2 rows: P10. Sl1P. yb. Sl1PB. yf. **Turn**. Knit to end of row.

Next row: Purl across all sts.

Note: To avoid a hole, work to the wrapped st. Pick up the wrapped yarn from behind into back loop and place on left needle. Purl it together with slipped st above.

Shorts: Right Leg (cont.)

Continue in Stockinette St until work along longest edge measures 8 (**8.25**-8.5-**9.25**) ins [20.5 (**21**-21.5-**23.5**) cm], ending with RS facing for next row.

***Shape Crotch:** Inc 1 st each end of needle on next and following 0 (**0-1-1**) alt row. Cast on 2 sts beginning next 2 rows. 64 (**68-70-78**) sts. Work 2 rows Stockinette St.

Shape Inseam: Dec 1 st each end of needle on next and following alt rows to 56 (**58-58-62**) sts.

Continue even in Stockinette St until work from crotch measures 3 (**3.5-4-5**) ins [7.5 (**9-10-12.5**) cm] ending with RS facing for next row.

Work in (K2. P2) ribbing for .75 ins [2cm], ending with RS facing for next row.

Bind off all sts. ***

Shorts: Left Leg

(Starting at the waist)

Using B, work from ** to ** as given for Shorts: Right Leg, only end with a RS facing for next row.

Shape Back:

Next 2 rows: K30. Sl1P. yf. Sl1PB. yb.
Turn. Purl to end of row.

Next 2 rows: K25. Sl1P. yf. Sl1PB. yb.
Turn. Purl to end of row.

Next 2 rows: K20. Sl1P. yf. Sl1PB. yb.
Turn. Purl to end of row.

Next 2 rows: K15. Sl1P. yf. Sl1PB. yb.
Turn. Purl to end of row.

Next 2 rows: K10. Sl1P. yf. Sl1PB. yb.
Turn. Purl to end of row.

Next row: Knit across all sts.

Note: To avoid a hole, work to the wrapped st. Pick up the wrapped yarn from below and knit it together with slipped st above.

Shorts: Left Leg (cont.)

Continue in Stockinette St across all sts until work along longest edge measures 8 (**8.25**-8.5-**9.25**) ins [20.5 (**21**-21.5-**23.5**) cm], ending with RS facing for next row.

Work from *** to *** as given for Shorts: Right Leg.

Shorts: Finishing

Sew inseams. Sew crotch seam. Fold waistband to inside and sew into place leaving an opening for elastic. Cut and insert elastic to fit, sewing ends of elastic tog. Sew up opening.

Suspenders (optional)

(To measure 14.5 (**16**-16.5-**17.5**) ins [37 (**40.5**-42-**44.5**) cm] long)

***With smaller needles and A, cast on 74 (**78**-82-**86**) sts.

Work 3 rows (K2. P2) ribbing as given for Jacket: Back.

Next row: Work 2 sts in ribbing. Bind off 2 sts. Work in ribbing to last 4 sts. Bind off 2 sts. Work in ribbing to end of row.

Next row: Work in ribbing, casting on 2 sts over bound off sts.

Work another 3 rows in ribbing. Bind off all sts. ***

Repeat from *** to *** with B, for 2nd suspender.

Sew buttons on at waistband. Button on suspenders crossing over at Back.

Hat

6-18 mos 16.25 ins [41.5cm], (**18mos-2 yrs**) **18.25 ins** [**46.5cm**].

With smaller needles and MC, cast on 102 (**110**) sts.

Work 1 in [2.5cm] in (K2. P2) ribbing as given for Jacket: Back, ending with RS facing for next row. Change to larger needles.

Work 10 rows in MC, dec 21 (**19**) sts evenly across 1st row. 81 (**91**) sts.

Next: Work 2 rows in A.

Next: Work 2 rows in MC.

Next: Work 2 rows in B.

Using MC, work in Stockinette St until work from beginning measures 4 (**5**) ins [10 (**12.5**) cm], ending with RS facing for next row.

Hat (cont.)

Shape top:

Row 1: K1 *K2tog. K6 (**7**); Rep from * to end of row. 71 (**81**) sts.

Row 2 and alt rows: Purl.

Row 3: K1. *K2tog. K5 (**6**); Rep from * to end of row. 61 (**71**) sts.

Row 5: K1. *K2tog. K4 (**5**); Rep from * to end of row. 51 (**61**) sts.

Continue in this manner, dec 10 sts every row until 11 sts remaining.

Next row: P1. *P2tog; Rep from * to end of row. 6 sts.

Change to dpn and work I-cord as follows:

I-cord: *K6. Slide sts to other end of needle. K6; Rep from * until I-cord is 3 ins [7.5cm] long. Break yarn. Draw end through remaining sts and fasten. Tie single knot in I-cord loosely.

Sew back seam.

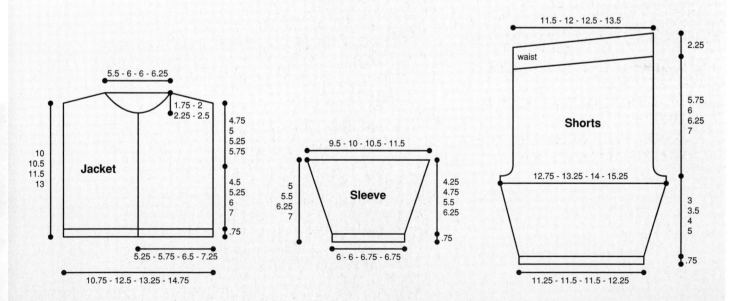

Chapter 4

After you become familiar with the basics of knitting, you can diversify your knitting repertoire by adding decorative touches to your projects. Adding ornamental elements to your projects gives them a more professional and polished look. In this chapter, you will learn how to knit with beads, create cable and lace designs and add decorative fringes, tassels and pompoms to your work.

Decorative Touches

In this Chapter...

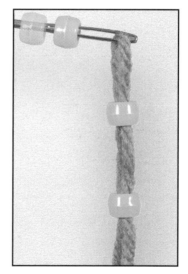

slip a stitch

Patterns may instruct you to slip a stitch, which simply means moving a stitch from the left needle to the right needle without knitting or purling the stitch. There are two ways you can slip a stitch—purlwise or knitwise. To slip a stitch purlwise, you insert the right needle into the front of the stitch as if you were going to purl the stitch (from right to left). To slip a stitch knitwise, you insert the right needle into the stitch as if you were going to knit the stitch (from left to right).

Patterns often use abbreviations for slipping a stitch (**sl st**) or more specifically, slipping a stitch purlwise

(**Sl1P**) and slipping a stitch knitwise (**Sl1K**). Some instructions may also use the phrases "slip stitch as if to purl" or "slip stitch as if to knit." If the instructions do not specify one way or the other, you should slip stitches purlwise to avoid twisting the stitches.

Slipping stitches is useful for creating different textured patterns.

SLIP A STITCH PURLWISE

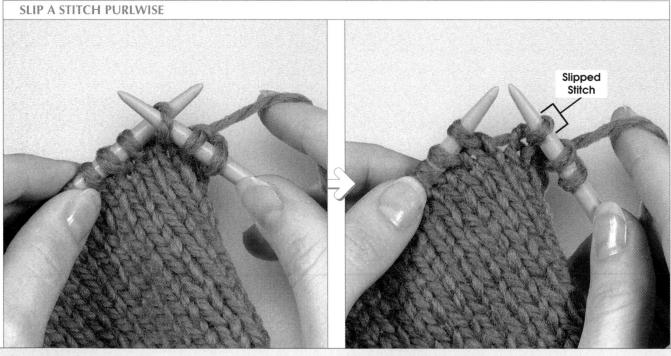

Slipped Stitch

1 Insert the tip of the right needle into the first stitch on the left needle purlwise, from right to left.

2 Slip the stitch onto the right needle by removing the stitch from the left needle.

Before slipping a stitch, where should I position the yarn I am working with?

Depending on the effect you want to create in your knitted fabric, you may need to position the yarn in front or at the back of your work before slipping a stitch. The pattern instructions may indicate where you should position the yarn. For example, the abbreviation **wyif** means "with yarn in front" and indicates that you should position the yarn in front of your work, as when purling, before slipping a stitch.

Similarly, the abbreviation **wyib** means "with yarn in back" and indicates that the yarn should be positioned at the back of your work, as when knitting.

SLIP A STITCH KNITWISE

Slipped Stitch

1 Insert the tip of the right needle into the first stitch on the left needle knitwise, from left to right.

2 Slip the stitch onto the right needle by removing the stitch from the left needle.

knit a stitch in the row below

Pattern instructions may require you to knit a stitch in the row below the row you are working on. Knitting a stitch in the row below will thicken your fabric in that location by doubling the strands of yarn at the base of the new stitch—one strand from the row below plus one strand from the row you are working on. You can knit several consecutive stitches in the row below to bulk up and add depth to your fabric, which can help enhance your project's visual appeal.

Pattern instructions abbreviate knitting a stitch in the row below as **k-b** or **k1b**. However, some patterns use the **k1b** abbreviation to mean "knit into the back of the next stitch," so you should double-check the pattern's stitch glossary to confirm the meaning of the abbreviation.

Step 2

1 Work to where you want to knit a stitch in the row below.

• The yarn should be toward the back of your work.

2 Insert the tip of the right needle through the middle of the stitch below the next stitch on the left needle, from front to back.

3 Wrap the yarn around the tip of the right needle, counterclockwise from back to front.

Would I ever need to knit a stitch in the row below on both the right and wrong sides of my work?

Knitting stitches in the row below on both sides of your work creates a thick, soft fabric. You can see a popular example of this effect in knitted fabrics made using the fisherman's rib pattern. The fisherman's rib pattern is a simple knit 1 purl 1 rib, but each knit stitch is knit in the row below instead of in the current row. This makes fisherman's rib deeper and softer than other kinds of ribbing.

New stitch

4 Slide the tip of the right needle and the wrapped yarn back through the stitch toward you.

5 Allow the stitch above the stitch you knitted to drop off the left needle.

• You have created a new stitch on the right needle.

twist stitches

Twisting to the Left

When you twist stitches, you cross one stitch over another stitch. You can create a series of twisted stitches to produce a cable-like pattern in your work. If you want to produce a cable-like pattern by crossing more than two stitches, you should use a cable needle as discussed on page 124.

You can twist stitches to the left when working on the knit side of your fabric. In pattern instructions, twisting stitches to the left is often abbreviated as **LT** (left twist) or **T2L** (twist to the left using two stitches).

Twisted stitches can pull your fabric together, making your knitted piece narrower than you expect. To make sure your project will be the correct width, you can make a gauge swatch of the twisted stitch design you will be using. To make and measure a gauge swatch, see page 62.

The method shown below is a popular method of twisting stitches to the left. If the pattern you are using provides instructions for another method, follow the instructions in the pattern.

1 Work to where you want to twist two stitches to the left.

2 Insert the tip of the right needle into the back of the second stitch on the left needle, from right to left.

3 Wrap the yarn around the tip of the right needle, counterclockwise from back to front.

4 Slide the tip of the right needle and the wrapped yarn back through the stitch. Leave the first and second stitches on the left needle.

What kind of design can I create by twisting stitches to the left?

You can create an attractive diagonal line that slopes to the left in your fabric. To create a left-sloping diagonal line, create a left twist one stitch farther to the left each time you work a row on the knit side of your fabric.

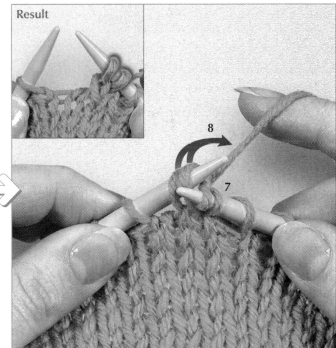

Result

5 Insert the tip of the right needle through the back of the first and second stitches on the left needle, from right to left.

6 Wrap the yarn around the tip of the right needle, counterclockwise from back to front.

7 Slide the tip of the right needle and the wrapped yarn back through the stitches toward you.

8 Slide the original two stitches off the left needle.

• You have created two new stitches that twist to the left on the right needle.

CONTINUED...

twist stitches
(continued)

Twisting to the Right

You can overlap two stitches in your work to twist the stitches. Twisting a series of stitches produces a cable-like pattern in your fabric.

You can twist stitches to the right when working on the knit side of your fabric. In pattern instructions, twisting stitches to the right is often abbreviated as **RT** (right twist). You may also see the abbreviation **T2R**, which stands for twisting two stitches to the right.

Twisted stitches can pull your fabric together, making your knitted piece narrower than you expect. To make

sure your project will be the correct width, you can make a gauge swatch of the twisted stitch design you will be using. To make and measure a gauge swatch, see page 62.

The method shown below is a popular method of twisting stitches to the right. If the pattern you are using provides instructions for another method, follow the instructions in the pattern.

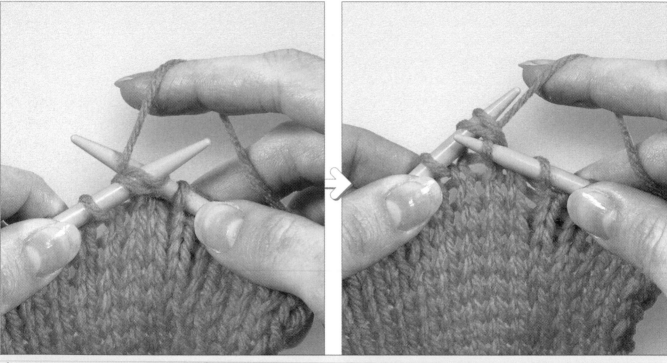

1 Work to where you want to twist two stitches to the right.

2 Insert the tip of the right needle into the front of the first and second stitches on the left needle, knitwise from left to right.

3 Wrap the yarn around the tip of the right needle, counterclockwise from back to front.

4 Slide the tip of the right needle and the wrapped yarn back through the stitches toward you. Leave the first and second stitches on the left needle.

What kind of design can I create by twisting stitches to the right?

You can create an attractive diagonal line that slopes to the right in your fabric. To create a right-sloping diagonal line, create a right twist one stitch closer to the right each time you work a row on the knit side of your fabric.

Result

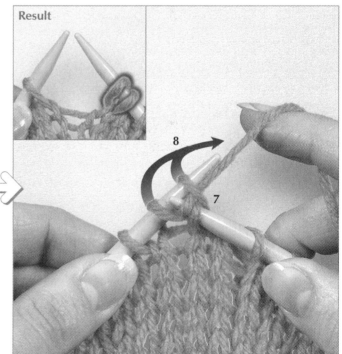

5 Insert the tip of the right needle into the front of the first stitch on the left needle, knitwise from left to right.

6 Wrap the yarn around the tip of the right needle, counterclockwise from back to front.

7 Slide the tip of the right needle and the wrapped yarn back through the stitch toward you.

8 Slide the original two stitches off the left needle.

• You have created two new stitches that twist to the left on the right needle.

decorative designs

Abbreviations used in decorative design patterns:

K2tog	Knit two stitches together. See page 88.
psso	Pass slipped stitch over.
SI	Slip a stitch. See page 114.
ssk	Slip slip knit. See page 90.

wyib	With yarn in back of work.
wyif	With yarn in front of work.
yo	Yarn over. See page 84.

Brick Stitch

INTERMEDIATE

Cast on a multiple of 4 stitches (4, 8, 12, etc.), plus 1 stitch.

Row 1 (RS): K4. *K1, winding yarn around needle twice. K3; Rep from * to last st, K1.

Row 2: P4. *Sl1 purlwise, dropping extra loop. P3; Rep from * to last st, P1.

Row 3: K4. *Sl1 purlwise. K3; Rep from * to last st, K1.

Row 4: K4. *Move yarn to front of work. Sl1 purlwise. Move yarn to back of work. K3; Rep from * to last st, K1.

Row 5: K2. *K1, winding yarn around needle twice. K3; Rep from * to last 3 sts, K1, winding yarn around needle twice. K2.

Row 6: P2. *Sl1 purlwise, dropping extra loop. P3; Rep from * to last 3 sts, Sl1 purlwise. P2.

Row 7: K2. *Sl1 purlwise. K3. Rep from * to last 3 sts, Sl1 purlwise. K2.

Row 8: K2. *Move yarn to front of work. Sl1 purlwise. Move yarn to back of work. K3; Rep from * to last 3 sts, move yarn to front of work. Sl1 purlwise. Move yarn to back of work. K2.

Rep Rows 1 to 8.

Baby Cable Ribbing

INTERMEDIATE

Cast on a multiple of 4 stitches (4, 8, 12, etc.), plus 2 stitches.

Row 1 (WS): K2. *P2. K2; Rep from * to end of row.

Row 2: P2. *K2. P2; Rep from * to end of row.

Row 3: As Row 1.

Row 4: P2. *K2tog, leaving on needles. Insert right needle between the 2 sts you just knitted together and knit the first st on left needle again. Then drop both stitches off needle. P2; Rep from * to end of row.

Rep Rows 1 to 4.

Quilted Lattice

ADVANCED

Cast on a multiple of 6 stitches (6, 12, 18, etc.), plus 3 stitches.

Row 1 and all wrong-side (WS) rows: Purl.

Row 2: K2. * Sl5 wyif. K1; Rep from * to last st, K1.

Row 4: K2. *Insert right needle under loose strand and knit the next stitch, bringing new stitch out from under strand. K5; Rep from * to last 4 sts, K4.

Row 6: K1. Sl3 wyif. *K1. Sl5 wyif; Rep from * to last 5 sts, K1. Sl3 wyif. K1.

Row 8: K1. *Insert right needle under loose strand and knit the next stitch, bringing new stitch out from under strand. K5; Rep from * to last st, K1.

Rep Rows 1 to 8.

Butterfly Stitch

ADVANCED

Cast on a multiple of 10 stitches (10, 20, 30, etc.), plus 9 stitches.

Rows 1, 3, 5, 7 and 9 (RS): K2. *Sl5 wyif. K5; Rep from * to last 7 sts, Sl5 wyif. K2.

Row 2, 4, 6 and 8: Purl.

Row 10: P4. *Insert right needle, from top to bottom, down through the 5 loose strands and slip them to the left needle. P5 strands and next stitch together to make one stitch. P9; Rep from * to last 4 sts, P4.

Row 11, 13, 15, 17 and 19: K7. *Sl5 wyif. K5. Rep from * to last 12 sts, Sl5 wyif. K7.

Row 12, 14, 16 and 18: Purl.

Row 20: P9. *Insert right needle, from top to bottom, down through the 5 loose strands and slip them to the left needle. P5 strands and next stitch together to make one stitch. P9. Rep from * to end of row.

Rep Rows 1 to 20.

create a cable

A cable is a set of stitches that cross in front or behind another set of stitches to form appealing designs in your fabric. Since the cable pattern is usually made up of knit stitches and the background is usually purl stitches, the cable really stands out in your work.

Cabling normally requires a cable needle, which is a small, double-pointed needle designed to hold stitches. When creating a simple cable design, the number of stitches you slip onto the cable needle represents half the width of the cable. For example, creating a cable that is six stitches wide (called a simple six-stitch cable) involves crossing three stitches on the cable needle with three stitches on the left needle.

There are many variations of cable designs that you can create. For example, you can create a cable that is two, four, six or more stitches wide or make the cable cross to the left or to the right. With the cable needle holding stitches in front of your work, the cable crosses to the left. With the cable needle holding stitches behind your work, the cable crosses to the right.

To repeat a cable design in your work, you cross a set of stitches at specific intervals. In other words, you create a cable, work a number of rows and then create a cable again.

- In this example, we make a simple six-stitch cable.

1 Work to where you want to make a cable.

2 Insert the tip of the cable needle into the front of the next stitch on the left needle, from right to left.

3 Slip the stitch onto the cable needle by removing the stitch from the left needle.

4 Repeat steps 2 and 3 for the next two stitches on the left needle.

5 Keep the cable needle at the front of your work.

- Make sure the stitches are in the center of the cable needle to help ensure they will not fall off the needle.

Do I have to knit from the cable needle when creating a cable?

No. When you are ready to knit the stitches on the cable needle, you can slip the stitches from the cable needle onto the left needle and knit them like regular stitches. This method takes longer, but is useful if you find it awkward to knit from the cable needle.

What do the cable abbreviations mean?

Cable instructions are often shown as abbreviations, such as **C4F** and **C4B**. "C" indicates that these are cable stitches. The number tells you how many stitches are involved. For example, if the number is 4, you cross two stitches on the cable needle with two stitches on the left needle. "F" or "B" means to hold the cable needle in front or back.

How do I create a cable that crosses to the right?

To create a cable that crosses to the right, perform steps **1** to **7** below, except keep the cable needle at the back of your work in step **5**.

Three knitted stitches

6 Using the right needle, knit the next three stitches on the left needle.

7 Using the right needle, knit the three stitches on the cable needle, beginning with the stitch at the right side of the cable needle.

- You have now created a cable.

- By keeping the cable needle at the front of your work, you have created a cable that crosses to the left.

cable
designs

To make the cable effect stand out, cable designs are often bordered on each side by purl stitches, also referred to as reverse stockinette stitch. The instructions for a cable panel specify how many stitches the cable design requires, including the purl stitches on each side of the cable.

Some cable designs are all-over patterns, which means you can repeat the design a number of times across your fabric to create an entire knitted piece. When the pattern instructions specify a multiple of a specific number of stitches, such as the Honeycomb Cable design on page 127, the design is an all-over pattern.

Abbreviations used in cable design patterns:

Sl	Slip a stitch. For more information, see page 114.
cn	Cable needle. For more information, see page 124.

Simple 4-Stitch Cable

Cast on 16 stitches.

Row 1 (WS): K6. P4. K6.

Row 2: P6. K4. P6.

Row 3: As Row 1.

Row 4: P6. Sl 2 sts to cn and hold in back of work, K2, K2 from cn (C4B). P6.

Rep Rows 1 to 4.

Note: To create the reverse of this cable pattern, hold the stitches on the cable needle in front of your work on Row 4 (C4F).

EASY

Braid Cable

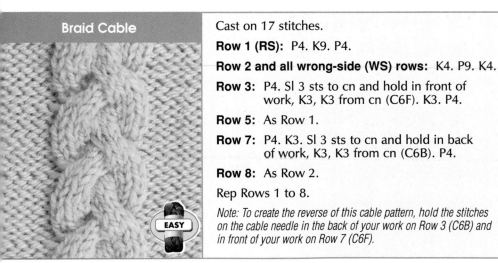

Cast on 17 stitches.

Row 1 (RS): P4. K9. P4.

Row 2 and all wrong-side (WS) rows: K4. P9. K4.

Row 3: P4. Sl 3 sts to cn and hold in front of work, K3, K3 from cn (C6F). K3. P4.

Row 5: As Row 1.

Row 7: P4. K3. Sl 3 sts to cn and hold in back of work, K3, K3 from cn (C6B). P4.

Row 8: As Row 2.

Rep Rows 1 to 8.

Note: To create the reverse of this cable pattern, hold the stitches on the cable needle in the back of your work on Row 3 (C6B) and in front of your work on Row 7 (C6F).

EASY

Staghorn Cable

Cast on 22 stitches.

Row 1 (RS): P3. K4. Sl 2 sts to cn and hold in back of work, K2, K2 from cn (C4B). Sl 2 sts to cn and hold in front of work, K2, K2 from cn (C4F). K4. P3.

Row 2 and all wrong-side (WS) rows: K3. P16. K3.

Row 3: P3. K2. Sl 2 sts to cn and hold in back of work, K2, K2 from cn (C4B). K4. Sl 2 sts to cn and hold in front of work, K2, K2 from cn (C4F). K2. P3.

Row 5: P3. Sl 2 sts to cn and hold in back of work, K2, K2 from cn (C4B). K8. Sl 2 sts to cn and hold in front of work, K2, K2 from cn (C4F). P3.

Row 6: As Row 2.

Rep Rows 1 to 6.

Honeycomb Cable

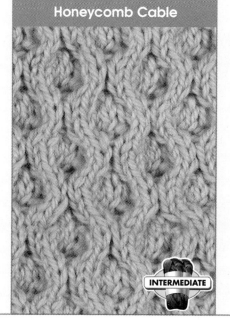

Cast on a multiple of 8 stitches (8, 16, 24, etc.).

Row 1 (RS): Knit.

Row 2 and all wrong-side (WS) rows: Purl.

Row 3: *Sl 2 sts to cn and hold in back of work, K2, K2 from cn (C4B). Sl 2 sts to cn and hold in front of work, K2, K2 from cn (C4F); Rep from * to end of row.

Row 5: Knit.

Row 7: *Sl 2 sts to cn and hold in front of work, K2, K2 from cn (C4F). Sl 2 sts to cn and hold in back of work, K2, K2 from cn (C4B); Rep from * to end of row.

Row 8: Purl.

Rep Rows 1 to 8.

knitting lace

Many people avoid knitting lace because the designs seem intricate and difficult. In reality, the hardest thing about knitting lace is keeping your place in the pattern.

Depending on the pattern and the type of yarn you use, lace can produce a variety of different looks, ranging from elaborate and delicate to rustic and modern. A lace pattern can

consist of scattered openings in a mostly solid fabric or the pattern can be airy with lots of openings.

You can use wool or synthetic yarn to create stylish garments, such as dresses and gloves, or use cotton to create beautiful, serviceable items such as placemats and curtains. Try to avoid using thick or fluffy yarns that may hide your lace design.

LACE EDGINGS AND INSERTIONS

In addition to creating an entire item in lace fabric, you can also accent other types of fabric using a lace edging or insertion.

Lace edging generally features one decorative shaped edge and one straight edge, which you use to attach the edging to another item. Lace edgings are often used to embellish items such as table linens, pillowcases and garments.

Lace edging can be made from different types of yarn, depending on the look you want to obtain. You may want to work with thin cotton yarn to make an attractive edging that you can starch to maintain the shape or you may want to use metallic yarn to add sparkle to edging used for shirt collars or cuffs.

Lace insertions are panels of lace that are inserted into a knitted piece to enhance an otherwise plain project. When knitting a lace panel into another piece, you must first check to see that the gauge of the lace insertion matches the gauge of the background stitch. The pattern for a project featuring a lace insertion will usually account for the gauge.

INCREASES AND DECREASES

You create lace by using the increase and decrease methods discussed in chapter 3 to form decorative holes in the fabric. You can create different patterns by varying how these holes are placed throughout the fabric.

To make the decorative holes in a lace fabric, you perform a yarn over increase. For information on yarn overs, see page 84. For every increase, you must perform a corresponding decrease, such as knitting two stitches together, to keep the total number of stitches the same. For information on decrease methods, see pages 88 to 93. The increase and corresponding decrease can be completed in the same row or the decrease can be completed in the following row.

When you first start knitting lace, you may find it easier to try lace patterns that require you to increase and decrease stitches only on the right side of the fabric. It is also a good idea to start with a simple item, such as a scarf, that does not require shaping.

TYPES OF LACE

There are several different types, or categories, of lace. Three of the most common types are discussed here.

Eyelet

Eyelet lace features a pattern of holes, called eyelets, scattered throughout a solid background. The background is usually worked in stockinette stitch (knit one row, purl one row). Compared to other types of lace, eyelet lace has more solid areas in the fabric and fewer holes.

To create an interesting effect in your fabric, you can work a horizontal row of eyelets and then weave a ribbon through the holes.

Open Lace

Open lace generally has a greater number of holes in the fabric than eyelet lace. This type of pattern creates a more traditional lace look and is often used for items such as shawls.

When creating open lace, you will need to keep careful track of the rows you work to help keep your place in the pattern.

Faggot Lace

Faggot lace is a simple lace pattern that is usually created by alternating a yarn over increase and a slip slip knit decrease. You can repeat this pattern to create an all over net-like fabric. Faggot lace may be used alone or used as a lace insertion in another fabric.

lace designs

Abbreviations used in lace design patterns:

K2tog	Knit two stitches together. See page 88.
Sl	Slip a stitch. See page 114.
ssk	Slip slip knit. See page 90.

psso	Pass slipped stitch over.
yo	Yarn over. See page 84.

Basic Faggoting

EASY

Cast on a multiple of 2 stitches (2, 4, 6, etc.).

Row 1: K1. *yo. ssk. Rep from * to last st, K1.

Rep Row 1.

Ridged Ribbon Eyelet

EASY

Cast on an odd number of stitches.

Row 1 (RS): Knit.

Row 2: Purl.

Row 3: Knit.

Row 4: Knit.

Row 5: *K2tog. yo; Rep from * to last st, K1.

Row 6: Knit.

Rep Rows 1 to 6.

Cloverleaf

INTERMEDIATE

Cast on a multiple of 8 stitches (8, 16, 24, etc.), plus 7 stitches.

Row 1 and all wrong-side (WS) rows: Purl.

Row 2: Knit.

Row 4: K2. yo. Sl1. K2tog. psso. yo. *K5. yo. Sl1. K2tog. psso. yo; Rep from * to last 2 sts, K2.

Row 6: K3. yo. ssk. *K6. yo. ssk; Rep from * to last 2 sts, K2.

Row 8: Knit.

Row 10: K1. *K5. yo. Sl1. K2tog. psso. yo; Rep from * to last 6 sts, K6.

Row 12: K7. *yo. ssk. K6; Rep from * to end of row.

Rep Rows 1 to 12.

Flemish Block Lace

INTERMEDIATE

Cast on a multiple of 14 stitches (14, 28, 42, etc.), plus 3 stitches.

Row 1 (RS): K2. *K2tog. yo. K1. yo. ssk. K3. K2tog. yo. K4; Rep from * to last st, K1.

Row 2 and all wrong-side (WS) rows: Purl.

Row 3: K1. *K2tog. yo. K3. yo. ssk. K1. K2tog. yo. K4; Rep from * to last 2 sts; K2.

Row 5: K2tog. yo. *K5. yo. Sl1. K2tog. psso. yo. K4. K2tog. yo; Rep from * to last st, K1.

Row 7: K2. *yo. ssk. K4. yo. ssk. K3. K2tog. yo. K1; Rep from * to last st, K1.

Row 9: K3. *yo. ssk. K4. yo. ssk. K1. K2tog. yo. K3; Rep from * to end of row.

Row 11: K4. *yo. ssk. K4. yo. K3tog. yo. K5; Rep from * to last 4 sts, K4.

Row 12: Purl.

Rep Rows 1 to 12.

Arrowhead Lace

INTERMEDIATE

Cast on a multiple of 10 stitches (10, 20, 30, etc.), plus 1 stitch.

Row 1 (WS): Purl.

Row 2: K1. *(yo. ssk) twice. K1. (K2tog. yo) twice. K1; Rep from * to end of row.

Row 3: Purl.

Row 4: K2. *yo. ssk. yo. Sl 2 knitwise. K1. Lift 2 slipped sts over the knit st and allow both to fall off needle (p2sso). yo. K2tog. yo. K3; Rep from * to last 2 sts, K2.

Rep Rows 1 to 4.

knit with beads

You can knit beads directly into your knitted work to embellish your project.

Before you begin knitting, you must thread all the beads you want to use onto your yarn. After you start knitting, the only way to add more beads to the yarn is to cut the yarn from the ball or unwind the ball so you can thread the beads onto the other end of the yarn.

Beads can be made from many different types of material, including glass, wood, plastic or clay. The beads you choose for your project must slide easily along the yarn you are using. When you knit beads into your work, the beads sit on top of your stitches, rather than between your stitches. You can space beads evenly or randomly throughout your knitted fabric.

The method of knitting with beads shown below is one popular method. If the pattern you are using provides instructions for another method of knitting with beads, follow the instructions provided by the pattern.

1 Before you begin your knitted piece, thread the yarn you will use for the piece through a tapestry needle.

Note: The needle must be small enough to fit through your beads but the eye of the needle must be large enough to allow the yarn to fit through.

2 Slide each bead you will use for your knitted piece over the needle and along the yarn.

3 Remove the tapestry needle from the yarn.

4 Work to where you want to place the first bead, with the right side of your work facing you.

5 Bring the strand of yarn between your needles to the front of your work.

6 Move the bead along the strand of yarn until it is close to the last stitch you knitted.

How do I work with small beads?

To create a professional-looking knitted project when working with small beads, you should slip the stitch purlwise, rather than knitwise, in the steps below. To slip the stitch purlwise, insert the right needle into the front of the first stitch on the left needle from right to left in step **7**.

Can I create a pattern using different colors of beads?

Yes. As long as you plan ahead, you can easily create a pattern using different colors of beads. Simply thread the beads onto your yarn in the correct order before you start knitting.

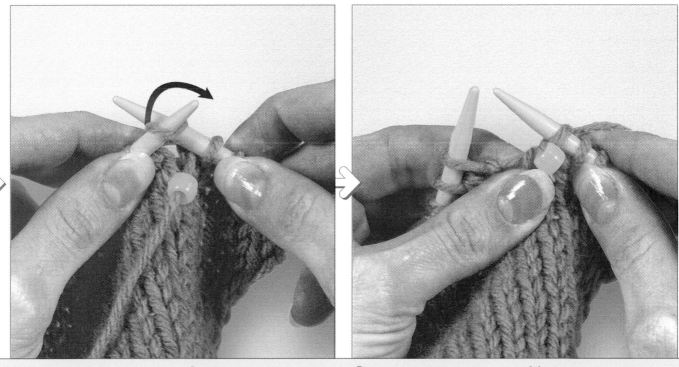

7 To slip the next stitch, insert the tip of the right needle into the front of the first stitch on the left needle, from left to right.

8 Slip the stitch onto the right needle by removing the stitch from the left needle.

9 Take the strand of yarn between your needles to the back of your work.

10 Push the bead in front of the stitch you slipped in steps **7** and **8**.

11 Knit the next stitch tightly to keep the bead in its proper location.

12 Continue working until you reach the location where you want to place the next bead. Then repeat steps **5** to **11**.

make a bobble

A bobble is a ball-shaped decoration that you can use to add texture and interest to your knitted projects. To create a bobble, you add several stitches to your project and then work those stitches back into a single stitch, forming a bulge on your fabric.

The size of a bobble depends on how many new stitches you add to the original stitch and how many new rows you create with the stitches. Bobble patterns often require you to create four rows with the stitches to create a bobble.

You can incorporate bobbles into any type of background stitch, such as cables, stockinette stitch or garter stitch. You can create bobbles in a background fabric to form a pattern or use bobbles randomly.

The directions for making a bobble are usually given in pattern instructions. The steps below give instructions for creating a bobble that is five stitches wide and four rows high, using stockinette stitch (knit 1 row, purl 1 row).

Step 4

Five new stitches

1 Knit the stitch where you want to make a bobble, but do not slide the original stitch off the left needle.

2 Insert the tip of the right needle into the back of the original stitch, from right to left.

3 Wrap the yarn around the right needle once, counterclockwise from back to front.

4 Slide the right needle and the wrapped yarn back through the stitch toward you. Do not slide the original stitch off the left needle.

5 Repeat steps 1 to 4.

6 Knit the original stitch on the left needle.

- Five new stitches are now on the right needle.

Can I make a bobble using reverse stockinette stitch?

Yes. Instead of creating a bobble using stockinette stitch as shown below, you can create a bobble using reverse stockinette stitch to give the bobble a different look. Perform the steps below, except knit the stitches when working on the wrong side of the fabric in step **8** and purl the stitches when the right side of the work is facing you in step **10**. For information on stockinette stitch and reverse stockinette stitch, see page 55.

Can I make a bobble using garter stitch?

Yes. To make a bobble in garter stitch, perform the steps below, except knit the stitches in every row in the bobble. This means you knit the stitches in step **8** and in step **10**. For information on garter stitch, see page 54.

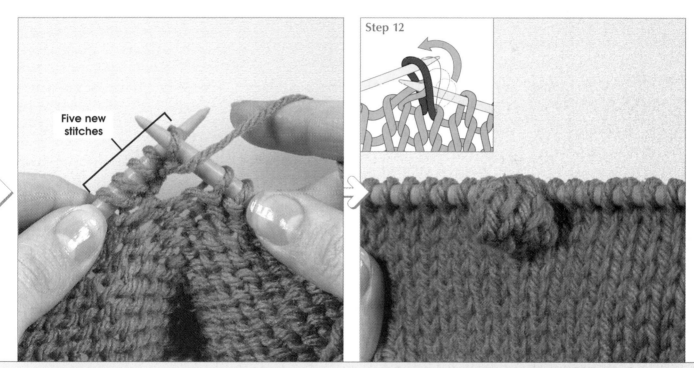

Five new stitches

Step 12

7 Turn your work so the wrong side is facing you and place each needle in the opposite hand.

8 Purl each of the five new stitches on the left needle.

9 Turn your work so the right side is facing you and place each needle in the opposite hand.

10 Knit each of the five new stitches on the left needle.

11 Repeat steps **7** to **10**.

12 Use the left needle to lift the second stitch on the right needle over the first stitch. Allow the second stitch to drop off both needles.

13 Repeat step **12** three times.

- One stitch of the bobble remains on the needle and the bobble is complete.

- You can now continue working the rows for your project.

make a fringe

Adding a fringe to a knitted piece is a quick and easy way to enhance the appearance of a piece, such as a scarf, shawl or afghan. To add a fringe to the edge of a knitted piece, all you need is yarn and a crochet hook.

You can customize the look of your fringe to suit your needs. The thickness and length of the fringe is determined by how many strands of yarn you use and the length of the strands. Your fringe can be

made from one color of yarn or you can use several different colors to create a multicolored fringe. If you have leftover yarn from a project, making a fringe to add to the project is a good way to use the remaining yarn.

Once you have completed your fringe, you can trim the fringe to create a neat edge.

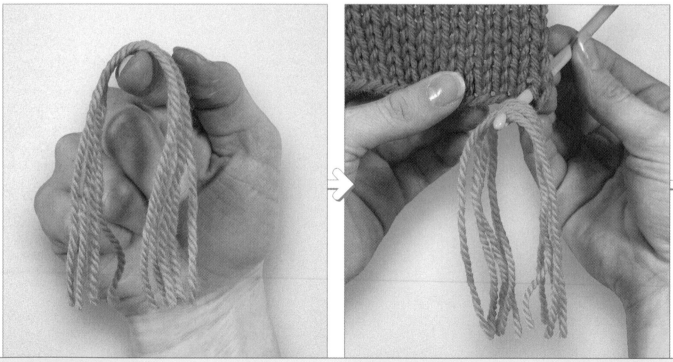

1 Cut strands of yarn slightly longer than double the length of the fringe you want to make.

Note: The number of strands you should cut depends on how thick you want the fringe to be.

2 Line up the strands of yarn.

3 Fold the strands of yarn in half.

4 With the right side of the knitted piece facing you, insert the crochet hook at the edge of your knitted piece where you want to add the fringe, from the wrong side to the right side.

5 With the crochet hook, catch the strands of yarn at the fold.

QUESTION & ANSWER

Can I make a more decorative fringe?

Yes. You can make an attractive knotted fringe. To make a knotted fringe, you will first need to perform the steps below to add a fringe to your knitted piece. In step **1**, cut longer strands of yarn to accommodate the knots. Take half of the strands of yarn from two neighboring sections of fringe and tie two knots, one on top of the other. Repeat this procedure for each of the remaining sections of fringe along the edge of the knitted piece. As long as you have enough yarn to work with, you can make additional rows of knots as far down the fringe as you want.

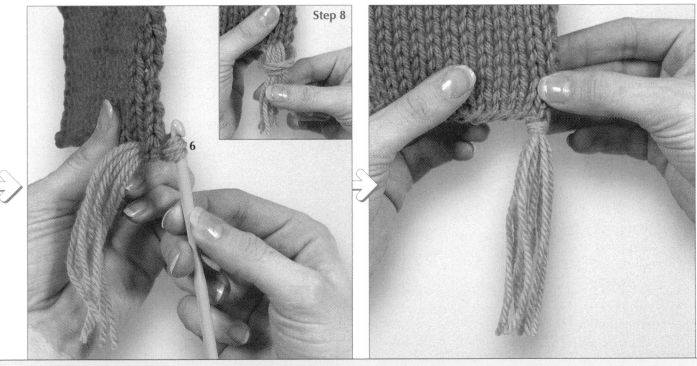

Step 8

6 Use the crochet hook to slide the strands of yarn through the knitted piece. The yarn forms a loop on the wrong side of the knitted piece.

7 Remove the crochet hook from the yarn.

8 Use your fingers to bring the ends of the yarn through the loop.

9 Pull the ends of the yarn to secure the fringe to the knitted piece.

10 Straighten and trim the fringe.

11 Repeat steps **1** to **10** for each section of fringe you want to add to the edge of your knitted piece.

make a tassel

Tassels are fun to make and can add a decorative element to your knitting projects. You can add tassels to many items, including blanket corners, scarves and the tops of hats. In addition to yarn and scissors, you will need a tapestry needle and a piece of cardboard to make a tassel.

Your tassel can be made from one color of yarn or you can use several different colors to create a multicolored tassel. If you have leftover yarn, making tassels to add to your projects is a good way to use the yarn.

You can make your tassel as long and as full as you like. Once you have completed your tassel, you can trim the bottom of the tassel to create a neat and even edge.

You can also use a tassel maker to create a tassel. Tassel makers are inexpensive and can be found at most knitting stores.

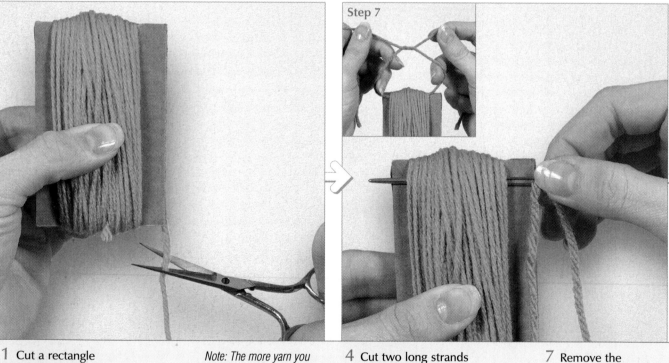

1 Cut a rectangle out of cardboard.

Note: The rectangle should be the same length as the tassel you want to make.

2 Wind the yarn around the rectangle.

Note: The more yarn you wind, the fuller the tassel will be.

3 When you finish winding the yarn, cut the yarn from the ball.

4 Cut two long strands of yarn from a ball.

5 Thread the first strand of yarn through a tapestry needle.

6 Insert the tapestry needle under all the loops of yarn on the rectangle.

7 Remove the tapestry needle and tie the strand of yarn into a tight knot, leaving ends of equal length.

8 Remove the rectangle.

How do I attach my tassel to a knitted piece?

You use the two strands of yarn dangling from the top of the tassel to attach the tassel to a knitted piece. Thread one strand of yarn through a tapestry needle and insert the tapestry needle from the right side to the wrong side of your project.

Wrong Side   Right Side

Repeat this process for the second strand of yarn, inserting the tapestry needle one or two stitches away from the first strand. Tie the strands of yarn into a tight knot on the wrong side of your project to secure the tassel firmly to the knitted piece.

Steps 11 & 12

Result

9 Wrap the second strand of yarn tightly around the tassel several times about half an inch from the top of the tassel.

10 Tie the strand of yarn into a tight knot.

11 Thread the ends of yarn through a tapestry needle.

12 Insert the tapestry needle through the tassel from top to bottom.

13 Remove the tapestry needle.

14 Cut the loops of yarn at the bottom of the tassel.

15 Trim the tassel to create an even edge.

make a pompom

Pompoms are easy to make and are ideal for decorating hats, sweaters and slippers. You can also use pompoms to make soft toys for children. To make a pompom, all you need is yarn, cardboard and a pair of scissors.

Some types of yarn are better for making pompoms than other types of yarn. For example, wool will create a fuller, fluffier pompom than cotton. Your pompom can be made from one color of yarn or you can use several different colors to create a

multicolored pompom. Making pompoms is a great way to use up any leftover yarn you may have.

You can make your pompoms as large and as full as you like. Once you complete a pompom, you can trim any strands of yarn that are sticking out to create a smooth, even pompom.

You can also use a pompom maker to create pompoms. Pompom makers are inexpensive and can be found at most knitting stores.

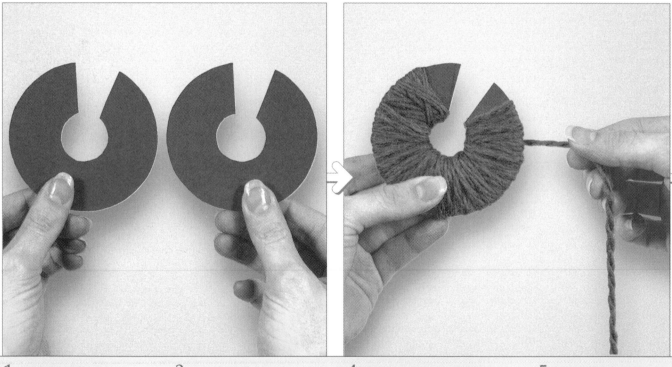

1 Cut two circles out of cardboard.

- The circles should be the same size and slightly larger than the pompom you want to make.

2 Cut a small section out of each circle.

3 Cut a hole out of the center of each circle.

4 Holding the two circles together, wind the yarn around the circles until the yarn covers the circles.

Note: The more yarn you wind, the fuller the pompom will be.

5 When you finish winding the yarn, cut the yarn from the ball.

How do I attach my pompom to a knitted piece?

You use the two long strands of yarn dangling from the pompom to attach the pompom to a knitted piece. Thread one strand of yarn through a tapestry needle and insert the tapestry needle from the right side to the wrong side of your project. Repeat this process for the second

Wrong Side   Right Side

strand of yarn, inserting the tapestry needle one or two stitches away from the first strand. Tie the strands of yarn into a tight knot on the wrong side of your project to secure the pompom firmly to the knitted piece.

Step 8

6 Insert one blade of the scissors between the circles and cut the loops of yarn all the way around the outside edge of the circles.

7 Separate the circles slightly.

8 Tie a long strand of yarn tightly between the two circles.

9 Remove the circles.

10 Fluff and trim the pompom.

decorative pillow

Easy Project

Decorative Pillow

Size

Approx. 14 ins (35.5cm) square.

Materials

Classic Elite Paintbox 3.5oz/100g, #6820 Cerulean Blue, 3 balls.

Pillow form 14 x 14 ins (35.5 x 35.5cm).

Size 11 US (8mm) knitting needles or size needed to obtain gauge.

Gauge

15 stitches (sts) and 21 rows = 4 ins (10cm) in pattern.

Instructions

Abbreviations: RS = right side; K = knit; Sl1 = slip one stitch.

Cast on 51 stitches.

Row 1 (RS): Knit.

Row 2: Knit.

Row 3: K1. *Sl1 purlwise. K1; Rep from * to end of row.

Row 4: K1. *Move yarn to front of work. Sl1 purlwise. Move yarn to back of work. K1; Rep from * to end of row.

Row 5: As Row 1.

Row 6: As Row 1.

Row 7: K2. *Sl1 purlwise. K1; Rep from * to last st, K1.

Row 8: K2. *Move yarn to front of work. Sl1 purlwise. Move yarn to back of work. K1; Rep from * to last st, K1.

These 8 rows form pattern.

Instructions (cont.)

Continue in pattern until work from beginning measures 28 ins (71cm).

Bind off all stitches.

Fold material in half and sew two sides together using whip stitch. Insert pillow form. Sew remaining side.

Tassel: (Make 4)
Cut a rectangle 6.5 ins (16.5cm) long out of cardboard. Wind yarn around rectangle 28 times and then cut yarn from ball. Then perform steps 4 to 15 starting on page 138 to create a tassel. Attach tassel to pillow corner.

Add a tassel to each pillow corner.

cell phone cozy

• Intermediate Project •

Cell Phone Cozy

Materials

Paton's Classic Merino Wool 3.5oz/100g,
#233 Blush, 1 ball.

Size 7 US (4.5mm) knitting needles or size needed
to obtain gauge.

One button.

Gauge:

20 stitches (sts) and 26 rows = 4 ins (10cm) in
Stockinette St (knit 1 row, purl 1 row).

Instructions

Abbreviations: RS = right side; WS = wrong side;
P = purl; K = knit; Sl1 = slip 1 stitch;
psso = pass slipped stitch over; yrn = yarn
round needle; P2tog = purl 2 stitches together.

Cast on 22 stitches.

Proceed as follows:

Row 1 (RS): P2. *Sl1. K2. psso. P2; Rep from * to
end of row.

Row 2: K2. *P1. yrn. P1. K2; Rep from * to end
of row.

Row 3: P2. *K3. P2; Rep from * to end of row.

Row 4: K2. *P3. K2; Rep from * to end of row.

These 4 rows form pattern.

Continue in pattern until work from beginning
measures 11 ins [28cm], ending with WS facing
for next row.
Note: You may lengthen according to the size of
your cell phone.

Antenna hole:

Bind off 6 sts. 16 sts.
Work in pattern to end of row. Work 3 more rows
in pattern. Cast on 6 sts. 22 sts. Continue in pattern
until work from beginning measures 13.75 ins [35cm]
ending with Row 3 of pattern facing for next row.

Instructions (cont.)

Make Buttonhole:

Row 1 (RS): Work in pattern 10 sts. Bind off 2 sts.
Work in pattern to end of row.

Next row: Work Row 4 of pattern, casting on 2 sts
over bound off sts. Work in pattern to
end of row.

Next row: (P2tog. Sl1. K2. psso) twice. P2tog.
(Sl1. K2. psso. P2tog.) twice. 17 sts.

Knit 2 rows.

Bind off all sts knitwise on WS.

Fold bottom edge up to
where first bind off is
and sew side seams.
Sew on button.

summer lacy vest

Intermediate Project

Summer Lacy Vest

Sizes

Bust measurement
Small   30-32 ins (76-81cm)
Medium   34-36 ins (86-91cm)
Large   38-40 ins (97-102cm)

Finished bust
Small   32.25 ins (84cm)
Medium   36.75 ins (89cm)
Large   41 ins (119.5cm)

Materials

Patons Grace 50g, #60901 Tangello
Sizes   S   M   L
          8   9   9   balls

Size 4 US (3.5mm) and size 7 US (4mm) circular knitting needles (90cm long) or size needed to obtain gauge.

Set of four size 4 US (3.5mm) double–pointed knitting needles.

One stitch holder.

5 buttons.

Gauge

24 stitches (sts) and 32 rows = 4 ins (10cm) with size 7 US (4mm) needles in Stockinette St (knit 1 row, purl 1 row).

Stitch Glossary

Abbreviations: WS=wrong side; RS=right side; K = knit; P= purl; yo = yarn over; ssk = slip slip knit; K2tog = knit two stitches together; dec = decrease.

Lace Pattern:

Row 1 (WS): Purl.

Row 2: K3. *yo. K2. ssk. K2tog. K2. yo. K1. Rep from * to last st, K1.

Row 3: Purl.

Row 4: K2. *yo. K2. ssk. K2tog. K2. yo. K1. Rep from * to last 2 sts, K2.

Instructions

Bracketed numbers are for sizes S (**M-L**).

With smaller circular needles, cast on 202 (**229**-256) stitches. **Do not join.** Working back and forth across needle:
Work 5 rows in Garter St (knit every row). Change to larger circular needles.

Next: Work in Lace Pattern until work from beginning measures 9 (**9.5**-9.75) ins [23 (**24**-25) cm], ending with RS facing for next row.

Divide for armholes:
Next row: Work 51 (**57**-64) sts in pattern (Right Front). **Turn.** Leave remaining sts on a spare needle.

Right Front

Continue in Lace Pattern and bind off next 6 sts (armhole edge) and dec 1 st at armhole edge on every following 5 (**11**-14) alt rows. 40 (**40**-44) sts. Continue even in pattern until armhole measures 4.5 ins [11.5cm], ending with RS facing for next row.

Neck shaping: Bind off next 8 (**6**-7) sts (neck edge). Work in pattern to end of row. Dec 1 st at neck edge on next 15 rows. 17 (**19**-22) sts. Continue even in pattern until armhole measures 8 ins [20.5cm], ending with WS facing for next row.

Shoulder shaping: Bind off 6 (**6**-7) sts beginning next and following alt row. Work 1 row even. Bind off remaining sts.

Divide for Back: Next row: With RS of work facing, join yarn to remaining sts on spare needle. Bind off 6 sts, work 94 (**109**-122) sts in Lace Pattern (including st on needle after bind off). (Back). **Turn.** Leave remaining sts on spare needle.

summer lacy vest

Left Front

With RS facing, join yarn to remaining sts on spare needle. Continue in Lace Pattern and bind off next 6 sts (armhole edge) and dec 1 st at armhole edge on every following 5 (**11**-14) alt rows. 40 (**40**-44) sts.

Continue even in pattern until armhole measures 4.5 ins [11.5cm], ending with WS facing for next row.

Neck shaping: Bind off next 8 (**6**-7) sts. (neck edge). Work in pattern to end of row. Dec 1 st at neck edge on next 15 rows. 17 (**19**-22) sts. Continue even in pattern until armhole measures 8 ins [20.5cm] ending with RS facing for next row.

Shoulder shaping: Bind off 6 (**6**-7) sts beginning of next and following alt row. Work 1 row even. Bind off remaining sts.

Back

Bind off 6 sts. Work in pattern to end of row. Keeping continuity of pattern, dec 1 st at each end of needle on next 5 (**11**-14) rows. 78 (**81**-88) sts. Continue even in pattern until armhole measures same length as Right Front, ending with RS facing for next row.

Shoulder shaping: Bind off 6 (**6**-7) sts beginning next 4 rows, then 5 (**7**-8) sts beginning of next 2 rows. Leave remaining 44 (**43**-44) sts on stitch holder.

Finishing

Buttonhole Band:
Sew shoulder seams.
With RS of work facing and smaller needles, pick up and knit 74 (**76**-78) sts up Right Front edge.

Working back and forth across needle in rows, proceed as follows:
Work 3 rows Garter St (knit every row).

Row 4 (RS): K2. * Bind off 2 sts. K17 (**17**-18) (including st on needle after bind off). Rep from * 2 more times. Bind off 2 sts. Knit to end of row.

Row 5: Knit, casting on 2 sts over bind off sts. Work 3 rows Garter St (knit every row).

Bind off knitwise on WS.

Finishing (cont.)

Button Band:
Work as for Buttonhole Band omitting all reference to buttonholes.
Sew buttons to correspond to buttonholes.

Neckband:
With RS facing and smaller needles, pick up and knit 28 sts up Right Front neck edge, knit across 44 (**43**-44) sts from Back neck St holder. Pick up and knit 28 sts down Left Front neck edge. 100 (**99**-100) sts.

Work 1 row Garter St and dec 1 st at center back neck. 99 (**98**-99) sts.

Next: K2. Bind off 2 sts. Knit to end of needle.

Next row: Knit, casting on 2 sts over bind off sts. Knit 1 row.

Bind off knitwise.

Armbands:
With RS facing and set of four needles, pick up and knit 91 sts evenly around armhole edge dividing sts evenly on 3 double-pointed needles. Join in round and placing a marker on first st, proceed as follows:
Rnd 1: Purl.
Rnd 2: Knit.
Rep last 2 rounds once more. Bind off purlwise.

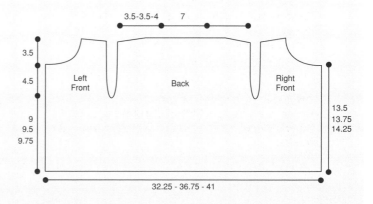

Chapter 5

During the course of knitting a project, it is possible that mistakes will occur. However, most mistakes are easy to prevent or correct. In this chapter, not only will you learn how to pick up a dropped stitch and how to rip out stitches to return to where you made a mistake, you will also learn how to prevent mistakes from happening in the first place.

Fixing Your Mistakes

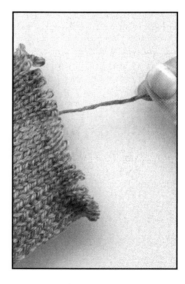

pick up a dropped stitch *(in the row below)*

If you count the stitches on your knitting needle and find you are missing a stitch, you may have dropped a stitch. A dropped stitch is a stitch that has slipped off the end of your needle. To help ensure you find a dropped stitch in your project as soon as possible, you should count your stitches often to make certain you always have the correct number. A dropped stitch is easy to correct when the stitch was dropped on the previous row and has not unraveled further down in the project.

When you find a dropped stitch in your work, you can use a safety pin to secure the stitch. The safety pin will prevent the dropped stitch from unraveling any further until you can work your way across the next row to pick up the stitch.

As a general rule, whether you need to pick up a dropped knit or purl stitch depends on which side of your work is facing you. If the knit side is facing you, you will usually pick up a knit stitch. If the purl side is facing you, you will usually pick up a purl stitch.

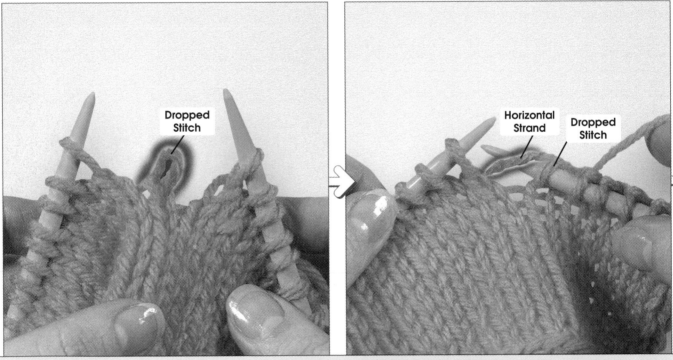

- When you find you are missing a stitch, you can perform the following steps to pick up a dropped knitted stitch in the row below.

1 Work to where the knitted dropped stitch is located.

2 Insert the right needle into the dropped stitch from front to back to help prevent the stitch from unraveling any further.

3 Insert the tip of the right needle under the horizontal strand of yarn behind the dropped stitch, from front to back.

How can I pick up a dropped purl stitch in the row below?

Perform steps **1** to **6** below, except insert the tip of the right needle from back to front in steps **2** and **3**. The horizontal strand of yarn should be in front of the dropped stitch.

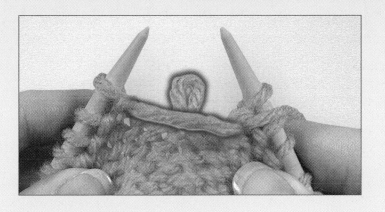

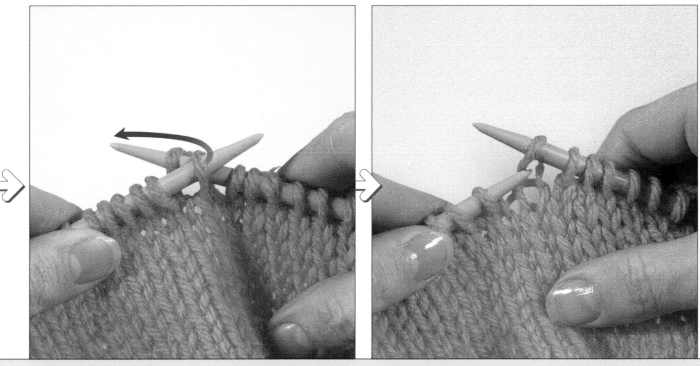

4 Insert the left needle into the front of the dropped stitch, from left to right.

5 Lift the dropped stitch over the horizontal strand of yarn and off the tip of the right needle. Allow the stitch to fall off the left needle.

● You have created a new stitch on the right needle.

6 Insert the left needle through the new stitch on the right needle from right to left and then move the stitch onto the left needle.

CONTINUED...

pick up a dropped stitch *(several rows below)*

You can pick up a dropped stitch several rows below in your knitting. This is useful if you did not notice that a stitch dropped before the stitch unraveled through several rows of your work.

You can tell where a stitch has dropped in your work by looking at your knitting project. If a series of horizontal strands of yarn appears in your project, you know a stitch has dropped through several rows. Each horizontal strand represents a row you have completed.

You can use a crochet hook to pick up a dropped stitch located several rows below where you are currently

working. You should choose a crochet hook that is no larger than the knitting needles you are using. The crochet hook should be large enough to catch the strand of yarn, but not so large that it stretches your stitches when you insert the crochet hook through a dropped stitch.

After you have picked up a dropped stitch, you should gently pull your knitting project in several directions to ensure the picked-up stitch takes on the same appearance as the rest of the stitches in your project.

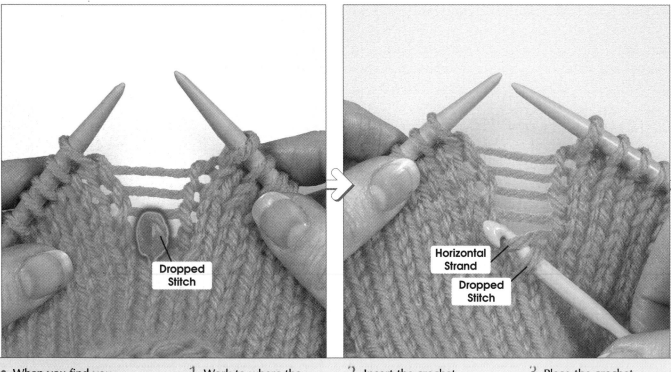

Dropped Stitch

Horizontal Strand

Dropped Stitch

- When you find you are missing a stitch, you can perform the following steps to pick up a dropped knitted stitch located several rows below.

1 Work to where the dropped knitted stitch is located.

2 Insert the crochet hook through the dropped stitch, from front to back.

3 Place the crochet hook under the first horizontal strand of yarn behind the dropped stitch and catch the yarn in the hook.

QUESTION & ANSWER

?

How can I pick up a dropped purl stitch several rows below?

1 Work to where the dropped purl stitch is located.

2 Turn your work around so the knit side of your work is facing you.

3 Perform steps 2 to 6 below, except insert the tip of the right needle through the stitch on the crochet hook from front to back in step 6.

4 Turn your work around so you can continue purling.

4 Pull the horizontal strand of yarn through the dropped stitch.

• You have created a new stitch on the crochet hook.

5 Repeat steps 3 and 4 for each horizontal strand of yarn above the dropped stitch.

6 Insert the tip of the left needle through the stitch on the crochet hook, from front to back, moving the stitch off the crochet hook and onto the left needle.

rip out
stitches

When you make a mistake, you can unravel, or rip out, your stitches until you get to the location of the mistake. You can then fix the mistake and continue knitting.

You can rip out stitches one stitch at a time or row by row. The point at which you discover your mistake will determine the most efficient way to rip out the stitches. If you are still on the same row where the mistake occurred, rip out one stitch at a time. If the mistake was made several rows before, it will be

faster to rip out stitches row by row. You may want to mark the row containing the mistake with a safety pin to help prevent you from ripping out more rows than you need to. To avoid damaging your work or ruining the yarn, unravel the stitches gently.

When replacing your stitches on the needle, you should make sure none of the stitches are twisted when you place them on the needle.

STITCH BY STITCH

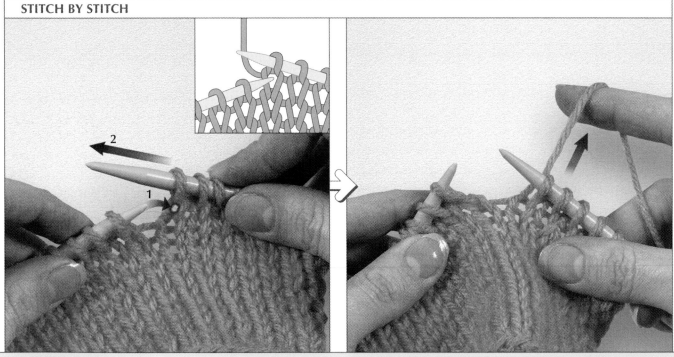

1 To fix a mistake you made in the current row, insert the left needle into the stitch directly below the first stitch on the right needle, from front to back.

Note: Make sure you keep the strand of yarn at the back of your work.

2 Gently pull the first stitch off the right needle.

3 Pull the yarn attached to the ball to pull the excess yarn through the stitch.

4 Repeat steps 1 to 3 until you reach the mistake. Then correct the mistake and continue knitting.

Is there another method I can use to rip out stitches row by row?

Yes. You can use another method to help you avoid dropping stitches when unraveling your work. Using a smaller size needle, weave the needle in and out of each stitch in the row below the row containing the mistake. From right to left, pass the needle under the right side and over the left side of each stitch. Then perform steps **1** and **2** below to unravel the rows.

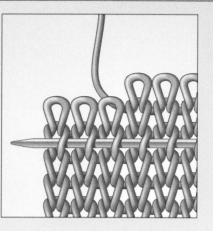

When you get to the location where you placed the needle, the last stitches will be on the needle. Replace the small needle with a needle of the correct size and then continue with your knitting. This method is most effective when working with the knit side of stockinette stitch.

ROW BY ROW

1 Carefully slide your needle out of all the stitches.

2 Gently pull the yarn attached to the ball away from the stitches to unravel each row until you unravel the row containing the mistake.

3 Hold your work in your left hand, with the yarn attached to the ball coming from the top left edge of your work.

4 Starting with the stitch at the right edge of your work, insert the needle into the first stitch from back to front.

5 Repeat step **4** until all the stitches are on the needle. Then re-knit the stitches you unraveled.

Note: Make sure the stitches are not twisted when you place them on the needle.

Chapter 6

While knitting flat pieces is fundamental to knitting, some projects, such as socks and sweaters, are easier to complete by knitting in a continuous tubular shape. This chapter teaches you how to knit in the round using circular needles and double-pointed needles. Knitting in the round creates a seamless tubular piece of fabric, which can save you from knitting separate pieces and sewing the pieces together later.

Knitting in the Round

In this Chapter...

Knit With Circular Needles

Knit With Double-Pointed Needles

Cozy Knit Socks

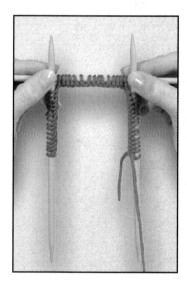

knit with circular needles

Circular needles consist of a pair of short, straight needles attached by a flexible cord. These needles allow you to knit in a circle, which is referred to as knitting in the round or circular knitting.

When creating large tubular items, such as the body of a sweater, circular needles are ideal. You can simply work continuously to create a seamless tube, instead of working the front and back separately with straight needles and then sewing the pieces together. Circular needles are also useful for working with repeating color patterns since the right side of your work always faces you.

To be able to work a knitted piece easily on circular needles, choose a needle length for your circular needles that is slightly smaller than the circumference of the piece. Most patterns will indicate the length of needles you require.

Casting on stitches to begin your project is the same on circular needles as on straight needles. When working with circular needles, you can create the same basic patterns of stockinette stitch and garter stitch, but the methods used to create the patterns are switched. You create stockinette stitch by knitting every row and garter stitch by knitting one row and then purling the next.

1 Cast on the number of stitches you require onto the circular needles. To cast on stitches, see pages 41 to 45.

2 Hold the needle containing the first stitch you cast on in your left hand.

3 Hold the needle containing the last stitch you cast on in your right hand.

- The ball of yarn should be attached to the first stitch on the needle in your right hand.

4 Line up the bumps at the bottom of each stitch along the needles to ensure the stitches are not twisted.

5 Place a stitch marker at the top of the stitches on the needle in your right hand. The stitch marker indicates the beginning of each round of knitting.

Note: You work "rounds" with circular needles compared to "rows" with straight needles.

How can I uncoil my circular needles?

If your circular needles are stiffly coiled, you can soak the needles in hot water for a couple of minutes to loosen the cord. Since the size of circular needles is not usually indicated on the needles, you may want to store your needles in their package, which means you may need to uncoil the needles before each use.

Can I use circular needles for knitting flat items?

Yes. Circular needles are also useful for knitting large, flat items that do not fit on straight needles, such as an afghan. Circular needles can hold a larger number of stitches than straight needles and you can still work back and forth across a piece, turning your work at the end of every row.

When knitting with circular needles, is there an advantage to knitting a garment starting from the top?

Some patterns will instruct you to knit with circular needles starting from the top of a garment. When knitting a garment such as a sweater, working from the top down allows you to try on the sweater as you make it to see when it is long enough. As a child grows, you can also easily add length to the bottom and sleeves of a sweater you knit for them.

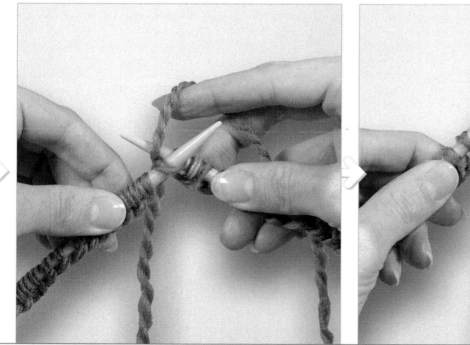

6 Using the needle in your right hand, work the first stitch on the needle in your left hand.

• You have now joined the first and last stitches that you cast on together, joining the round of stitches.

7 Continue to work every stitch in the round to create a tube shape.

Note: When working the first round of stitches, repeat step 4 throughout the round to ensure the stitches are not twisted.

8 When you complete all the stitches in the round and reach the stitch marker, slip the stitch marker from the left needle to the right needle.

• Work the following rounds in the same way.

knit with double-pointed needles

You can use double-pointed needles to knit small, seamless, tubular items, such as socks and mittens. Double-pointed needles are straight needles that have a point at each end. Knitting with double-pointed needles is referred to as knitting in the round or circular knitting.

Double-pointed needles are often used in sets of four. To get started, you evenly distribute your stitches among three of the needles. The fourth, empty needle is your working needle, which you will use to knit the stitches onto. When you have knit all the stitches onto your working needle, the new empty needle becomes

your working needle. To avoid holes in your work, try to keep the tension on the yarn even as you switch between needles.

When working with double-pointed needles, you always work on the right side of your work and you work in "rounds" compared to "rows" with single-pointed needles. You can create the same basic patterns of stockinette stitch and garter stitch as on single-pointed needles, but the methods used to create the patterns are switched. You create stockinette stitch by knitting every row and garter stitch by knitting one row and then purling the next.

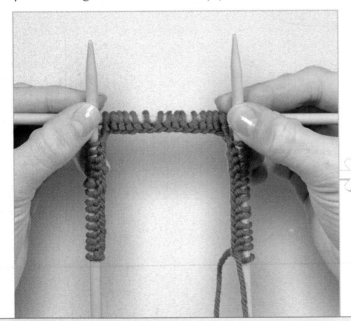
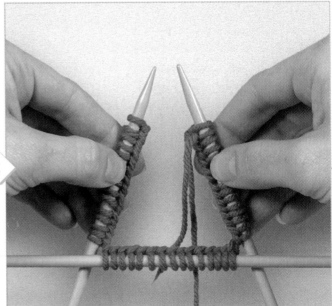

1 Cast on the total number of stitches you require onto one double-pointed needle. To cast on stitches, see pages 42 to 45.

2 Starting with the last stitch you cast on, slip one-third of the stitches purlwise onto an empty double-pointed needle. To slip stitches purlwise, see page 114.

3 Slip the next one-third of the stitches purlwise onto a second, empty double-pointed needle.

- You have now evenly distributed the stitches on three needles.

4 Hold the needles to form a triangle. The first stitch you cast on should be at the top of the left needle. The last stitch you cast on should be at the top of the right needle.

Note: You can use a stitch marker or strand of yarn to keep track of the location of the first stitch you cast on. For more information, see the top of page 163.

5 To ensure the stitches are not twisted around the needles, line up the bumps at the bottom of each stitch toward the inside of the triangle.

The stitches keep falling off my double-pointed needles. What can I do?

The double-pointed needles you are using may be too short. Try using longer double-pointed needles or switch to circular needles described on page 160. If the stitches fall off your double-pointed needles when you put down your work, you can place point protectors on the ends of your needles to keep the stitches in place. For more information on point protectors, see page 33.

How do I keep track of the beginning of each round?

Loosely tie a short strand of yarn in a different color around the tip of the right needle before knitting the first stitch in step 6 below. When you complete all the stitches in the round and reach the strand of yarn, slip the yarn marker from the left needle to the empty needle and then work the next round.

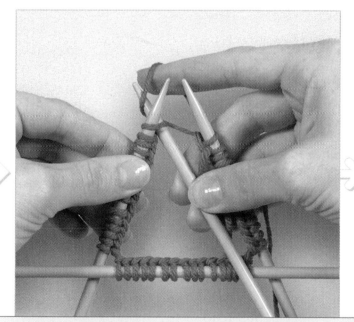

6 With a fourth, empty double-pointed needle, knit the first stitch on the left needle.

7 After you work the first stitch, gently pull the yarn attached to the ball to tighten the strand between the needles to prevent holes in your work.

• You have now joined the first and last stitches that you cast on together, joining the round of stitches.

8 Repeat step 6 until you have finished knitting all the stitches on the left needle.

9 To continue, place the empty needle in your right hand and repeat steps 6 to 8 to knit each stitch on the needle to the left. Repeat this step to move around the stitches.

Note: You may find the first round or two of stitches awkward to knit. After you knit a few rounds, the weight of your knitting will help keep the needles in position.

cozy knit
socks

Intermediate Project

Cozy Knit Socks

Sizes

Finished Foot Length

Small   9 ins (23cm)
Medium 9.5 ins (24cm)
Large   10.5 ins (26.5cm)

Materials

Stahl Socka Color 50g, #2419 Kolibri **or** #2414 Holz, 2 balls.

Set of four double-pointed needles size 1 US (2.25mm) or size needed to obtain gauge.

Kolibri

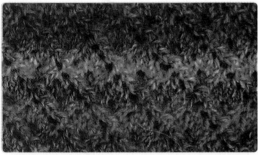

Holz

Gauge

38 stitches (sts) and 52 rows = 4 ins (10cm) in Stockinette St (knit 1 row, purl 1 row).

Instructions

Abbreviations: K = knit; P = purl; yo = yarn over; ssk = slip slip knit; K2tog = knit two stitches together; P2tog = purl two stitches together; psso = pass slipped stitch over; inc = increase; dec = decrease; Sl1 = slip one stitch purlwise; RS = right side; WS = wrong side.

Bracketed numbers are for sizes S (**M**-L).

Cast on 76 stitches loosely. Divide sts into 26 sts on 1 needle and 25 sts on each of next 2 needles. Mark the first st with contrasting thread.
Work in (K1. P1) ribbing for 1 (**1.5**-1.5) ins [2.5 (**4**-4) cm] dec 13 sts evenly on last round (rnd). 63 sts.

Proceed in Lace Pattern as follows:

1st and alt rnds: Knit.

2nd rnd: K1. *yo. ssk. K1. yo. K2tog. K1. Rep from * to last 2 sts, yo. ssk.

4th rnd: K2. *yo. ssk. K1. K2tog. yo. K1. Rep from * to last st, K1.

6th rnd: K3. *yo. Sl1. K2tog. psso. yo. K3. Rep from * to end of rnd.

8th rnd: K1. *yo. K2tog. K1. yo. ssk. K1. Rep from * to last 2 sts, yo. K2tog.

10th rnd: K2. *K2tog. yo. K1. yo. ssk. K1. Rep from * to last st, K1.

12th rnd: K1. K2tog. yo. *K3. yo. Sl1. K2tog. psso. yo. Rep from * to last 6 sts, K3. yo. ssk. K1.

These 12 rounds form Lace Pattern.

Continue in pattern until sock from beginning measures approx 6 (**6.5**-6.5) ins [15 (**16.5**-16.5) cm] ending with a knit round. Inc 12 sts across last round as follows:
(K1. Inc 1) 6 times on first 12 sts of 1st needle. Work 2nd needle even. (K1. Inc 1) 6 times on last 12 sts of 3rd needle. 75 sts. Cut yarn.

cozy knit socks

Make Heel

Slip last 17 sts of last round and first 17 sts of first round onto one needle for heel, having contrast thread at center and leaving 41 sts on 2 needles for instep.

With WS of work facing, join yarn and proceed across heel sts as follows:

Row 1: Sl1. Purl to end of row.

Row 2: *Sl1. K1. Rep from * to end of row.

Rep these 2 rows until heel measures 2.25 ins [5.5cm] ending on a Row 2.

Shape Heel

Row 1: P17. P2tog. P1. **Turn.**

Row 2: Sl1. K2. Sl1. K1. psso. K1. **Turn.**

Row 3: Sl1. P3. P2tog. P1. **Turn.**

Row 4: Sl1. K4. Sl1. K1. psso. K1. **Turn.**

Row 5: Sl1. P5. P2tog. P1. **Turn.**

Row 6: Sl1. K6. Sl1. K1. psso. K1. **Turn.**

Row 7: Sl1. P7. P2tog. P1. **Turn.**

Row 8: Sl1. K8. Sl1. K1. psso. K1. **Turn.**

Row 9: Sl1. P9. P2tog. P1. **Turn.**

Row 10: Sl1. K10. Sl1. K1. psso. K1. **Turn.**

Row 11: Sl1. P11. P2tog. P1. **Turn.**

Row 12: Sl1. K12. Sl1. K1. psso. K1. **Turn.**

Row 13: Sl1. P13. P2tog. P1. **Turn.**

Row 14: Sl1. K14. Sl1. K1. psso. K1. **Turn.**

Row 15: Sl1. P15. P2tog. P1. **Turn.**

Row 16: Sl1. K16. Sl1. K1. psso. 18 sts.

With RS facing and 1st needle, pick up and knit 16 sts along left side of heel. With 2nd needle, work next 41 sts of instep in Lace Pattern at next appropriate row. With 3rd needle, pick up and knit 16 sts along right side of heel. Knit first 9 sts from heel onto end of 3rd needle. Slip remaining 9 sts from heel onto beginning of 1st needle. 91 sts are now divided onto 3 needles (25-41-25) sts on 3 needles.

Shape Heel (cont.)

1st rnd:	**1st needle:**	Knit to last 3 sts, K2tog. K1.
	2nd needle:	Work next row in Lace Pattern.
	3rd needle:	K1. Sl1. K1. psso. Knit to end of needle.
2nd rnd:	**1st needle:**	Knit.
	2nd needle:	Work next row in Lace Pattern.
	3rd needle:	Knit.
3rd rnd:	**1st needle:**	Knit to last 3 sts, K2tog. K1.
	2nd needle:	Work next row in Lace Pattern.
	3rd needle:	K1. Sl1. K1. psso. Knit to end of needle.
4th rnd:	**1st needle:**	Knit.
	2nd needle:	Work next row in Lace Pattern.
	3rd needle:	Knit.

Continue in Lace Pattern on 2nd needle while **AT THE SAME TIME** dec 1 st on 1st and 3rd needles, as before, on every alt rnd to 75 sts (17-41-17) sts on 3 needles.

Continue even until foot from picked up sts at heel measures 5 (**6**-7) ins [12.5 (**15**-16) cm].

Next rnd: Knit dec 3 sts around by dec 1 st off each of the 3 needles. 72 sts.

Slip last 2 sts on 2nd needle onto beginning of 3rd needle. Slip 1st 2 sts on 2nd needle onto end of 1st needle. Sts are now divided as (18-36-18) sts on needles.

Shape Toe

1st rnd:	**1st needle:**	Knit to last 3 sts, K2tog. K1.
	2nd needle:	K1. Sl1. K1. psso. Knit to last 3 sts, K2tog. K1.
	3rd needle:	K1. Sl1. K1. psso. Knit to end of needle.

Knit 1 rnd even.

Rep last 2 rnds until 28 sts remaining. Knit sts from 1st needle onto 3rd needle. Cut yarn leaving long end.

Graft 2 sets of 14 sts together for toe.

167

Chapter 7

One of the easiest and most attractive ways to embellish a knitted project is to add color. This chapter teaches you two different techniques for knitting with multiple color—Fair Isle and intarsia knitting. Knowing how to knit in color using the Fair Isle and intarsia techniques will allow you to add a wide range of colored patterns to your fabric.

Knitting With Color

In this Chapter...

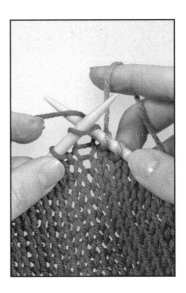

knit in color
using fair isle

Strand Yarn Between Color Changes

Fair Isle is a color knitting technique in which you frequently change between two or more colors of yarn in each row to create a pattern. Fair Isle garments are typically worked in the basic stockinette stitch pattern and are often knitted on circular needles.

Since Fair Isle knitting involves frequent color changes, you carry the yarn you are not currently working with across the wrong side of your work. There are two methods of carrying yarn—stranding and weaving. You use the stranding method when you will use a yarn color again within four or fewer stitches. If you need

to carry yarn across more than four stitches, you should use the weaving method.

When you change from one yarn color to another color using the stranding method, you bring the new yarn color above or below the old yarn color to prevent holes from appearing in your knitted fabric.

Fair Isle designs are usually presented in charts that show you which color to use for every stitch in a colored area. For information on reading charts, see page 70.

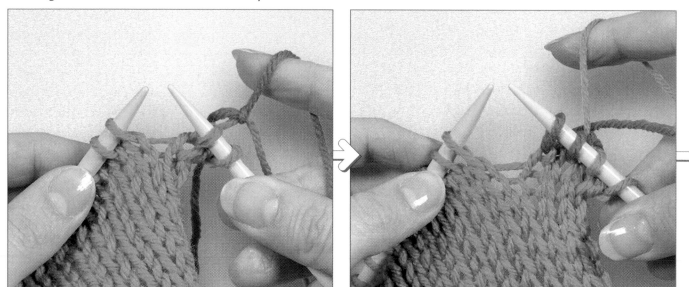

- When changing colors, if you have used the same yarn color four or fewer stitches ago, you can strand the yarn between color changes.

1 Work to where you want to use a different color of yarn.

2 To add a new color, tie the new color of yarn loosely around the yarn you are currently working with near the first stitch on the right needle. Leave a tail approximately 6 inches long.

3 Use the new yarn color to work stitches until you reach the location of the next color change in the row.

4 If you used the yarn color you want to change to four or fewer stitches ago, bring the yarn color you want to change to **above** the yarn color you are currently using.

5 Use the new yarn color to work stitches until you reach the location of the next color change in the row.

QUESTION & ANSWER ?

What should I keep in mind when stranding yarn between color changes?

You want to make sure the yarn you are stranding is not too tight. If the stranded yarn is too tight, your work will gather and not lie flat. Just before making a color change, gently stretch apart the first several stitches on the right needle. Stretching apart these stitches and gently extending the new yarn over them before you work the next stitch ensures the stranded yarn will not be too tight.

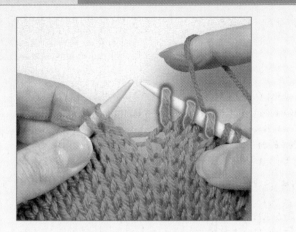

6 If you used the yarn color you want to change to four or fewer stitches ago, bring the yarn color you want to change to **below** the yarn color you are currently using.

7 Use the new yarn color to work stitches until you reach the location of the next color change in the row.

8 Repeat steps **4** to **7** until you complete all the color changes in your pattern. Each time you add a brand new color to your work, perform steps **2** and **3**.

*Note: When you become comfortable with Fair Isle knitting, you may want to skip step **2** to avoid creating knots in your work.*

• When you finish all the rows in your pattern, cut the colored yarn, leaving a tail approximately 6 inches long.

Note: When you finish your project, you can untie any knots and weave in the yarn ends. For information on weaving in yarn ends, see the top of page 175.

CONTINUED...

knit in color using fair isle (continued)

Weave in Yarn Between Color Changes

When knitting in color using Fair Isle, you use the weaving method when you want to carry colored yarn across more than four stitches. You weave in strands of colored yarn every three or four stitches to avoid having long strands of yarn floating across the knitted fabric. Long strands of yarn can get caught on jewelry or fingers and be pulled out of position, damaging your knitted piece.

Weaving in yarn across the wrong side of your work creates an additional layer of yarn in your fabric,

making your knitted project thicker and warmer.

When you knit a Fair Isle project, your knitted pieces may end up narrower than if you were knitting with only one color of yarn. You should make a gauge swatch in the Fair Isle pattern you will use for your project to ensure the project will be the correct size when it is complete. For information on making a gauge swatch, see page 62.

- When changing colors, if you will not use a yarn color again within four or fewer stitches, you should weave in the yarn between color changes.

1 Work to where you want to use a different color of yarn.

2 To add a new color, tie the new color of yarn loosely around the yarn you are currently working with near the first stitch on the right needle. Leave a tail approximately 6 inches long.

3 Hold the new yarn color in your right hand.

4 Hold the yarn color you just finished working with in your left hand.

5 Use the new yarn color to work the next three stitches on the left needle.

How will I know if I am weaving in the strands of yarn correctly?

Each strand of yarn you weave in correctly will be worked into the knitted fabric every three stitches and will not show through on the right side of your fabric.

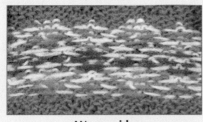

Wrong side

How can I avoid creating knots in my work when joining new colors of yarn?

Once you become comfortable with Fair Isle knitting, you can skip steps **2** to **5** below when you add a brand new color of yarn to avoid creating knots in your work. To secure the new color of yarn without tying a knot, work to the stitch before where you want to change yarn colors. Insert the right needle into the front of the stitch on the left needle knitwise and lay the new yarn color across the tip of the right needle. Then finish working the stitch with the current yarn color. You can then perform steps **3** to **8** below, using the new yarn color to work the next stitches on the left needle.

6 To knit the next stitch, insert the right needle into the front of the next stitch on the left needle, knitwise from left to right.

7 Lay the yarn you are holding in your left hand across the tip of the right needle, from back to front.

*Note: To purl the stitch in steps **6** and **7**, insert the right needle into the stitch purlwise from right to left in step **6**. Then lay the yarn across the tip of the needle from front to back in step **7**.*

8 Finish working the stitch.

Note: Make sure you do not pull the yarn color you are holding in your left hand through the stitch.

9 Repeat steps **3** to **8** to weave in the yarn every three stitches until you reach the next color change in the row.

10 Repeat steps **3** to **9** each time you want to change colors. To add a brand new color to your work, repeat steps **2** to **9**.

- When you finish all the rows in your pattern, cut the colored yarn, leaving a tail approximately 6 inches long.

Note: When you finish your project, you can untie any knots and weave in the yarn ends. For information on weaving in yarn ends, see the top of page 175.

knit in color using intarsia

Intarsia is a knitting method that involves using different colored yarns in your fabric to create attractive geometric designs and pictures. Intarsia knitting is ideal when working with large areas of color.

With intarsia knitting, you use a new ball of yarn or long strand of yarn for every area of color. The amount of yarn you need for an area of color depends on the size of the colored area. When you introduce a new color, you twist the old and new colors of yarn together to avoid creating a gap in your work where you change colors.

Unlike Fair Isle knitting, the intarsia method does not require you to carry strands of yarn across the rows in your work. You start a new ball of yarn for each color change in a row, even if you have previously used the color in the row. As a result, fabrics knit using the intarsia method tend to be less thick than fabrics knit using the Fair Isle method. For information on Fair Isle knitting, see page 170.

Intarsia designs are usually presented in charts that show you which color to use for every stitch in a colored area. For information on reading charts, see page 70.

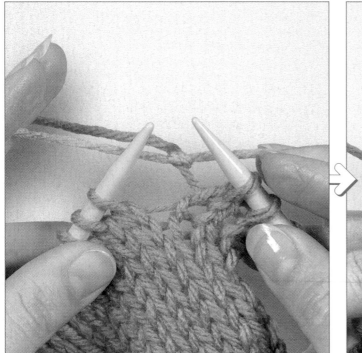

1 Work to where you want to use a different color of yarn.

2 Tie the new color of yarn loosely around the yarn you are currently working with near the first stitch on the right needle. Leave a tail approximately 6 inches long.

Note: When you become comfortable with intarsia knitting, you may want to skip step 2 to avoid creating knots in your work.

3 Bring the yarn color you are currently working with above the new yarn color and toward the left side of your work.

4 Pick up the new yarn color and work the next stitch.

174

QUESTION & ANSWER

When I finish my project, how do I weave in the colored yarn ends?

To prevent the yarn ends from showing on the right side of the fabric, you need to weave in each yarn end into stitches of the same color on the wrong side. Untie any knots you tied when starting a new color. Then thread a yarn end through a tapestry needle. Insert the tapestry needle under the upper bumps of the purl stitches along the border of the area that is the same color as the yarn.

5 Continue working with the new yarn color until you reach the location of the next color change in the row.

6 Repeat steps 2 to 5 for each color change in the current row.

Note: Each time you change yarn colors in the row, you must start a new ball or strand of yarn, even if you have previously used the same color in the row.

- When you work the next rows, perform steps 3 to 6 for each color change, picking up the colored yarn you used in the previous row.

- When you finish all the rows for a colored area, cut the colored yarn, leaving a tail approximately 6 inches long.

sweet dreams blanket

· Intermediate Project ·

Sweet Dreams Blanket

Size

Approx. 26 x 34 ins (66 x 86.5cm).

Materials

Dale of Norway Baby Ull
MC (Main Color) = Pink, 2 balls
Contrast A = Blue, 2 balls
Contrast B = Yellow, 2 balls
Contrast C = Green, 2 balls

Size 2 US (2.75mm) knitting needles or size
needed to obtain gauge.

Gauge

27 stitches (sts) and 46 rows = 4 ins (10cm) in
Seed St.

Stitch Glossary

Abbreviations: K = knit; P = purl; RS=right side.

Seed St:
Row 1: K1. *P1. K1; Rep from * to end of row.

Instructions

While this is an intermediate pattern, it is very
time consuming due to the small needles.

Note: When changing colors, use the intarsia
method as discussed on page 174.

With B, cast on 25 stitches (sts). With A, cast on
25 sts. With MC, cast on 25 sts. With C, cast on
25 sts. With B, cast on 25 sts. With A, cast on
25 sts. With MC, cast on 25 sts. 175 sts total.

Row 1 (RS): With MC, work 25 sts in Seed St.
Change to A and work 25 sts in Seed St.
Change to B and work 25 sts in Seed St.
Change to C and work 25 sts in Seed St.
Change to MC and work 25 sts in Seed St.
Change to A and work 25 sts in Seed St.
Change to B and work 25 sts in Seed St.
Continue in Seed St for 42 rows (approx
3.75 ins [9cm]), keeping continuity of colors,
ending with RS facing for next row.

Next Row: Starting with C, continue in Seed St
following Chart A to end of chart, changing colors
every 42 rows, as shown.

Bind off all stitches in Seed St.

Block to measurements.

Chart A

KEY								
MC=Pink	B	A	MC	C	B	A	MC	Row 378
A=Blue	C	B	A	MC	C	B	A	Row 336
B=Yellow	MC	C	B	A	MC	C	B	Row 294
C=Green	A	MC	C	B	A	MC	C	Row 252
	B	A	MC	C	B	A	MC	Row 210
	C	B	A	MC	C	B	A	Row 168
	MC	C	B	A	MC	C	B	Row 126
	A	MC	C	B	A	MC	C	Row 84
	B	A	MC	C	B	A	MC	Row 42
								Start Here

child's colorful
sweater

· Intermediate Project ·

Child's Colorful Sweater

Sizes

Chest measurement

2	22 ins (56cm)
4	24 ins (61cm)
6	26 ins (66cm)

Finished chest

2	25 ins (63.5cm)
4	29 ins (73.5cm)
6	31.5 ins (80cm)

Materials

Paton's Classic Merino Wool (3.5oz/100g)

Sizes	2	4	6	
MC (Main Color)=213 Blueberry	2	3	3	balls
Contrast A=202 Aran	1	1	1	ball
Contrast B=210 Petal Pink	1	1	1	ball

Sizes 6 US (4mm) and 7 US (4.5mm) knitting needles or size needed to obtain gauge.

2 stitch holders.

Gauge

20 stitches (sts) and 26 rows = 4 ins (10cm) with larger needles in Stockinette St (knit 1 row, purl 1 row).

Stitch Glossary

Abbreviations: RS = right side; WS = wrong side; K = knit; P = purl; P2tog = purl two stitches together; dec = decrease; inc = increase.

M1P = Make one stitch by picking up the horizontal loop lying before the next stitch and purling into the back of loop.

Square A:

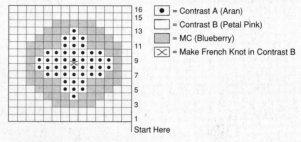

Square B: (Striped Pattern)

(worked over 13 sts in Stockinette St (knit 1 row, purl 1 row))

Work 1 row in MC.

Work 1 row in A.

Work 1 row in B.

Rep these 3 rows until a total of 16 rows have been worked.

Square C:

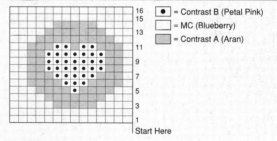

Square D:

(worked over 13 sts)

Foundation Row (RS): With A, knit.

Row 1: P1. M1P. (K2. P2) 3 times.

Row 2: (K2. P2) 3 times. K2.

Row 3: As Row 2.

Row 4: (P2. K2) 3 times. P2.

Row 5: As Row 4.

Row 6-13: Rep Rows 2 to 5 twice.

Row 14: As Row 2.

Row 15: As Row 2.

Row 16: (P2. K2) 3 times. P2tog.

These 16 rows form Square D.

child's colorful sweater

Instructions

When working from charts, wind small balls (or bobbins) of the colors to be used, one for each separate area of color in the design. Start new colors at appropriate points. To change colors, twist the 2 colors around each other where they meet, on wrong side, to prevent a hole.

Bracketed numbers are for sizes 2 (**4**-6).

Back

With smaller needles and MC, cast on 62 (72**-78) stitches (sts).

Row 1: *K1. P1; Rep from * to end of row.

Row 2: Purl the knit sts and knit the purl sts.

These two rows form Seed St.

Repeat these 2 rows for 1 in [2.5cm], ending with RS facing for next row.

Change to larger needles and proceed in pattern as follows:

NOTE: Squares A and C are in chart form.

Row 1 (RS): With MC, Seed St 2 (**4**-4) sts. Work Row 1 of Square A across next 13 sts. With MC, Seed St 2 (**4**-6) sts. Work Row 1 of Square B across next 13 sts. With MC, Seed St 2 (**4**-6) sts. Work Row 1 of Square C across next 13 sts. With MC, Seed St 2 (**4**-6) sts. Work Row 1 of Square D across next 13 sts. With MC, Seed St to end of row.

Row 2: With MC, Seed St 2 (**4**-4) sts. Work Row 2 of Square D. With MC, Seed St 2 (**4**-6) sts. Work Row 2 of Square C. With MC, Seed St 2 (**4**-6) sts. Work Row 2 of Square B. With MC, Seed St 2 (**4**-6) sts. Work Row 2 of Square A. With MC, Seed St to end of row.

Row 3: With MC, Seed St 2 (**4**-4) sts. Work Row 3 of Square A. With MC, Seed St 2 (**4**-6) sts. Work Row 3 of Square B. With MC, Seed St 2 (**4**-6) sts. Work Row 3 of Square C. With MC, Seed St 2 (**4**-6) sts. Work Row 3 of Square D. With MC, Seed St to end of row.

Row 4: With MC, Seed St 2 (**4**-4) sts. Work Row 4 of Square D. With MC, Seed St 2 (**4**-6) sts. Work Row 4 of Square C. With MC, Seed St 2 (**4**-6) sts. Work Row 4 of Square B. With MC, Seed St 2 (**4**-6) sts. Work Row 4 of Square A. With MC, Seed St to end of row.

Squares A, B, C and D are now in position.

Back (cont.)

Continue in pattern, keeping continuity of Squares and Seed St as established above, until Row 16 of all squares has been worked.

Next: With MC, work 6 rows in Seed St.

Proceed as follows:

Row 1 (RS): With MC, Seed St 2 (**4**-4) sts. Work Row 1 of Square B. With MC, Seed St 2 (**4**-6) sts. Work Row 1 of Square C. With MC, Seed St 2 (**4**-6) sts. Work Row 1 of Square D. With MC, Seed St 2 (**4**-6) sts. Work Row 1 of Square A. With MC, Seed St to end of row.

Row 2: With MC, Seed St 2 (**4**-4) sts. Work Row 2 of Square A. With MC, Seed St 2 (**4**-6) sts. Work Row 2 of Square D. With MC, Seed St 2 (**4**-6) sts. Work Row 2 of Square C. With MC, Seed St 2 (**4**-6) sts. Work Row 2 of Square B. With MC, Seed St to end of row.

Squares B, C, D and A are now in position.

Continue in this manner, following Diagram 1 for square placement. With MC, work 6 rows of Seed St between each row of squares, until 4 (**4**-5) rows of complete squares from Diagram 1 have been worked, ending with RS facing for next row.**

With MC, work in Seed St until work from beginning measures 14.75 (**15.75**-18.5) ins [37.5 (**40**-47) cm], ending with RS facing for next row.

DIAGRAM 1

D	C	B	A
C	B	A	D
B	A	D	C
A	D	C	B
D	C	B	A

START HERE

Shoulder shaping: Bind off 8 (**10**-11) sts beginning next 2 rows, then 9 (**11**-11) sts beginning following 2 rows. Leave remaining 28 (**30**-34) sts on a stitch holder.

Front

Work from ** to ** as given for Back.

With MC, work in Seed St until work from beginning measures 13.25 (**13.75**-16.5) ins [33.5 (**35**-42) cm], ending with RS facing for next row.

Neck shaping: Next row: Work in pattern across 22 (**26**-27) sts (neck edge). **Turn.** Leave remaining sts on a spare needle. Continue in Seed St and dec 1 st at neck edge on next 3 rows, then following alt rows twice. 17 (**21**-22) sts. Continue in Seed St until work from beginning measures 14.75 (**15.75**-18.5) ins [37.5 (**40**-47) cm], ending with RS facing for next row.

child's colorful sweater

Front (cont.)

Bind off 8 (**10**-11) sts beginning next row. Work 1 row even. Bind off remaining 9 (**11**-11) sts.

Slip next 18 (**20**-24) sts onto a stitch holder and Seed St to end of row.
Continue in Seed St and dec 1 st at neck edge on next 3 rows, then following alt rows twice. 17 (**21**-22) sts.
Continue in Seed St until work from beginning measures 14.75 (**15.75**-18.5) ins [37.5 (**40**-47) cm], ending with WS facing for next row.

Shoulder shaping: Bind off 8 (**10**-11) sts beginning next row. Work 1 row even. Bind off remaining 9 (**11**-11) sts.

Sleeves

With smaller needles and MC, cast on 35 (**41**-41)sts. Work in Seed St for 1 in [2.5cm] as given for Back.

Change to larger needles and work Striped pattern as given for Square B, **at the same time**, inc 1 st at each end of needle on 3rd and following 4th (**6th**-6th) rows to 55 (**61**-65) sts, taking increased sts into pattern.

Continue in Striped pattern until work from beginning measures 7 (**10.5**-12) ins [18 (**26.5**-30.5) cm] ending with RS facing for next row.

Bind off all stitches.

Finishing

Pin to measurements and cover with damp cloth, leaving to dry on garment.

Roll Collar: Sew right shoulder seam. With RS facing, MC and larger needles, pick up and knit 11 sts down left front neck edge. Knit across 18 (**20**-24) sts from front neck stitch holder. Pick up and knit 11 sts up right front neck edge. Knit across 28 (**30**-34) sts from back neck stitch holder. 68 (**72**-80) sts.

Beginning with a purl row, work in Stockinette St (knit 1 row, purl 1 row) for 3 ins [7.5cm], ending with RS facing for next row.
Bind off all stitches.

Sew left shoulder and collar seam, reversing seam to allow it to roll forward. Measure 5.5 (**6**-6.5) ins [14 (**15**-16.5) cm] down from shoulder and place marker. Sew in sleeves between markers. Sew side and sleeve seams.

Using B, embroider French Knots in Square A, as illustrated.

Finishing (cont.)

French Knot:
Thread tapestry needle with strand of B. Insert tapestry needle through fabric from back to front. Wrap yarn around tapestry needle twice, keeping yarn tight. Reinsert tapestry needle through the fabric from front to back one stitch away, creating knot on fabric.

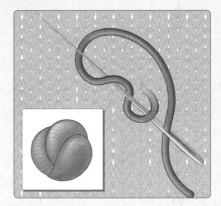

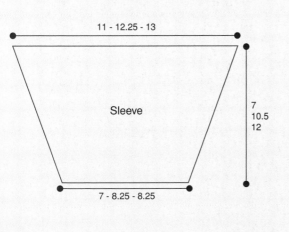

Sleeve

11 - 12.25 - 13

7 - 8.25 - 8.25

7
10.5
12

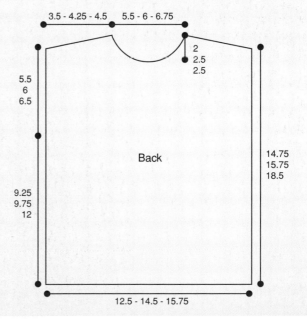

3.5 - 4.25 - 4.5   5.5 - 6 - 6.75

2
2.5
2.5

5.5
6
6.5

Back

14.75
15.75
18.5

9.25
9.75
12

12.5 - 14.5 - 15.75

zip-neck sweater

· Intermediate Project ·

Zip-Neck Sweater

Sizes

Bust/chest measurement

Small	30-32 ins (76-81cm)
Medium	34-36 ins (86-91cm)
Large	38-40 ins (97-102cm)
X-Large	42-44 ins (107-112cm)

Finished bust/chest

Small	38 ins (96.5cm)
Medium	42 ins (106.5cm)
Large	46 ins (117cm)
X-Large	50 ins (127cm)

Materials

Alafoss Lopi Lite 50g

Sizes	S	M	L	XL	
MC (Main Color) = #9443 Blue	10	11	11	12	balls
Contrast A = #0051 Aran	1	1	1	1	ball
Contrast B = #9432 Indigo	1	1	1	1	ball

Sizes 8 US (5mm) knitting needles and 8 US (5mm) circular knitting needles (40cm long) or size needed to obtain gauge.

2 stitch holders.

Closed ended zipper 3 ins (7.5cm) long (find a shop that will cut zippers to size for you).

Gauge

18 stitches (sts) and 24 rows = 4 ins (10cm) in Stockinette St (knit 1 row, purl 1 row).

Stitch Glossary

Abbreviations: WS = wrong side; RS = right side; K = knit; P = purl; Sl = slip stitch; wyif=with yarn in front; inc = increase; dec = decrease.

Stitch Glossary (cont.)

Pattern St:

Rows 1 and 3 (WS): K2. *P5. K3; Rep from * to last 7 sts, P5. K2.

Row 2: K2. *Sl5 wyif. K3; Rep from * to last 7 sts, Sl5 wyif. K2.

Row 4: K4. *Insert needle knitwise under loose strand and knit the next st, bringing st out under strand. K7; Rep from * to last 5 sts. Insert needle knitwise under loose strand and knit the next st, bringing st out under strand. K4.

These 4 rows form pattern st.

Instructions

Bracketed numbers are for sizes S (**M**-L-**XL**)

Back

With MC, cast on 81 (89**-97-**105**) sts.

Work in pattern st until work from beginning measures 15 (**15.5**-16-**16.5**) ins [38 (**39.5**-40.5-**42**) cm], ending with RS facing for next row and inc 22 (**26**-28-**32**) sts evenly across last row. 103 (**115**-125-**137**) sts.

zip-neck sweater

Back (cont.)

Next row: Work 1st row of Chart A (beginning where indicated for size, repeating 12 st repeat, and ending where indicated for size) in Stockinette St to **end** of chart, reading knit rows from right to left and purl rows from left to right.

Next row: Purl, dec 22 (**26**-28-**32**) sts evenly across last row. 81 (**89**-97-**105**) sts.**

Continue in pattern st until work from beginning measures 23.5 (**24.5**-25.5-**26**) ins [59.5 (**62**-65-**66**) cm], ending with RS facing for next row.

Shoulder shaping: Bind off 8 (**9**-10-**12**) sts beginning next 4 rows, then 7 (**9**-11-**11**) sts beginning following 2 rows. Leave remaining 35 sts on stitch holder.

Chart A

KEY

 = MC (Blue #9443)

□ = Contrast A (Aran #0051)

⊡ = Contrast B (Indigo # 9432)

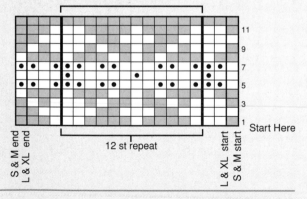

11
9
7
5
3
1 Start Here

S & M end
L & XL end

12 st repeat

L & XL start
S & M start

Front

Work from ** to ** as given for Back.

Continue in pattern st until work from beginning measures 20.5 (**21.5**-22.5-**23**) ins [52 (**54.5**-57-**58.5**) cm], ending with RS facing for next row.

Front (cont.)

Neck shaping:
Next row: Work in pattern st across 35 (**39**-43-**47**) sts (neck edge). **Turn.** Leave remaining sts on a stitch holder. Dec 1 st at neck edge on next 12 rows.

Continue in pattern st until work from beginning measures 23.5 (**24.5**-25.5-**26**) ins [59.5 (**62**-65-**66**) cm], ending with RS facing for next row.

Shoulder shaping:
Bind off 8 (**9**-10-**12**) sts beginning and following alt row. Work 1 row even. Bind off remaining 7 (**9**-11-**11**) sts.

Slip next 11 sts onto a stitch holder and work to end of row. Dec 1 st at neck edge on next 12 rows.

Continue in pattern st until work from beginning measures 23.5 (**24.5**-25.5-**26**) ins [59.5 (**62**-65-**66**) cm], ending with WS facing for next row.

Shoulder shaping:
Bind off 8 (**9**-10-**12**) sts beginning and following alt row. Work 1 row even. Bind off remaining 7 (**9**-11-**11**) sts.

Sleeves

With MC, cast on 41 sts. Work pattern st and AT THE SAME TIME inc 1 st each end of needle on 3rd and following 4th rows to 55 (**59**-65-**71**) sts, then every 6th row to 77 (**81**-85-**89**) sts, taking inc sts into pattern.

Continue in pattern st until work from beginning measures 17 (**18**-19-**20**) ins [43 (**45.5**-48-**51**) cm], ending with RS facing for next row.

Bind off all sts.

Finishing

Collar:
Sew shoulder seams. With RS of work facing, slip first 5 sts from front stitch holder onto spare needle.

With circular needle, join yarn to remaining sts and bind off next st. Knit remaining 5 sts from front st holder. Pick up and knit 19 st up right front neck edge. Knit across 35 sts from back neck st holder, dec 1 st at center. Pick up and knit 19 sts down left front neck edge. Knit remaining 5 sts from spare needle. 82 sts.

Work back and forth across needle as follows:

Row 1: P2. *K2. P2; Rep from * to end of row.

Row 2: K2. *P2. K2; Rep from * to end of row.

These 2 rows form (K2. P2) ribbing.

Continue in (K2. P2) ribbing for 6 ins [15cm], ending with RS facing for next row.

Bind off all stitches in ribbing.

Place markers on front and back side edges 9 (**9.5**-10-**10.5**) ins [23 (**24**-25.5-**26.5**) cm] down from shoulder seams. Sew in sleeves between markers.

Finishing (cont.)

Zipper edging:
With RS facing and MC, pick up and knit 27 sts down left side of Collar. Pick up and knit 1 st from Neckline. Pick up and knit 27 sts up right side of Collar. 55 sts. Bind off all sts knitwise.

Sew zipper to foldline of Collar. Fold Collar along foldline to WS and sew into position.

Sew side and sleeve seams.

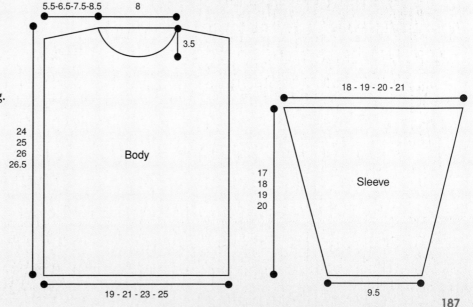

Chapter 8

When you have finished knitting all the pieces in your project, there are several finishing touches you may need to perform to complete the project. This chapter teaches you how to create buttonholes, weave in yarn ends and attach knitted pieces together. You will also learn different techniques for blocking knitted pieces, which helps you ensure that the knitted pieces have the correct dimensions before you sew them together.

Finishing Your Knitted Projects

In this Chapter...

make a buttonhole

Make a Horizontal Buttonhole

You can create a buttonhole in your knitwear. A horizontal buttonhole requires two rows to complete and is often referred to as a two-row buttonhole. In the first row, you create a gap by binding off (removing) a certain number of stitches in the row. In the following row, you cast on (add) new stitches overtop of the gap, leaving a hole between the rows. Using the single cast on method to add stitches provides a clean edge to close the buttonhole.

The size of the buttons and the thickness of the yarn you use determine how many stitches you need to bind off and cast on to create a buttonhole. For example, you need to bind off more stitches if you use larger buttons. Most knitting patterns provide directions for creating a buttonhole.

When creating a buttonhole, your goal should be to create a buttonhole that is not too loose for the button. Knitted fabric is flexible, so if a buttonhole is too loose, the button may slip out.

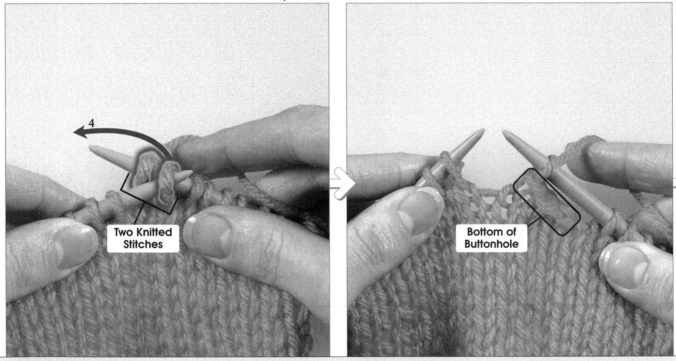

Two Knitted Stitches

Bottom of Buttonhole

- In this example, we create a buttonhole that is 3 stitches wide.

1 With the right side of your work facing you, work to where you want to create a buttonhole.

2 Knit the next two stitches on the left needle.

3 Insert the left needle into the front of the first stitch you knitted in step 2, from left to right.

4 Using the left needle, lift the stitch over the second stitch you knitted and allow the stitch to drop off both needles.

5 Knit the next stitch on the left needle.

6 Repeat steps 3 to 5 twice, leaving out step 5 the last time you repeat the steps.

7 Continue working to the end of the row.

What types of buttons should I choose for my knitwear?

Make sure the buttons you choose have rounded edges and smooth surfaces. If you use buttons with elaborate designs or rough edges, they may snag on the yarn in your garment. Larger buttons are ideal for use with heavier yarn weights while smaller buttons work well on baby garments.

How can I make sure my buttonhole will turn out the way I want?

You should knit a sample piece in the stitch pattern you are using for your project and include a test buttonhole. This will help you make sure the buttonhole will turn out the way you want in the stitch pattern. You can also verify that the hole is big enough or small enough for the buttons you want to use.

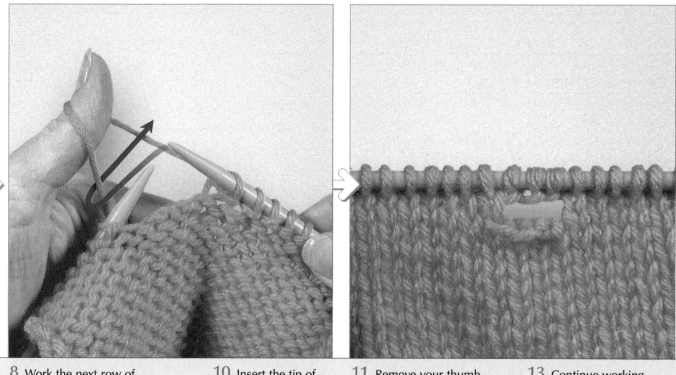

8 Work the next row of stitches until you reach the edge of the buttonhole.

9 Wrap the strand of yarn connected to the ball around your left thumb, clockwise from front to back and use the fingers of your left hand to hold the strand loosely in your palm.

10 Insert the tip of the right needle between your thumb and the strand of yarn, from bottom to top.

11 Remove your thumb from the loop of yarn and gently pull on the strand of yarn to tighten the stitch on the right needle.

12 Repeat steps 9 to 11 twice.

13 Continue working to the end of the row.

• You have now created a horizontal buttonhole.

CONTINUED...

Make a Vertical Buttonhole

You can create a vertical buttonhole in your knitwear by using two balls of yarn. A vertical buttonhole is essentially created by dividing a series of rows into two sides, so you will need one ball of yarn to knit each side.

Vertical buttonholes are more flexible than horizontal buttonholes so buttons tend to slip out more easily. As a result, vertical buttonholes are mainly used to enhance the visual appeal of a garment as opposed to functioning as fasteners. Vertical buttonholes work

well with many stitch patterns, but you may not want to place them in plain stockinette stitch patterns as the edges of the hole may curl towards the wrong side of your fabric.

You should make a test buttonhole to ensure your buttons will fit in the buttonholes and to double check the number of rows you will have to create to make the buttonholes.

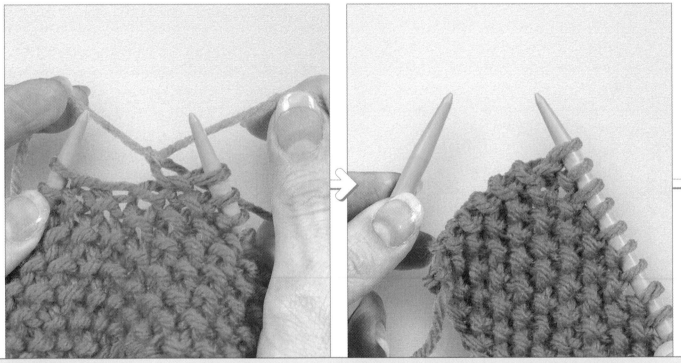

1 With the right side of your work facing you, work to where you want to create a buttonhole.

2 Drop the yarn you are currently using.

3 Tie a new strand of yarn around the original yarn near the first stitch on the right needle. Leave approximately 6 inches of a tail.

4 Continue working across the row with the new yarn until you complete the row.

Note: We use two different colors of yarn to clearly show the two balls of yarn. Normally, you would use two balls of yarn in the same color.

Is there any other way to make a buttonhole?

There are several ways to create buttonholes. Another popular method is to use the yarn over technique to create an intentional hole, called an eyelet, in your work.

To create an eyelet buttonhole in stockinette stitch, work to where you want to create a

buttonhole. Knit the next two stitches on the left needle together as shown on page 88. Then make a yarn over (**yo**) between two knit stitches as shown on page 84. You can then continue working the rest of the row.

5 Work across the next row with the new yarn. When you reach the location of the buttonhole, drop the yarn.

6 Pick up the original yarn again and finish working the row.

7 Repeat steps **1** to **6**, leaving out step **3**, until the buttonhole is the length you want.

8 Cut the strand of yarn attached to the new ball of yarn. Leave approximately 6 inches of a tail.

9 Work all the stitches in the remaining rows with the original ball of yarn.

• You have now created a vertical buttonhole.

pick up stitches

Picking up stitches allows you to create new stitches along a finished edge. You can then use the new stitches to knit an additional piece onto the original piece. For example, you can use picked-up stitches to knit a collar directly onto a sweater instead of knitting the collar separately and then sewing the collar onto the sweater.

You can pick up stitches along a bound-off edge (commonly used for adding a collar to a sweater) or along a side edge of your work (commonly used for adding a band for buttons to a cardigan).

When picking up stitches, you work from right to left along the edge of the completed, knitted fabric, pulling loops from a new ball of yarn through the existing stitches to create new stitches on your needle.

Most pattern instructions tell you how many stitches you need to pick up along a finished edge of your work. Since you usually do not pick up every stitch along a finished edge, make sure you leave an equal amount of space between each stitch you pick up or your knitted fabric will not lie flat.

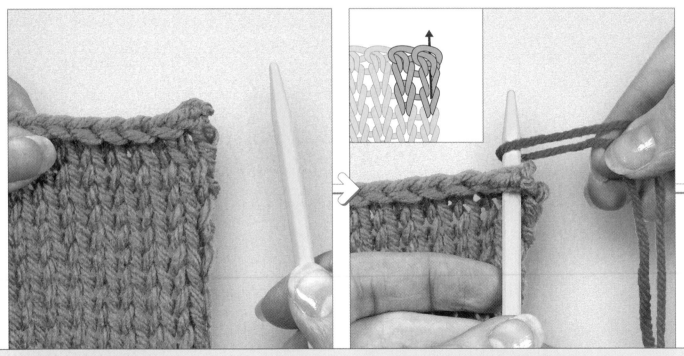

1 Hold the completed, knitted fabric in your left hand with the right side of the fabric facing you and the edge where you want to pick up stitches at the top.

2 Hold a knitting needle in your right hand.

3 Insert the tip of the needle through the first stitch in the fabric where you want to start picking up stitches, from front to back.

4 With the ball of yarn you will use to knit the new piece, wrap a strand of yarn around the tip of the needle, leaving a tail approximately 6 inches long.

Note: We use a different color of yarn to more clearly show the example. You should use the same yarn you used to knit the piece.

Can I pick up stitches along an edge that is not straight?

Yes. You can pick up stitches on curved edges, such as necklines. Follow the curve of the piece you are working on, making sure to pick up stitches evenly along the curve.

How can I make sure I pick up stitches evenly along my work?

You can fasten stitch markers or tie strands of yarn along the edge of your work every 2 inches to help you evenly space the stitches you pick up. Check the pattern instructions for the number of stitches you need to pick up. Divide this number by the number of 2-inch sections you have. The resulting number will tell you the number of stitches you need to pick up in each 2-inch section.

5 Slide the tip of the needle and the wrapped yarn back through the stitch toward you.

• You have picked up one stitch on the needle.

6 Repeat steps 3 to 5 for each stitch you want to pick up, wrapping the yarn around the tip of the needle counterclockwise in step 4.

Note: Most patterns tell you how many stitches you need to pick up along an edge. Make sure you leave an equal amount of space between each stitch you pick up.

block knitted pieces

Wet Blocking

Before sewing together the knitted pieces of a project, you should block each piece. Blocking knitted pieces helps you even out stitches, flatten curling edges and make sure that the pieces have the correct dimensions. When blocking a knitted piece, you can make minor adjustments to the shape and size of a piece.

There are two main types of blocking—wet blocking and steam blocking. When wet blocking, a knitted piece is soaked in water, reshaped and then allowed to

dry thoroughly. Wet blocking is suitable for knitted pieces made from colorfast yarns and fuzzy yarns. Wet blocking is also the best blocking method for garments with cabled or highly textured patterns.

When blocking a knitted piece, you use rust-proof pins to fasten the piece to a flat, padded surface such as an ironing board or a flat surface covered with a towel. The pins help keep the knitted piece in its proper shape and size until it dries.

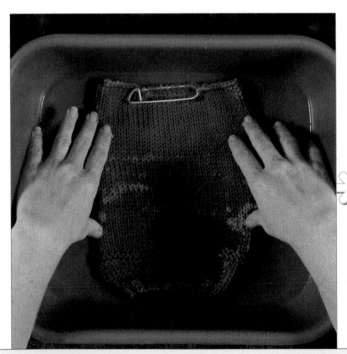 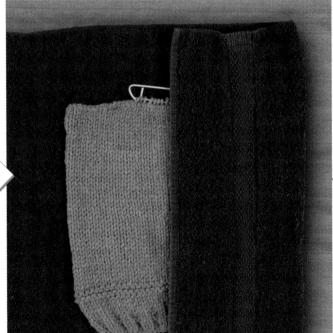

- To wet block a knitted piece, you will need a basin or sink, a towel, a flat surface that is padded or covered with a towel, rust-proof pins and a tape measure.

1 Fill a basin or sink with cool water and completely wet the knitted piece you want to block. Do not wring or rub the knitted piece.

2 Drain the water from the basin and gently press on the knitted piece to remove the excess water.

3 Lift the knitted piece out of the basin without allowing any part of the piece to stretch.

4 Spread out the knitted piece right-side up on a clean, dry towel without stretching the piece.

5 Fold the ends of the towel over the knitted piece.

Can I block all my knitted pieces?

You should check the yarn label for the yarn you used to knit your pieces. If the yarn label indicates that you can wash the fabric in water, you can safely use the wet blocking method for your knitted pieces. If your knitted pieces are composed of different types of yarns, use the blocking method suitable for the most delicate type of yarn used. To ensure that wet blocking will not ruin your knitted pieces, you can first try wet blocking your gauge swatch. For information on gauge swatches, see page 62.

Can I use a bit of detergent when wet blocking?

Yes. To wash out any dirt in your knitted pieces, you can soak the pieces in water that contains a small amount of mild detergent. After you empty the water from the basin, gently press on the pieces to remove excess water. To rinse, refill the basin with clean water and repeat the previous step until soap residue does not appear on the knitted pieces and the water in the basin is clear. You can also use this method to wash your knitted garment after wearing it.

6 Loosely roll up the towel.

Note: Rolling the towel too tightly may cause creases in your knitted piece.

7 Gently press on the rolled towel to absorb water from the knitted piece.

8 Unroll the towel.

9 Lay the knitted piece on a flat surface that is padded or covered with a clean, dry towel.

10 Starting at the center of the knitted piece, spread out the piece to the correct dimensions as specified in the pattern instructions.

11 To keep the knitted piece at its correct dimensions, use rust-proof pins to pin the knitted piece to the padding or towel.

Note: The knitted piece may take a day or more to dry completely. You should not unpin or move the piece until it is dry.

block knitted
pieces (continued)

Steam Blocking

Before sewing together the knitted pieces of a project, you should block each piece. Blocking knitted pieces helps you make sure that each piece has the correct dimensions and allows you to make minor adjustments to the shape and size of each piece. Blocking also helps to even out stitches and flatten curling edges in your work.

When steam blocking, a knitted piece is pinned to its specified shape and size, covered with a damp cloth

and very gently pressed with an iron. Steam blocking is quicker and easier than wet blocking.

Steam blocking is suitable for knitted pieces made from yarns such as cotton and wool. Knitted pieces made from synthetic or fuzzy yarns should not be steam blocked. Always check the pattern instructions or the yarn label to see whether an iron can be used on the yarn you knitted the piece with.

- To steam block a knitted piece, you will need a flat surface that is padded or covered with a towel, rust-proof pins, a tape measure, a damp cloth and an iron.

1 Lay the knitted piece you want to block right-side up on a flat surface that is padded or covered with a towel.

2 Starting at the center of the knitted piece, spread out the piece to the correct dimensions as specified in the pattern instructions.

3 To keep the knitted piece at its correct dimensions, use rust-proof pins to pin the knitted piece to the padding or towel.

What types of knitted pieces should not be steam blocked?

Steam blocking should not be used on knitted pieces with cabled or highly textured patterns. Even gently holding an iron on such pieces can squash textures, distort details and change the appearance of the patterns. Ribbing may also become less stretchy if even gently pressed with an iron. Knitted pieces with cabled or textured patterns should be wet blocked instead.

Can I use a steam iron to steam block my knitted pieces?

Yes. You should use a steam iron for delicate yarns and knitted items you could distort by holding an iron on the fabric. First, pin a knitted piece to its correct dimensions by performing steps 1 to 3 below. Then hold a steam iron several inches above the knitted piece and use the steam from the iron to dampen the piece. Make sure you do not touch the steam iron to your knitted piece. After dampening the entire piece using the steam from the iron, allow the piece to dry thoroughly before unpinning the piece.

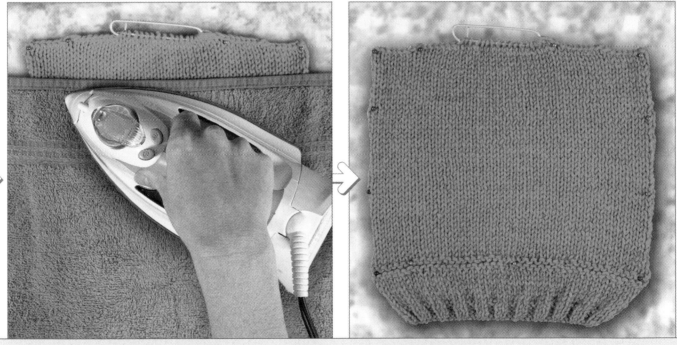

4 Cover the knitted piece with a damp cloth.

5 Using an iron set to the correct temperature, lightly hold the iron on one area of the knitted piece for a few seconds.

Note: The pattern instructions or yarn label may indicate whether you should use a cool, warm or hot iron.

6 Lift the iron and then move the iron to the next area you want to block.

7 Repeat steps 5 and 6 until you have blocked the entire knitted piece.

• When you have finished blocking the entire knitted piece, leave the piece pinned to the surface until the piece is completely dry.

sew knitted pieces together

Using the Mattress Stitch

Once you have finished knitting all the pieces in your project, you can sew the pieces together, known as sewing seams or seaming. There are three commonly used stitches for sewing knitted pieces together—mattress stitch, backstitch and whip stitch. The mattress stitch, also called the invisible seam, is often the best stitch to use for seaming garments as it produces a flexible, almost undetectable seam.

To use the mattress stitch, your knitted pieces should have approximately the same number of rows.

Before you start, you should align the rows in the knitted pieces. You can use straight pins to hold the knitted pieces in place as you sew. Since the mattress stitch allows you to join knitted pieces row by row, this seaming method helps conceal any uneven stitches on the edges of your work.

When using the mattress stitch, the right side of your work faces you, allowing you to see how the seam will look when finished. You can later weave in the yarn ends left over from sewing the seam.

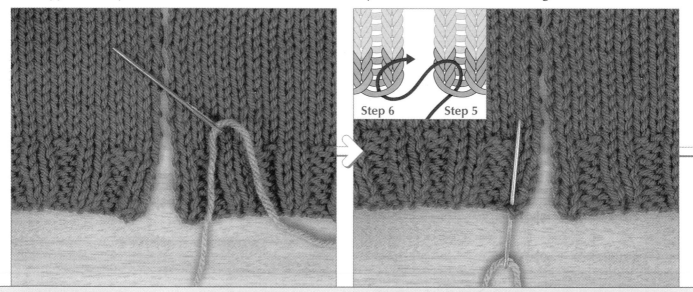

1 Place the two knitted pieces you want to sew together side by side with the right sides facing you, the bottom edges at the bottom and the rows lined up.

2 Cut a strand of yarn long enough to sew the knitted pieces together.

3 Thread the strand of yarn through a tapestry needle, leaving a tail approximately 6 inches long.

Note: We use a different color of yarn to sew the knitted pieces together to more clearly show the example. You should use the same yarn you used to knit the pieces.

4 On the bottom right corner of the left knitted piece, insert the needle between the two bottom corner stitches, from back to front. Then pull the yarn through.

5 On the bottom left corner of the right knitted piece, insert the needle between the two bottom corner stitches, from back to front. Then pull the yarn through.

6 On the bottom right corner of the left knitted piece, insert the needle between the two bottom corner stitches again, from back to front. Then pull the yarn through to secure the yarn.

QUESTION & ANSWER

Can I sew knitted pieces together without using a new strand of yarn?

Yes. If a knitted piece has a long tail, you can use the tail for sewing a seam using the mattress stitch. Position the knitted pieces as described in step **1** below, with the tail you will use to sew the pieces attached to the bottom left corner of the right knitted piece. Thread the end of the tail through a tapestry needle and then perform steps **4** to **11** below to sew the knitted pieces together.

How can I sew knitted pieces together more quickly?

If you find that sewing your knitted pieces together by catching a single horizontal strand of yarn between the stitches is too time consuming, you may want to try catching two horizontal strands on each side instead. Perform steps **1** to **11** below, except bring the tip of the needle back to the front of the knitted piece just above the next higher horizontal strand of yarn in steps **8** and **10**.

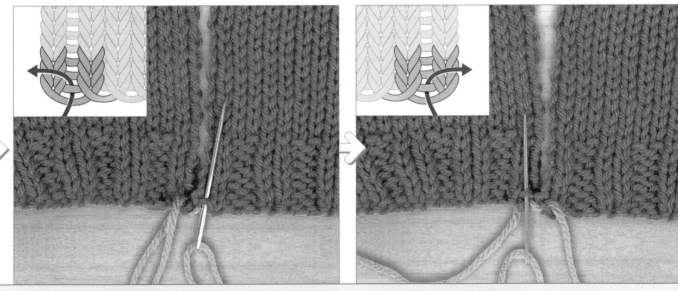

7 On the bottom left corner of the right knitted piece, insert the needle just below the horizontal strand of yarn that connects the first two stitches, from front to back.

Note: To help locate the horizontal strand of yarn that connects the two stitches, gently pull the stitches away from each other.

8 Bring the tip of the needle back to the front of the knitted piece, just above the same horizontal strand of yarn. Then pull the yarn through.

9 On the bottom right corner of the left knitted piece, insert the needle just below the horizontal strand of yarn that connects the first two stitches, from front to back.

10 Bring the tip of the needle back to the front of the knitted piece, just above the same horizontal strand of yarn. Then pull the yarn through.

11 Repeat steps **7** to **10**, moving up one row at a time on each knitted piece, until you have sewed the entire edge.

Note: To weave in the yarn ends left over from sewing the knitted pieces together, see page 208.

CONTINUED...

sew knitted pieces together

Using the Backstitch

When you are ready to assemble your knitted project, you can sew the individual pieces together. The backstitch is an ideal stitch to use when you are sewing curved edges together, such as attaching a sleeve to the body of a sweater. Compared to the mattress stitch, the backstitch produces a stronger, less flexible and more noticeable seam.

When using the backstitch, you hold the knitted pieces together with the right sides facing each other and the edges lined up. You may want to pin the pieces together to make sure they do not move while you sew the seam. You sew the seam from right to left, using a strand of the same yarn you used to knit the pieces. You can later weave in the yarn ends left over from sewing the seam.

Since the backstitch is worked with the wrong side of your work facing you, you cannot see what the seam will look like when finished as you sew the seam.

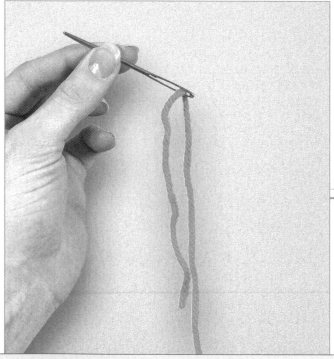

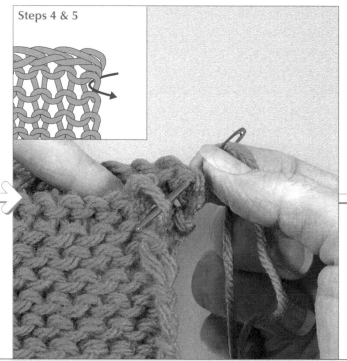

Steps 4 & 5

1 Cut a strand of yarn long enough to sew the knitted pieces together.

2 Thread the strand of yarn through a tapestry needle, leaving a tail approximately 6 inches long.

Note: We use a different color of yarn to sew the knitted pieces together to more clearly show the example. You should use the same yarn you used to knit the pieces.

3 Hold the two knitted pieces you want to sew together with the right sides facing each other and the edges lined up. Make sure the edges you want to sew together are at the top.

4 At the top right corner of both knitted pieces, insert the needle through the first stitch, from back to front. Then pull the yarn through.

5 Bring the needle and yarn to the right of the knitted pieces and then repeat step 4 to secure the yarn.

When should I not use the backstitch?

The backstitch produces a thick seam and should be used only when sewing together knitted pieces made with lightweight yarn. You should not use the backstitch when working with medium-to-heavy or heavy weight yarn. For information on yarn weights, see page 24.

Why are there holes between the knitted pieces I sewed together?

You may have inserted the needle more than two stitches to the left in step 6 below, making the stitches in your seam too large. If you notice holes between the knitted pieces, you should pull out the stitches and sew the seam again.

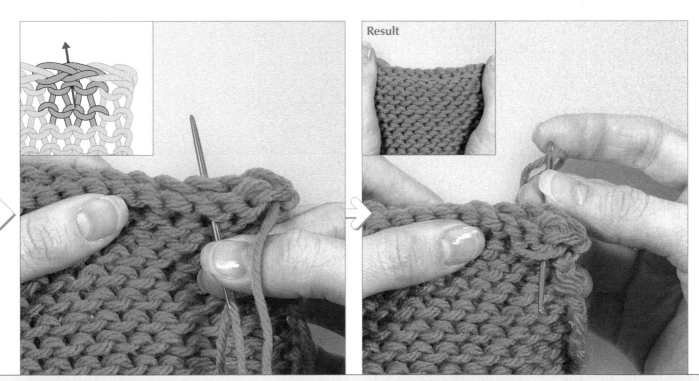

Result

6 On the front knitted piece, insert the needle two stitches to the left and through both knitted pieces, from front to back. Then pull the yarn through.

7 On the back knitted piece, insert the needle one stitch to the right and through both knitted pieces, from back to front. Then pull the yarn through.

8 Repeat steps 6 and 7 until you have sewed the entire edge.

Note: To weave in the yarn ends left over from sewing the knitted pieces together, see page 208.

CONTINUED...

sew knitted
pieces together

Using the Whip Stitch

You can use the whip stitch, also called overcasting, to sew your knitted pieces together. The whip stitch is often used when you need a strong seam, such as when creating knitted bags or purses. The whip stitch creates a bulky seam and is not commonly used to join knitted pieces of a garment.

When using the whip stitch, you normally hold your knitted pieces with the right sides facing each other and the edges lined up. You can pin the pieces

together to make sure they do not move while you sew the seam. You sew the seam from right to left, using a strand of the same yarn you used to knit the pieces. After you complete the seam, there will be ends of yarn hanging from your project. You can later weave the yarn ends into your project.

Since the whip stitch is worked with the wrong side of your work facing you, you cannot see what the seam will look like when finished as you sew the seam.

Step 4

1 Cut a strand of yarn long enough to sew the knitted pieces together.

2 Thread the strand of yarn through a tapestry needle, leaving a tail approximately 6 inches long.

Note: We use a different color of yarn to sew the knitted pieces together to more clearly show the example. You should use the same yarn you used to knit the pieces.

3 Hold the two knitted pieces you want to sew together with the right sides facing each other and the edges lined up. Make sure the edges you want to sew together are at the top.

4 At the top right corner of both knitted pieces, insert the needle through the first stitch, from back to front. Then pull the yarn through.

Can I use the whip stitch on the right side of my fabric?

Yes. You can use the whip stitch to create an attractive, decorative seam on the right side of your fabric. For maximum effect, you can use a thick yarn in a color that contrasts with the color of your knitted pieces. Perform the steps below, except hold the two knitted pieces you want to sew together with the wrong sides facing each other in step 3.

5 Bring the needle and yarn over the top edges of the knitted pieces.

6 Repeat steps 4 and 5, moving one stitch to the left each time, until you have sewed the entire edge.

Note: To weave in the yarn ends left over from sewing the knitted pieces together, see page 208.

graft two knitted pieces together

When you are ready to finish your project, grafting allows you to join two edges that contain stitches that are not yet bound off, also called live stitches. Grafting, which is also called the Kitchener stitch, is ideal for finishing sweater shoulders, sock toes and mitten tips.

The grafting technique creates a smooth, flexible seam and if done correctly, the seam will appear as a row of knit stitches. When grafting two knitted pieces together, you should aim for the same tension as the stitches in your knitted fabric. Do not pull the yarn too tight or leave the yarn too loose.

When grafting two knitted pieces together as shown below, the two pieces you are joining must have the same number of stitches. To join the pieces, you will need a tapestry needle and a strand of yarn. The yarn you use for grafting should measure about 1.5 inches for each stitch you are joining.

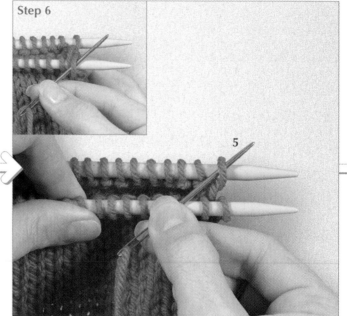

Step 6

1 For the two knitted pieces you want to graft together, cut the yarn from each ball of yarn, leaving one long strand for grafting.

2 Thread the strand of yarn through a tapestry needle.

3 Hold the two knitted pieces with the wrong sides facing each other and the tips of the needles pointing to the right.

4 Insert the tapestry needle into the front of the first stitch on the front needle, purlwise from right to left. Then pull the yarn through.

5 Insert the tapestry needle into the front of the first stitch on the back needle, knitwise from left to right. Then pull the yarn through.

6 Insert the tapestry needle into the front of the first stitch on the front needle, knitwise from left to right. Then pull the yarn through.

7 Slip the first stitch off the front needle.

How can I hold the two knitted pieces with the wrong sides facing each other and the tips of the needles pointing to the right?

To have the wrong sides of the fabric together and the tips of both needles pointing to the right in step **3** below, you may need to knit one fewer rows for one of the knitted pieces or slip each stitch from one needle onto a spare needle before you begin. Your pattern should instruct you on which method to use for your project.

Do I have to graft with the strand of yarn attached to one of my knitted pieces?

No. You can graft with an entirely new piece of yarn. When using a new piece of yarn, do not pull the yarn all the way through the first stitch in step **4** below. Leave a 6-inch tail that you can weave in later.

How can I remember the grafting technique?

When performing steps **6** to **11** below, you can use these instructions to remember which needle holds the stitch to work with, how to insert the needle and when to slip a stitch off the needle.

1	Front needle, knitwise, off.
2	Front needle, purlwise.
3	Back needle, purlwise, off.
4	Back needle, knitwise.

Step 9

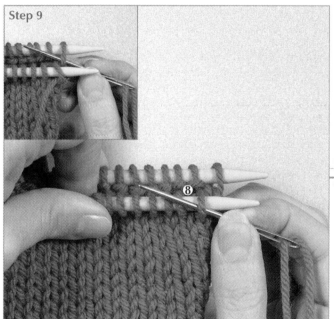

Step 12

8 Insert the tapestry needle into the front of the new first stitch on the front needle, purlwise from right to left. Then pull the yarn through.

9 Insert the tapestry needle into the front of the first stitch on the back needle, purlwise from right to left. Then pull the yarn through.

10 Slip the stitch off the back needle.

11 Insert the tapestry needle into the front of the new first stitch on the back needle, knitwise from left to right. Then pull the yarn through.

12 Repeat steps **6** to **11** until you have grafted all the stitches. You will have one stitch left on a needle. To finish grafting, slip the stitch off the needle.

Note: When you finish grafting, you can weave in the loose yarn ends. To weave in yarn ends, see page 208.

weave in yarn ends

After you finish a project, you need to conceal all the dangling ends of yarn left over from casting on stitches, binding off stitches and starting any new balls of yarn. Weaving in yarn ends allows you to incorporate the loose ends of yarn seamlessly into your knitted fabric.

You can weave yarn ends at the edge of your work vertically into the sides of your fabric. You can also weave yarn ends in the middle of your work horizontally across your fabric. Weaving yarn ends horizontally is slightly more secure than weaving

yarn ends vertically and is great for yarn ends left when you started a new yarn color.

If a knot where you added a new ball of yarn is not on a side edge, you may want to untie the knot before weaving in the yarn ends to prevent the knot from causing discomfort. Otherwise, leave knots tied to help ensure the fabric does not unravel when washed.

As you weave in yarn ends, you should check that there are no bulges or yarn ends showing through on the right side of the fabric.

WEAVING YARN ENDS INTO THE SIDES

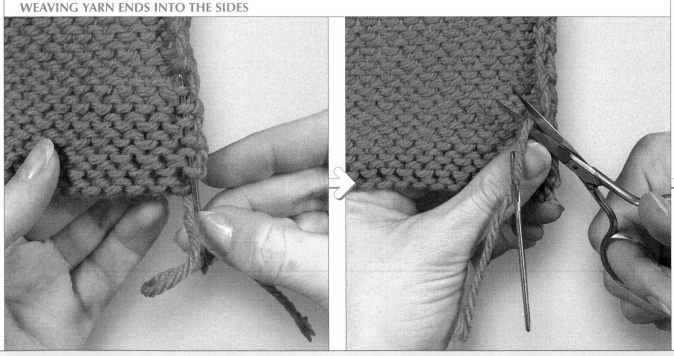

1 Thread the yarn end through a tapestry needle.

2 Insert the tapestry needle through the loops along the edge of your knitted piece.

Note: If your yarn is slippery, insert the needle through the loops in one direction, reverse the direction of the needle, skip a loop and then insert the needle through the loops in the opposite direction to weave in the yarn end more securely.

3 Cut the end of the yarn close to the surface of your work.

4 Gently stretch your work in each direction to pull the yarn end into the work.

5 Repeat steps 1 to 4 for each yarn end you want to weave into the sides of your work.

Note: You should weave each yarn end in the opposite direction from the last yarn end you weaved.

Is there another way to weave in yarn ends?

Yes. You can weave in yarn ends while you work instead of waiting until the end of the project. Weaving in yarn ends as you work is useful when you start a new ball of yarn or change colors in the middle of a row. To weave in a yarn end as you work, twist the yarn end around the yarn you are knitting with every three or four stitches to secure the yarn end within your work. To prevent the yarn ends from showing through on the right side of your work, make sure you twist the yarn ends around the yarn only when working stitches that are in the same color.

WEAVING YARN ENDS ACROSS YOUR WORK

1 Thread the yarn end through a tapestry needle.

2 Weave the tapestry needle in and out of the lower bumps of the purl stitches.

Note: If your yarn is slippery, weave in the yarn end in one direction and then back in the opposite direction to weave the yarn end in more securely.

3 Cut the end of the yarn close to the surface of your work.

4 Gently stretch the work in each direction to pull the yarn end into the work.

5 Repeat steps 1 to 4 for each yarn end you want to weave across your work.

Note: You should weave each yarn end in the opposite direction from the last yarn end you weaved.

little sweetheart
purse

· Easy Project ·

Little Sweetheart Purse

Size

Approx. 8 x 8 ins (20.5 x 20.5cm).

Materials

S. R. Kertzer's Butterfly Super 3 125g
MC (Main Color) = #3947 Violet, 1 hank.
Contrast A = #3459 Peony, 1 hank.

Sizes 7 US (4.5mm) and 8 US (5mm) knitting
needles or size needed to obtain gauge.

Gauge

18 stitches (sts) and 24 rows = 4 ins (10cm) with
larger needles in Stockinette St (knit 1 row, purl 1
row).

Instructions

Abbreviations: K = knit; P = purl;
RS = right side; WS = wrong side.

Seed St:

Row 1: *K1. P1. Rep from * to end of row.
Row 2: *P1. K1. Rep from * to end of row.
Rep these 2 rows.

Bag

With MC and larger needles, cast on 36 stitches.

Work in Stockinette St (knit 1 row, purl 1
row) until work from beginning measures
6.5 ins (16.5cm), ending with RS facing for
next row.

Change to smaller needles and work 1.5 ins (4cm)
in Seed St, ending with WS facing for next row.

Bind off in Seed St.

Front piece of bag is complete. Repeat steps
above to make another identical piece for back
piece of bag.

Pocket

With A and larger needles, cast on 17 stitches.

Work 6 rows in Stockinette St (knit 1 row,
purl 1 row), ending with RS facing for next row.
Next row: K4. Work Row 1 of Chart A. K4.
Next row: P4. Work Row 2 of Chart A. P4.

Chart A is now in position. Continue to end of
Chart A, reading rows from right to left on RS
rows and left to right on WS rows.

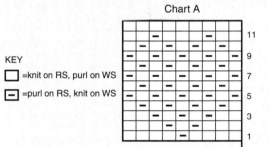

Chart A

KEY

☐ =knit on RS, purl on WS

⊟ =purl on RS, knit on WS

Start Here

Work 2 rows in Stockinette St (knit 1 row, purl 1
row). Change to smaller needles and work 3
rows in Seed St.

Bind off in Seed St.

Strap

With A and smaller needles cast on 10 stitches.
Work in Seed St until strap measures
46 ins (117cm).

Bind off all stitches.

Finishing

Sew pocket to front piece.
Sew strap together and then sew to 3 sides of front
piece of the purse, placing center seam at center
bottom of purse.
Sew back piece of purse to strap.

weekend pullover

• *Easy Project* •

Weekend Pullover

Sizes

Bust/chest measurement

Small 30-32 ins (76-81cm)
Medium 34-36 ins (86-91cm)
Large 38-40 ins (97-102cm)
X-Large 42-44 ins (107-112cm)

Finished bust/chest

Small 38.5 ins (98cm)
Medium 41 ins (104cm)
Large 45 ins (114.5cm)
XLarge 49 ins (124.5cm)

Materials

Classic Elite Two.Two 50g, #1558 Barn Red

Sizes	S	M	L	XL	
	9	10	10	11	hanks

Sizes 11 US (8mm) and 13 US (9mm) knitting needles or size needed to obtain gauge.

Four stitch holders.

Gauge

12 stitches (sts) and 18 rows = 4 ins (10cm) in Stockinette St (knit 1 row, purl 1 row) using larger needles.

Stitch Glossary

Abbreviations: P = purl; K = knit; psso = pass slipped stitch over; K2tog = knit two sts together; Sl1K = slip one st knitwise; RS = right side; P2tog = purl two sts together; P3tog = purl three sts together; WS = wrong side; P2togtbl=purl two sts together through back loops.

Instructions

Bracketed numbers are for sizes S (**M-L-XL**).

Back

With smaller needles, cast on 50 (58**-**62**-**70**) sts.

Row 1: P2. *K2. P2; Rep from * to end of row.

Row 2: K2. *P2. K2; Rep from * to end of row.

These two rows form (K2. P2) ribbing.

Continue in ribbing for 2.5 (**2.5**-3-**3**) ins [6 (**6**-7.5-**7.5**) cm], inc 8 (**4**-6-**4**) sts evenly across last row. 58 (**62**-68-**74**) sts.

Change to larger needles and work in Stockinette St (knit 1 row, purl 1 row) until work from beginning measures 13 (**14**-14.5-**15.5**) ins [33 (**38**-38-**39.5**) cm].

Raglan shaping:
Bind off 2 sts beginning next 2 rows. 54 (**58**-64-**70**) sts.

Next row (RS): K2. Sl1K. K1. psso. Knit to last 4 sts, K2tog. K2.

Next row: Purl.**

Rep last 2 rows 13 (**13**-18-**21**) times more. 26 (**30**-26-**26**) sts.

Next row: K2. Sl1K. K1. psso. Knit to last 4 sts, K2tog. K2.

Next: Work 3 rows even in Stockinette St.

Rep last 4 rows 2 (**3**-1-**0**) time(s) more. Leave remaining 20 (**22**-22-**24**) sts on a stitch holder.

weekend
pullover

Front

Work from ** to ** as given for Back.
52 (**56**-62-**68**) sts.

Rep last 2 rows 13 (**13**-16-**17**) times more.
26 (**30**-30-**34**) sts.

Medium only:
Next row: K2. Sl1K. K1. psso. Knit to last 4 sts, K2tog. K2. (**28**) sts.

Next: Work 3 rows even in Stockinette St.

Small & Medium only:
Neck shaping:

Next row (RS): K2. Sl1K. K1. psso. K3. K2tog (neck edge). **Turn**. Leave remaining sts on spare needle.

Row 2: Purl.
Row 3: Knit to last 2 sts, K2tog. 6 sts.
Row 4: Purl.
Row 5: K2. Sl1K. K1. psso. K2tog. 4 sts.
Row 6: Purl.
Row 7: Knit.
Row 8: Purl.
Row 9: K2. K2tog. 3 sts.
Row 10: Purl.
Row 11: K2tog. K1. 2 sts.
Row 12: P2tog.
Fasten off.

Large & X-Large only:
Neck shaping:

Next row (RS): K2. Sl1K. K1. psso. K4. K2tog (neck edge). **Turn**. Leave remaining sts on spare needle.

Row 2: Purl.
Row 3: Knit to last 2 sts, K2tog. 7 sts.
Row 4: Purl.
Row 5: K2. Sl1K. K1. psso. K2tog. 5 sts.
Row 6: Purl.
Row 7: Knit.
Row 8: Purl.
Row 9: K3. K2tog. 4 sts.

Front (cont.)

Row 10: Purl.
Row 11: K2tog. K2. 3 sts.
Row 12: P3tog.
Fasten off.

All sizes: With RS facing slip next 8 (**10-10-14**) sts from spare needle onto a stitch holder. Join yarn to remaining sts.

Small & Medium only:

Row 1 (RS): Sl1K. K1. psso. K3. K2tog. K2. 7 sts.
Row 2: Purl.
Row 3: Sl1K. K1. psso. Knit to end of needle. 6 sts.
Row 4: Purl.
Row 5: Sl1K. K1. psso. K2. K2tog. 4 sts.
Row 6: Purl.
Row 7: Knit.
Row 8: Purl.
Row 9: Sl1K. K1. psso. K2. 3 sts.
Row 10: Purl.
Row 11: K1. K2tog. 2 sts.
Row 12: P2tog.
Fasten off.

Large & X-Large only:

Row 1 (RS): Sl1K. K1. psso. K4. K2tog. K2. 8 sts.
Row 2: Purl.
Row 3: Sl1K. K1. psso. Knit to end of needle. 7 sts.
Row 4: Purl.
Row 5: Sl1K. K1. psso. K1. K2tog. K2. 5 sts.
Row 6: Purl.
Row 7: Knit.
Row 8: Purl.
Row 9: Sl1K. K1. psso. K2. 4 sts.
Row 10: Purl.
Row 11: K2. K2tog. 3 sts.
Row 12: P3tog.
Fasten off.

weekend
pullover

Sleeves

With smaller needles, cast on 28 (**30**-30-**32**) sts.
Work 2 ins (5cm) in (K2. P2) ribbing as given
for Back, ending with RS facing for next row.

Change to larger needles and proceed in
Stockinette St, inc 1 st each end of needle on
3rd and following 6th (**4th**-4th-**6th**) rows
5 (**1**-3-**10**) time(s) to 40 (**34**-38-**54**) sts.
Then inc 1 st each end of needle on every
8th (**6th**-6th-**8th**) row to 50 (**56**-58-**58**) sts.

All sizes: Continue even in Stockinette St, until
work from beginning measures 17 (**17**-17.5-**18**) ins
[43 (**43**-44.5-**45.5**) cm], ending with RS facing for
next row.

Raglan shaping:

Bind off 2 (**3**-3-**3**) sts beginning next 2 rows.
46 (**50**-52-**52**) sts.

Small, Medium & Large only:

Next row (RS):   K2. Sl1K. K1. psso. Knit to last
4 sts, K2tog. K2.

Next row: P2. P2tog. Purl to last 4 sts, P2togtbl. P2.
42 (**46**-48) sts.

All Sizes:

Next row (RS):   K2. Sl1K. K1. psso. Knit to last 4 sts,
K2tog. K2.

Next row: Purl.

Rep last 2 rows 18 (**20**-21-**23**) times to 4 sts.
Leave remaining 4 sts on a stitch holder.

Finishing

Sew raglan seams leaving back raglan seams open.

Collar:
With RS of work facing and larger needles,
Knit 4 sts from left sleeve stitch holder. Pick up and knit 8 sts down left front neck. Knit 8 (**10**-10-**14**) sts across front neck stitch holder. Pick up and knit 8 sts up right front neck edge. Knit 4 sts from right sleeve stitch holder. Pick up and knit 20 (**22**-22-**24**) sts across back stitch holder. 52 (**56**-56-**62**) sts on needle.

Next row (WS): Purl.

Beginning with a knit row, continue in Stockinette St for 3 ins (7.5cm), ending with RS facing for next row.

Bind off all sts.

Sew left back raglan and collar seam, reversing seam for curl back edge.

Sew side and sleeve seams.

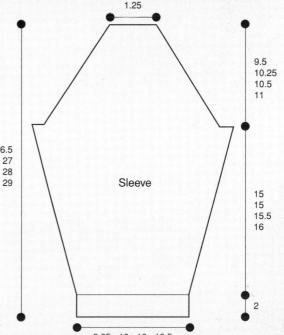

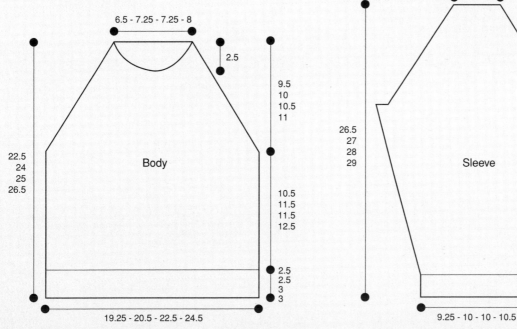

Body

6.5 - 7.25 - 7.25 - 8

2.5

9.5
10
10.5
11

22.5
24
25
26.5

10.5
11.5
11.5
12.5

2.5
2.5
3
3

19.25 - 20.5 - 22.5 - 24.5

Sleeve

1.25

9.5
10.25
10.5
11

26.5
27
28
29

15
15
15.5
16

2

9.25 - 10 - 10 - 10.5

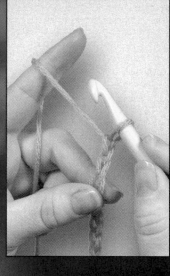

Chapter 9

This chapter will introduce you to the fundamental techniques and terms used in crocheting. You will learn how to hold the yarn and crochet hook as well as how to make a foundation chain. This chapter also explains how to read a crochet pattern, so you can quickly get started on your crochet projects.

Crochet Basics

In this Chapter...

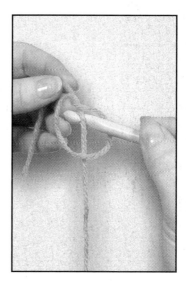

introduction to crochet

Crocheting is a fun activity that is easy to learn and requires only a ball of yarn and a crochet hook to practice. You can quickly create a variety of useful crochet projects ranging from decorative items, such as lace doilies, to more functional items, such as scarves, sweaters or blankets.

Crocheting and Knitting: What's the Difference?

Crocheting and knitting are similar in that both create fabric by interlacing a series of loops to form stitches. However, there are several differences between the two crafts.

Crocheting is generally faster than knitting and is considered by many to be easier to learn. You use one crochet hook to create stitches, instead of the two needles required for knitting. In crochet, only

one loop is active at a time, while in knitting, an entire row of stitches is usually active.

Crochet stitches are a different size and shape than stitches created by knitting, therefore the fabrics produced by each craft differ in appearance and texture. Crocheted fabrics tend to be bulkier and drape less freely than knitted fabrics.

Why Crochet?

There are many reasons you might want to learn to crochet. In today's fast-paced world, crochet is an ideal hobby, as it is a creative and satisfying craft that can help you relax. Crocheting has been likened to meditation in the way the repetitive movements of the crochet hook and yarn relieve stress. Another emotional benefit is the pride and pleasure you can derive from a completed crochet project that you can use or give as a gift.

Crocheting is convenient for a busy lifestyle, as you can complete a project over time, putting the project aside and resuming whenever you like. Crochet is also a portable pastime. You can take your project with you and work on the project while on the bus or train or during your lunch break at work.

Crochet: The New Generation

Although no longer practiced out of the necessity to produce garments and other items for personal use, crochet is still a very popular craft. Today, many people crochet simply for the joy of it. Once the domain of grandmothers, crocheting has, in recent years, become a trendy pastime for people of all ages. Of the thousands of new people learning to crochet each year, most are in their 20s and 30s.

Crochet and the Internet

The Internet is a valuable resource for new and experienced crochet enthusiasts who want information about crocheting and the opportunity to interact and share ideas with others around the world. The following are some popular Web sites devoted to sharing information about crocheting.

Popular Crochet Web Sites	
Crochet Guild of America	crochet.org
Craft Yarn Council of America	www.craftyarncouncil.com
The National NeedleArts Association	www.tnna.org
YarnStandards.com	www.yarnstandards.com
CrochetAndKnitting.com	www.crochetandknitting.com
Crochet 'N' More	www.crochetnmore.com
The Red Sweater	www.theredsweater.com/tips.html
Needlepointers.com	www.needlepointers.com
Learn to Knit and Crochet	www.learntoknit.com
By The Hook	www.angelfire.com/biz/bythehook

all about
crochet hooks

You require only two items to crochet—the yarn of your choice and a crochet hook. With these simple tools you can create many beautiful crocheted pieces.

Crochet hooks are available in various materials, including steel, plastic, aluminum, wood and bamboo. Steel crochet hooks are small and are often used to crochet intricate items, such as lace doilies, with fine yarn or cotton. Larger crochet hooks are usually made from lightweight materials such as plastic or aluminum.

Although most crochet hooks are similar in length (approximately 6 inches) and appearance, the shape of the hook at the end of a crochet hook can vary slightly between manufacturers. For example, some hooks are more rounded while others are pointier. You can experiment with different brands to find the crochet hooks you prefer.

CROCHET HOOK SIZES

There are three systems commonly used to classify crochet hook sizes—US, metric and UK. The US system classifies crochet hook sizes using a letter and/or a number.

You will usually select your crochet hook based on the size suggested in your pattern. When choosing a crochet hook, it is important to remember that different manufacturers may label the same crochet hook size differently.

The following chart is a guideline for aluminum and plastic crochet hook sizes. Sizes for steel crochet hooks range from 14US (¾ mm) to 00US (3½ mm).

Aluminum and Plastic Crochet Hook Sizes

US	Metric	UK
B/1	2¼ mm	12
C/2	2¾ mm	11
D/3	3¼ mm	10
E/4	3½ mm	9
F/5	3¾ mm	8
G/6	4¼ mm	7
H/8	5mm	6
I/9	5½ mm	5
J/10	6mm	4
K/10½	6½ mm	2
L/11	8mm	
N/15	9mm	
P	10mm	
Q	16mm	
S	19mm	

hold a crochet hook

You can hold a crochet hook in one of two ways. Both positions provide good support and allow you to work comfortably and quickly. You can try both positions to determine which one best suits you.

The most popular method is to hold the crochet hook as if you were holding a pencil, using your thumb and index finger to grip the flat area of the crochet hook. Alternatively, you can hold the crochet hook as if you were holding a knife, using your thumb, index finger and middle finger to hold the flat area of the crochet hook. Your free hand is used to hold the yarn.

If you are left-handed, you can hold a crochet hook in your left hand using either of the positions discussed here. Since this book is written for right-handed people, if you are left-handed, substitute right for left and left for right throughout the steps in this book.

POSITION 1

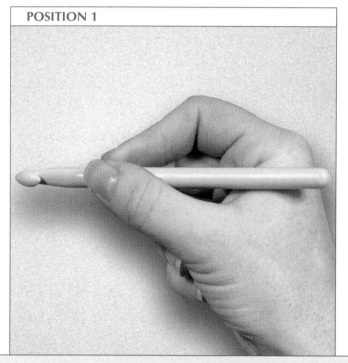

1 Hold the crochet hook in your right hand as if you were holding a pencil. Your thumb and index finger hold the flat section of the crochet hook.

POSITION 2

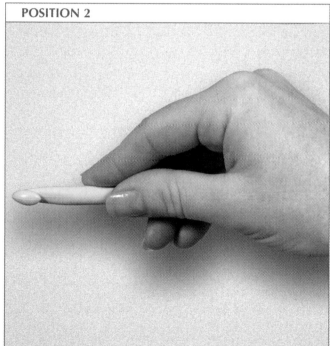

1 Hold the crochet hook in your right hand as if you were holding a knife. Your thumb, index finger and middle finger hold the flat section of the crochet hook.

• Your other fingers can help support the crochet hook.

make a slip knot

To begin crocheting, you must first make a slip knot to secure the yarn to the crochet hook. Making a slip knot around a crochet hook is similar to making a slip knot around a knitting needle.

When you make a slip knot, you create a loop with your yarn, leaving a "tail" that measures about 6 inches between the loop and the end of the yarn. You then use the crochet hook to pull the strand of yarn connected to the ball through the loop.

The final step is pulling the two yarn ends away from each other to tighten the slip knot around the crochet hook.

Unlike knitting, where a slip knot acts as your first stitch, a slip knot in crochet does not act as the first chain stitch. For more information on chain stitches, see page 226.

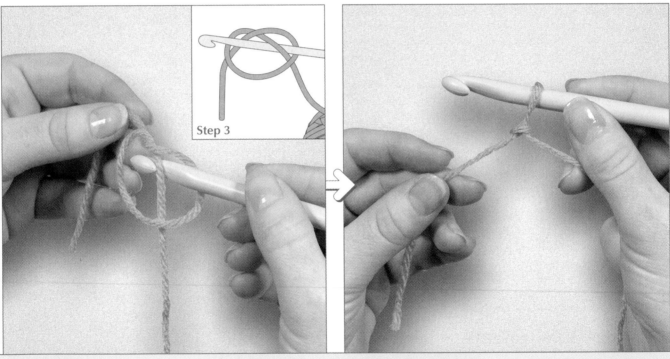

Step 3

1 Make a loop with your yarn, allowing the strand of yarn connected to the ball to hang down behind the loop.

2 Insert the crochet hook through the loop, from front to back.

3 Catch the strand of yarn hanging behind the loop with the crochet hook and pull the yarn through the loop.

4 Gently pull both ends of the yarn In opposite directions to tighten the slip knot around the crochet hook.

5 Slide the slip knot up the crochet hook until the slip knot is 1 or 2 inches from the hook.

• You are now ready to begin crocheting.

hold the yarn

One of the most basic steps when crocheting is learning to hold the yarn. Holding the yarn properly will allow you to maintain even tension on the yarn. As you crochet, you hold the crochet hook in your right hand and the yarn in your left hand.

To hold the yarn, you wrap the yarn around the fingers of your left hand. You can adjust the yarn until it lies comfortably around your fingers. As you

crochet, you use your left index finger to control the tension of the yarn and your left thumb and middle fingers to hold your work.

The ideal yarn tension is neither too tight nor too loose. The yarn should be tight enough so that you can easily grab the yarn with the crochet hook and loose enough so that you can easily pull the yarn and hook through your stitches.

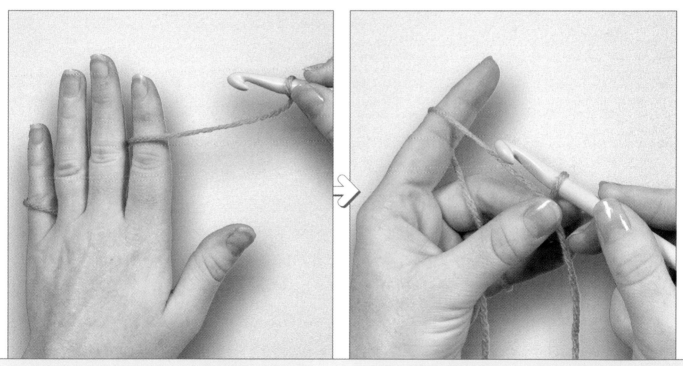

1 Hold the crochet hook in your right hand.

2 With the yarn in your left hand, place the yarn between your pinky and ring fingers. Then wrap the yarn counterclockwise around your pinky finger.

3 Weave the yarn under your ring and middle fingers and then over your index finger.

4 To start crocheting, grasp the slip knot on the crochet hook using the thumb and middle finger of your left hand.

Note: For information on making a slip knot, see page 224.

- Use your pinky, ring and middle fingers to hold the yarn loosely in your left hand.

- You can lift and lower your left index finger to control the tension of the yarn.

make a chain

To start your crochet project, you need to make chain stitches, which are often called chains. The first row of chain stitches you complete is called the foundation chain and will form the bottom edge of your crochet project. You will crochet all the other rows in your project on top of the foundation chain.

A yarn over is the basic movement used to create chain stitches and every other crochet stitch. A yarn over involves bringing the yarn over the crochet hook and catching the yarn with the hook. In instructions, the yarn over is represented by the abbreviation **yo**.

Chain stitches are not only created for the foundation chain. You can create chain stitches at any location in your project. You should work your chain stitches at the thickest part of the crochet hook, usually 1 or 2 inches from the hook. This will help ensure your chain stitches are not too tight. In patterns, the chain stitch is represented by the abbreviation **ch**. For example, **ch12** indicates that you should make 12 chain stitches.

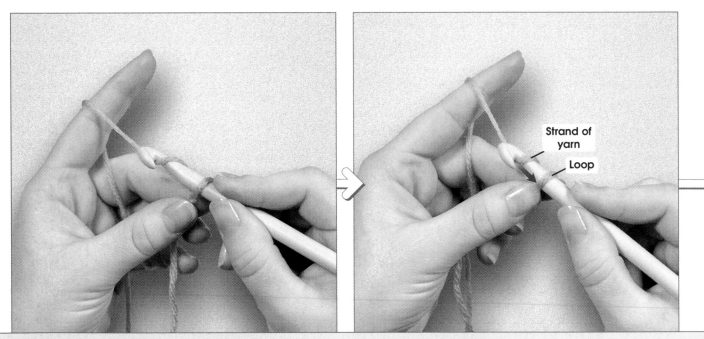

Strand of yarn

Loop

1 Make a slip knot on the crochet hook. To make a slip knot, see page 224.

2 Hold the crochet hook in your right hand, with the yarn wrapped around the fingers of your left hand.

Note: To hold the crochet hook and wrap the yarn around your fingers, see pages 223 and 225.

3 Bring the yarn over the crochet hook from back to front.

4 Catch the yarn with the crochet hook.

*Note: Bringing the yarn over the crochet hook and catching the yarn with the hook is known as a yarn over (**yo**).*

5 Slide the hook and the strand of yarn through the loop on the crochet hook, allowing the loop to fall off the crochet hook.

How do I count chain stitches?

Counting chain stitches is an essential part of any crochet project. To count the chain stitches in your foundation chain, make sure the front of the foundation chain is facing you. The front of the foundation chain displays a row of Vs and is flat. The back of the foundation chain is bumpy. Starting with the last chain stitch you completed, count every chain stitch in the foundation chain. Do not count the loop on the crochet hook as a chain stitch or the slip knot you made to secure the yarn to the crochet hook.

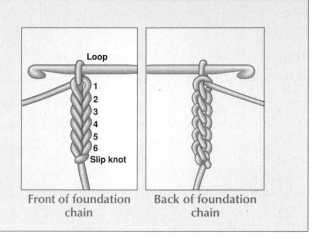

Front of foundation chain

Back of foundation chain

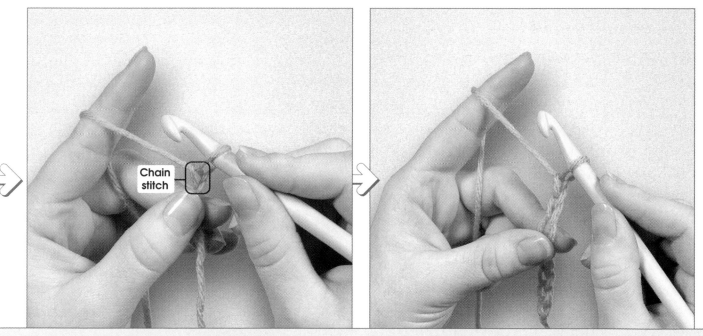

- You have created one chain stitch.
- A loop remains on the crochet hook.

6 Slide the loop down the crochet hook until the loop is 1 or 2 inches from the hook.

7 Repeat steps 3 to 6 for each chain stitch you want the foundation chain to contain.

- As you make new chain stitches, move your thumb and middle finger up the foundation chain to hold your work.

Note: The foundation chain will become the bottom edge of your work.

read a
crochet pattern

Crochet patterns provide you with all the information you need to create a crocheted project, including detailed instructions that use abbreviations, symbols and terms. With practice, you will be able to read crochet pattern instructions quickly and easily. Before beginning a project, you should read all the instructions included in the pattern so you have a good understanding of how the entire project will be made.

Size

A crochet pattern usually specifies the approximate dimensions of the finished project. When a project can be made in multiple sizes, the pattern specifies the additional sizes in brackets, such as "Small (Medium, Large)." Throughout the pattern, you will find the instructions for the additional sizes in brackets. For example, a pattern may specify "ch 30 (32, 34)," which means you should crochet 30 chain stitches for the small size, 32 chain stitches for the medium size or 34 chain stitches for the large size.

Materials

A pattern will tell you the type, color, weight and amount of the yarn you will need. A pattern will also indicate the crochet hook size you should use and include information about any additional materials you will need, such as buttons.

Gauge

A pattern indicates the gauge, or "tension," required to ensure your finished project will be the correct size. Gauge is the number of stitches and rows you should have in a sample piece of crocheted fabric when you use the same crochet hook and yarn you will use for the project.

Abbreviations

Pattern instructions are written using abbreviations. A list of abbreviations used in the pattern you are following may be included in the pattern. The following is a list of some commonly used crochet abbreviations. For a more extensive list, see page 284.

ch(s)	chain(s)
dc	double crochet
hdc	half double crochet
sc	single crochet
sl st	slip stitch
st(s)	stitch(es)
tr	triple crochet

Symbols

Here are some commonly used symbols you will find in crochet patterns.

*

An asterisk (*) marks the beginning of a set of instructions you will repeat. You work the instructions following the asterisk once and then repeat the instructions the specified number of times. For example, a pattern may specify "*sc in next 2 sts, ch 2, rep from * 4 times," which means you work the instructions following the first asterisk a total of five times.

** **

Double asterisks (**) mark a long section of instructions that you will be asked to repeat later in the pattern. For example, if a section of the front of a sweater is worked the same as the back of a sweater, the instructions for the back are enclosed in double asterisks. The instructions for the front may state "Work from ** to ** as given for Back."

( ) or [ ]

You work the instructions enclosed in brackets as many times as indicated by the number immediately following the brackets. For example, if a pattern states "(3 dc in next ch st. Ch 1) 3 times," you work the instructions enclosed in the brackets three times. Brackets can also indicate that you should work all the instructions into one stitch. For example, if a pattern states "(hdc, ch 2, hdc) in the next st," you work all the instructions enclosed in the brackets into the next stitch.

Terms

Here are some commonly used terms you will find in crochet patterns.

Back loop - Of the two top horizontal strands of a stitch, the strand that is farthest away from you.

Front loop - Of the two top horizontal strands of a stitch, the strand that is closest to you.

Post - The vertical part of a stitch. Also called a leg or bar.

Work even or **Work straight** - Work in the established pattern without increasing or decreasing stitches.

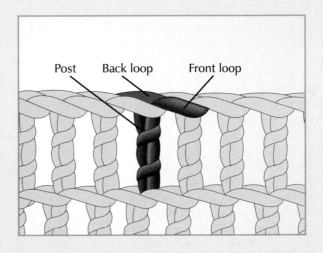

Post   Back loop   Front loop

Chapter 10

Once you are comfortable with the fundamentals of crocheting, you are ready to work with crochet stitches. This chapter teaches you how to make the basic crochet stitches, including single, half-double, double and triple crochet stitches. You will also learn how to shape your work by increasing and decreasing stitches, how to crochet in rounds as well as techniques for finishing your work.

Working With Crochet Stitches

In this Chapter...

single crochet

Row 1

The single crochet stitch is a short stitch that creates a tightly woven fabric. In patterns, the single crochet stitch is abbreviated as **sc**. A row may be made up entirely of single crochet stitches or a combination of different stitches.

To work a row of single crochet stitches into the foundation chain, you work the first single crochet stitch into the second chain stitch. Skipping the first chain stitch allows the row of single crochet stitches to stand at its proper height.

When locating the second chain stitch, make sure the front of the foundation chain is facing you. The front of the foundation chain displays a row of Vs. Also, make sure you do not count the loop on the crochet hook as a chain stitch.

Since you skip the first chain stitch, the number of single crochet stitches in the completed row will be one less than the number of chain stitches in the foundation chain. For example, if you have 10 chain stitches in the foundation chain, you will have nine single crochet stitches in the finished row.

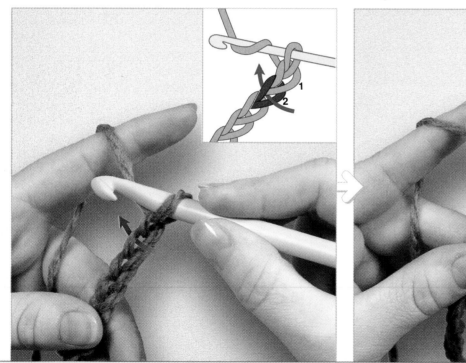

Strand of yarn

Loops

1 Make a foundation chain to start your crochet project. To make a foundation chain, see page 226.

2 Locate the second chain stitch from the crochet hook.

3 Insert the crochet hook under the top loop of the chain stitch from front to back.

4 Bring the yarn over the crochet hook from back to front.

5 Catch the yarn with the hook of the crochet hook.

6 Slide the hook and the strand of yarn through the first loop on the crochet hook, allowing the loop to fall off the crochet hook.

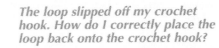

The loop slipped off my crochet hook. How do I correctly place the loop back onto the crochet hook?

If the loop slips off the crochet hook while you are crocheting, make sure the front of your work is facing you. Then insert the crochet hook through the front of the loop. Before inserting the crochet hook through the loop, make sure the loop is not twisted.

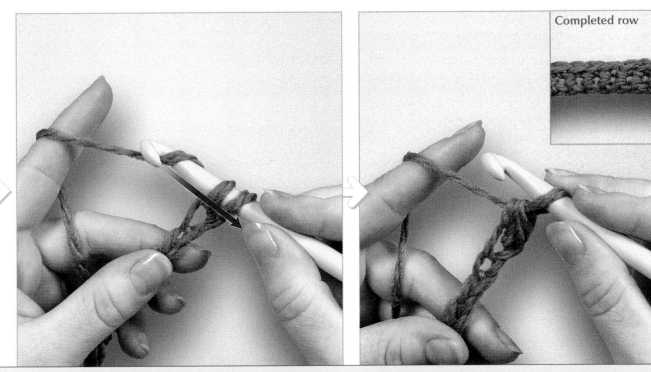

Completed row

- You now have two loops on the crochet hook.

7 Bring the yarn over the crochet hook from back to front.

8 Catch the yarn with the hook of the crochet hook.

9 Slide the hook and the strand of yarn through the two loops on the crochet hook, allowing the two loops to fall off the crochet hook.

- You now have one loop on the crochet hook.

- You have created one single crochet stitch.

10 To complete a row of single crochet stitches, repeat steps 3 to 9 for each of the following chain stitches in the foundation chain.

CONTINUED...

Row 2

After you work the first row of single crochet stitches into the foundation chain, you can work a new row of single crochet stitches back across the first row. You can continue working rows of single crochet stitches back and forth across your crochet piece to create as many rows as you need.

To start a new row of single crochet stitches, you must first make one chain stitch. This chain stitch is called a turning chain and raises the yarn up to the

proper height for the new row of single crochet stitches. After you make a turning chain, you must turn your work so you can crochet back across the previous row.

The chain stitch you make at the beginning of each new row of single crochet stitches is not considered a stitch in the row. When creating rows of single crochet stitches, you do not work into the chain stitch.

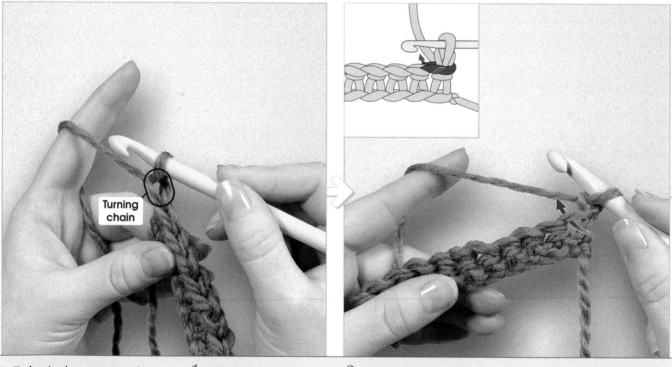

Turning chain

- To begin the next row of single crochet stitches, you must first make a turning chain to raise the yarn to the required height for the next row. The turning chain for the single crochet stitch is one chain stitch.

1 To make a turning chain, make one chain stitch. To make a chain stitch, see page 226.

2 Turn your work around so you can crochet back across the previous row.

3 Locate the first single crochet stitch in the previous row. The top of each single crochet stitch has two horizontal strands, shaped like a V.

Note: Do not count the base of the turning chain as the first single crochet stitch.

4 Insert the crochet hook under the top two horizontal strands of the single crochet stitch from front to back.

QUESTION & ANSWER

When I complete a new row of single crochet stitches, how can I make sure I still have the correct number of stitches?

After you complete a row of single crochet stitches, you should count the number of stitches in the row to make sure you have the correct number. Counting stitches will help ensure you have not worked two stitches into one stitch or skipped a stitch. To count single crochet stitches, place your work on a flat surface and count the vertical part of each stitch, called the post. A space separates each stitch in a row.

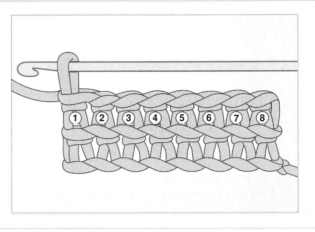

5 Complete the single crochet stitch.

Note: To complete a single crochet stitch, perform steps 4 to 9 starting on page 232, sliding the crochet hook through the first two loops in step 6.

6 Repeat steps 4 and 5 for each of the following single crochet stitches in the row.

7 To work additional rows of single crochet stitches, repeat steps 1 to 6 for each row you want to complete.

half double crochet

Row 1

The half double crochet stitch is a basic stitch that creates a moderately dense fabric. The half double crochet stitch is slightly taller than the single crochet stitch. In patterns, the half double crochet stitch is abbreviated as **hdc**. A row may be made up entirely of half double crochet stitches or a combination of different stitches.

You work the first row of half double crochet stitches into the foundation chain. The first half double crochet stitch is worked into the third chain stitch. You skip the first two chain stitches in the foundation chain to allow the row of half double crochet stitches to stand at its proper height.

The skipped chain stitches stand up alongside the half double crochet stitches and are considered the first half double crochet stitch in the row.

When locating the third chain stitch, make sure the front of the foundation chain is facing you. The front of the foundation chain displays a row of Vs and is flat. Also, make sure you do not count the loop on the crochet hook as a chain stitch.

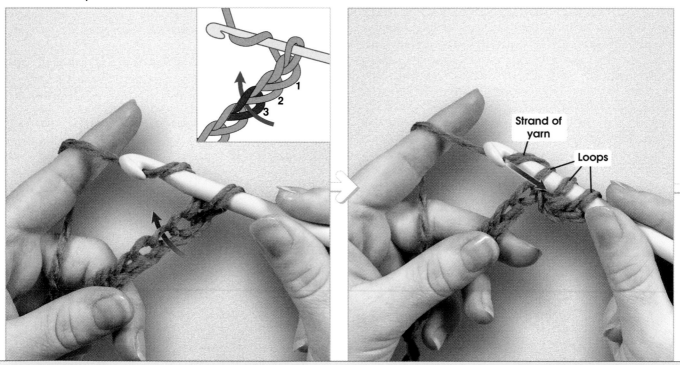

1 Make a foundation chain to start your crochet project. To make a foundation chain, see page 226.

2 Locate the third chain stitch from the crochet hook.

3 Bring the yarn over the crochet hook from back to front.

4 Insert the crochet hook under the top loop of the chain stitch, from front to back.

5 Bring the yarn over the crochet hook from back to front.

6 Catch the yarn with the hook of the crochet hook.

7 Slide the hook and the strand of yarn through the first loop on the crochet hook, allowing the loop to fall off the crochet hook.

Why do I have a different number of half double crochet stitches than chain stitches?

Skipped chain stitches

When you create the first half double crochet stitch, you skip the first two chain stitches and work into the third chain stitch in the foundation chain. This results in fewer half double crochet stitches than chain stitches. For example, if you have 10 chain stitches in the foundation chain, you will create eight half double crochet stitches in the row. The skipped chain stitches count as one half double crochet stitch, making a total of nine half double crochet stitches in the first row.

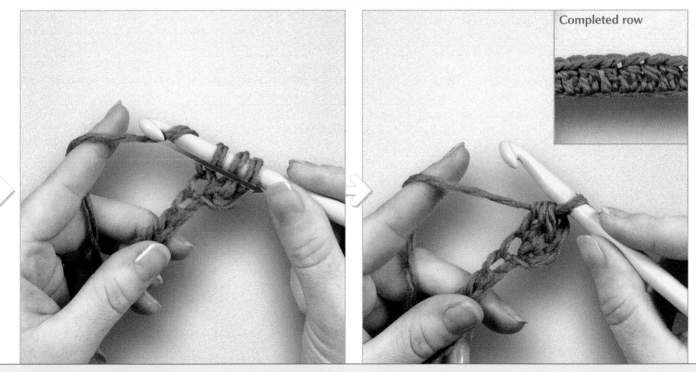

Completed row

- You now have three loops on the crochet hook.

8 Bring the yarn over the crochet hook from back to front.

9 Catch the yarn with the hook of the crochet hook.

10 Slide the hook and the strand of yarn through the three loops on the crochet hook, allowing the three loops to fall off the crochet hook.

- You now have one loop on the crochet hook.

- You have created one half double crochet stitch.

11 To complete a row of half double crochet stitches, repeat steps 3 to 10 for each of the following chain stitches in the foundation chain.

CONTINUED...

half double crochet (continued)

Once you have worked the first row of half double crochet stitches, you can work a new row of stitches back across the first row. You can continue working rows of half double crochet stitches to create as many rows as you need.

To start a new row of half double crochet stitches, you must first make two chain stitches. These chain stitches are called a turning chain and raise the yarn up to the proper height for the new row of half

double crochet stitches. You must then turn your work around so you can crochet back across the previous row.

The turning chain you make at the beginning of each new row of half double crochet stitches is considered the first half double crochet stitch in the row. At the end of each row of half double crochet stitches, make sure you work a stitch into the top chain stitch of the turning chain from the previous row.

ROW 2

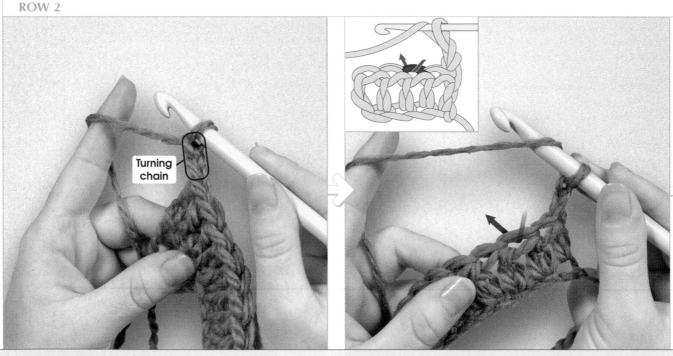

Turning chain

- To begin the next row of half double crochet stitches, you must first make a turning chain to raise the yarn to the required height for the next row. The turning chain for the half double crochet stitch is two chain stitches. The turning chain counts as the first half double crochet stitch in the row.

1 To make a turning chain, make two chain stitches. To make a chain stitch, see page 226.

2 Turn your work around so you can crochet back across the previous row.

3 Locate the second half double crochet stitch in the previous row. The top of each half double crochet stitch has two horizontal strands, shaped like a V.

4 Bring the yarn over the crochet hook from back to front.

5 Insert the crochet hook under the top two horizontal strands of the half double crochet stitch from front to back.

How can I remind myself to work a stitch into the turning chain?

When working in rows of half double crochet stitches, you can use a safety pin to mark the top chain stitch in a turning chain you make. This will remind you to work a stitch into the turning chain when you reach the turning chain at the end of a row.

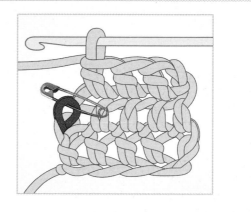

6 Complete the half double crochet stitch.

Note: To complete a half double crochet stitch, perform steps 5 to 10 starting on page 236, sliding the crochet hook through the first two loops in step 7.

7 To complete a row of half double crochet stitches, repeat steps 4 to 6 for each of the following half double crochet stitches in the row.

ROW 3 AND ALL REMAINING ROWS

1 To work additional rows of half double crochet stitches, repeat steps 1 to 7 for each row you want to complete.

• When you reach the end of each row, make sure you work a stitch into the top chain stitch of the turning chain in the previous row.

double crochet

Row 1

The double crochet stitch is a tall, commonly used stitch that creates a more open fabric than the single crochet stitch.

To work a row of double crochet stitches into the foundation chain, you work the first stitch into the fourth chain stitch. Skipping the first three chain stitches allows the row of double crochet stitches to stand at its proper height. The skipped chain stitches stand up alongside the double crochet stitches and are considered the first double crochet stitch in the row.

When locating the fourth chain stitch in the foundation chain, make sure the front of the foundation chain is facing you. The front of the foundation chain displays a row of Vs and is flat. Also, make sure you do not count the loop on the crochet hook as a chain stitch.

In patterns, the double crochet stitch is abbreviated as **dc**. A row may be made up entirely of double crochet stitches or a combination of different stitches.

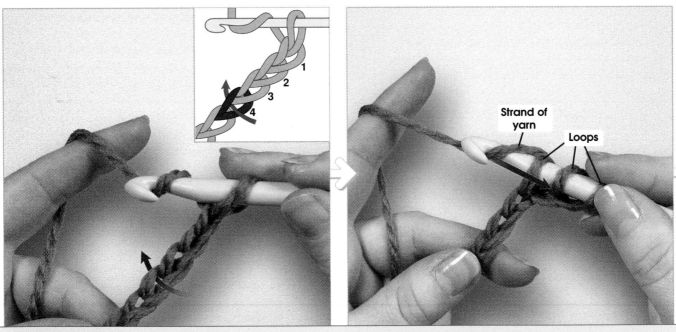

Strand of yarn

Loops

1 Make a foundation chain to start your crochet project. To make a foundation chain, see page 226.

2 Locate the fourth chain stitch from the crochet hook.

3 Bring the yarn over the crochet hook from back to front.

4 Insert the crochet hook under the top loop of the chain stitch from front to back.

5 Bring the yarn over the crochet hook from back to front.

6 Catch the yarn with the hook of the crochet hook.

7 Slide the hook and the strand of yarn through the first loop on the crochet hook, allowing the loop to fall off the crochet hook.

Why do I have a different number of double crochet stitches than chain stitches?

When you create the first double crochet stitch, you skip the first three chain stitches and work into the fourth chain stitch in the foundation chain. This results in fewer double crochet stitches than chain stitches. For example, if you have 10 chain stitches

Skipped chain stitches

in the foundation chain, you will create seven double crochet stitches in the row. The skipped chain stitches count as one double crochet stitch, making a total of eight double crochet stitches in the first row.

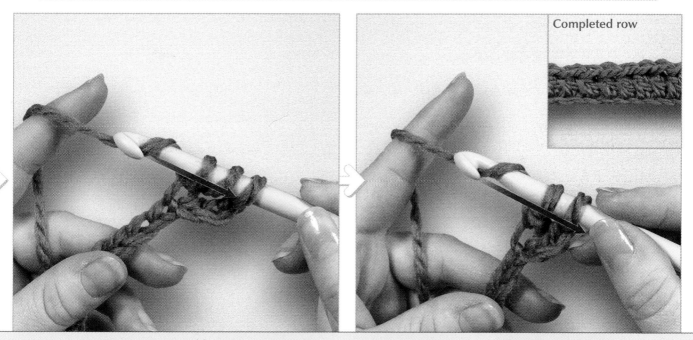

Completed row

- You now have three loops on the crochet hook.

8 Bring the yarn over the crochet hook from back to front.

9 Catch the yarn with the hook of the crochet hook.

10 Slide the hook and the strand of yarn through the first two loops on the crochet hook, allowing the two loops to fall off the crochet hook.

- You now have two loops on the crochet hook.

11 Bring the yarn over the crochet hook from back to front.

12 Catch the yarn with the hook of the crochet hook.

13 Slide the hook and the strand of yarn through the two loops, allowing the two loops to fall off the crochet hook.

- You have created one double crochet stitch.

14 To complete a row of double crochet stitches, repeat steps 3 to 13 for each of the following chain stitches in the foundation chain.

241

double crochet

(continued)

After you work the first row of double crochet stitches, you can work a new row of double crochet stitches back across the first row. You can continue working rows of double crochet stitches back and forth across your piece to create as many rows as you need.

To start a new row of double crochet stitches, you must first make three chain stitches. These chain stitches are called a turning chain and raise the yarn up to the proper height for the new row of double crochet stitches. After you make a turning chain, you must turn your work around so you can crochet back across the previous row.

At the beginning of each new row of double crochet stitches, the turning chain you make is considered the first double crochet stitch in the row. As you crochet rows of double crochet stitches, you work a double crochet stitch into the top chain stitch of each turning chain.

ROW 2

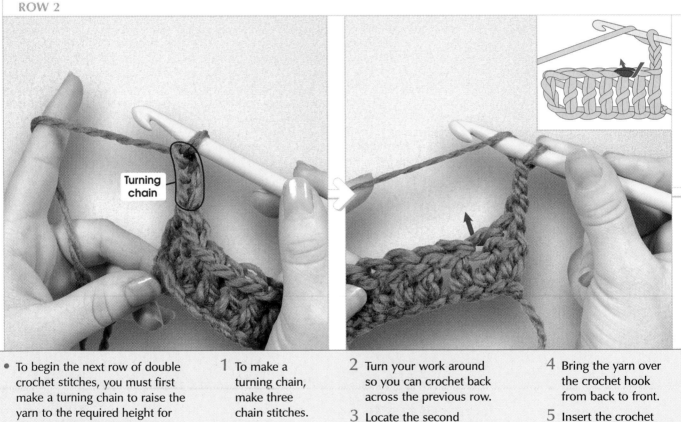

Turning chain

- To begin the next row of double crochet stitches, you must first make a turning chain to raise the yarn to the required height for the next row. The turning chain for the double crochet stitch is three chain stitches. The turning chain counts as the first double crochet stitch in the row.

1 To make a turning chain, make three chain stitches. To make a chain stitch, see page 226.

2 Turn your work around so you can crochet back across the previous row.

3 Locate the second double crochet stitch in the previous row. The top of each double crochet stitch has two horizontal strands, shaped like a V.

4 Bring the yarn over the crochet hook from back to front.

5 Insert the crochet hook under the top two horizontal strands of the double crochet stitch from front to back.

How do I correct a mistake?

To correct a mistake, remove the loop from the crochet hook. Then gently pull on the strand of yarn connected to the ball of yarn to unravel your stitches until you reach the first stitch past the mistake. With the front of your crochet piece facing you, re-insert the crochet hook into the front of the loop and begin crocheting again.

Unravel to here

Mistake

ROW 3 AND ALL REMAINING ROWS

Turning chain

6 Complete the double crochet stitch.

Note: To complete a double crochet stitch, perform steps 5 to 13 on page 240, sliding the crochet hook through the first two loops in step 7.

7 To complete a row of double crochet stitches, repeat steps 4 to 6 for each of the following double crochet stitches in the row.

1 To work additional rows of double crochet stitches, repeat steps 1 to 7 for each row you want to complete.

• When you reach the end of each row, make sure you work a stitch into the top chain stitch of the turning chain in the previous row.

triple crochet

Row 1

The triple crochet stitch, also known as the treble crochet stitch, is one of the tallest crochet stitches and creates an airy, delicate fabric. In patterns, the triple crochet stitch is abbreviated as **tr**.

You work the first row of triple crochet stitches into the foundation chain. The first triple crochet stitch is worked into the fifth chain stitch. Skipping the first four chain stitches allows the row of triple crochet stitches to stand at its proper height.

When locating the fifth chain stitch, make sure the front of the foundation chain is facing you and you do not count the loop on the crochet hook as a chain stitch. The front of the foundation chain displays a row of Vs.

After you complete the first row of triple crochet stitches, you should count the stitches in the row to ensure you have the correct number. Make sure you count the skipped chain stitches as one triple crochet stitch. You will have fewer triple crochet stitches than chain stitches in the foundation chain. For example, if you have 10 chain stitches, you will have seven triple crochet stitches.

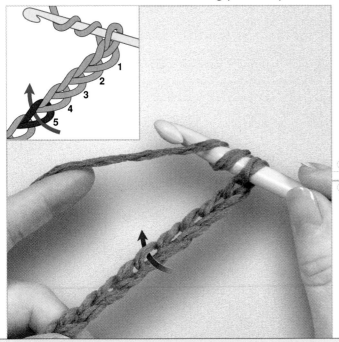

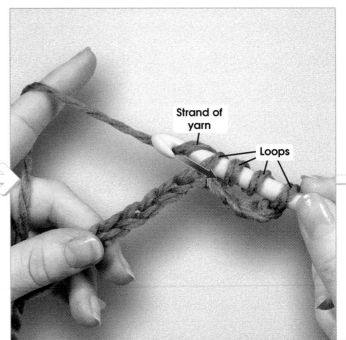

Strand of yarn

Loops

1 Make a foundation chain to start your crochet project. To make a foundation chain, see page 226.

2 Locate the fifth chain stitch from the crochet hook.

3 Bring the yarn over the crochet hook twice, from back to front.

4 Insert the crochet hook under the top loop of the chain stitch from front to back.

5 Bring the yarn over the crochet hook from back to front.

6 Catch the yarn with the hook of the crochet hook.

7 Slide the hook and the strand of yarn through the first loop on the crochet hook, allowing the loop to fall off the crochet hook.

Are there variations of the triple crochet stitch?

Yes. One common variation of the triple crochet stitch is the double triple crochet stitch (**dtr**). To make a double triple crochet stitch, perform steps **1** to **11** below, locating the sixth chain stitch in step **2** and bringing the yarn over the crochet hook three times in step **3**. After you complete the steps, you will have

two loops remaining on the crochet hook. Bring the yarn over the crochet hook once again and then slide the hook through the two loops. You have created one double triple crochet stitch. When working in rows of double triple crochet stitches, you will need to make five chain stitches for the turning chain.

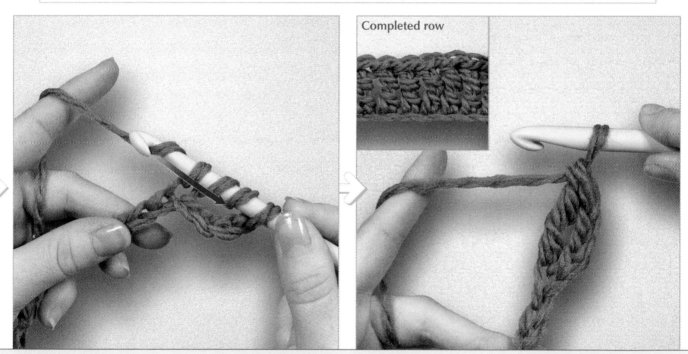

Completed row

• You now have four loops on the crochet hook.

8 Bring the yarn over the crochet hook from back to front.

9 Catch the yarn with the hook of the crochet hook.

10 Slide the hook and the strand of yarn through the first two loops on the crochet hook, allowing the two loops to fall off the crochet hook.

11 Repeat steps **8** to **10** twice to end up with one loop on the crochet hook.

• You now have one loop on the crochet hook.

• You have created one triple crochet stitch.

12 To complete a row of triple crochet stitches, repeat steps **3** to **11** for each of the following chain stitches in the foundation chain.

CONTINUED...

triple crochet *(continued)*

After working the first row of triple crochet stitches, you can work the second row of triple crochet stitches back across the first row. You can continue working rows of triple crochet stitches back and forth across the piece to create as many rows as you need.

To start a new row of triple crochet stitches, you must first make four chain stitches. These chain stitches are called a turning chain and raise the yarn up to the proper height for the new row of triple

crochet stitches. After you make the turning chain, you must turn your work around so you can crochet back across the previous row.

At the beginning of each new row of triple crochet stitches, the turning chain you make is considered the first triple crochet stitch in the row. As you crochet rows of triple crochet stitches, you work a triple crochet stitch into the top chain stitch of each turning chain.

ROW 2

Turning chain

- To begin the next row of triple crochet stitches, you must first make a turning chain to raise the yarn to the required height for the next row. The turning chain for the triple crochet stitch is four chain stitches. The turning chain counts as the first triple crochet stitch in the row.

1 To make a turning chain, make four chain stitches. To make a chain stitch, see page 226.

2 Turn your work around so you can crochet back across the previous row.

3 Locate the second triple crochet stitch in the previous row. The top of each triple crochet stitch has two horizontal strands, shaped like a V.

4 Bring the yarn over the crochet hook twice, from back to front.

5 Insert the crochet hook under the top two horizontal strands of the triple crochet stitch from front to back.

Do I have to make a turning chain at the beginning of each new row?

Yes. You must make a turning chain at the beginning of each new row of stitches. If you do not make a turning chain, the yarn will not be raised up to accommodate the height of the new row of stitches and the edges of your work will become compressed. For the triple, double and half double crochet stitches, your rows will also be short a stitch, causing the edges of your work to slope inward. The graphic to the right shows the height of the basic crochet stitches and the height of the turning chain required by each stitch.

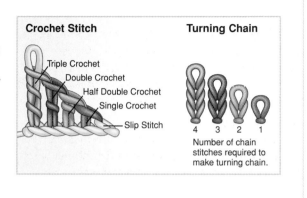

Crochet Stitch

- Triple Crochet
- Double Crochet
- Half Double Crochet
- Single Crochet
- Slip Stitch

Turning Chain

4 3 2 1

Number of chain stitches required to make turning chain.

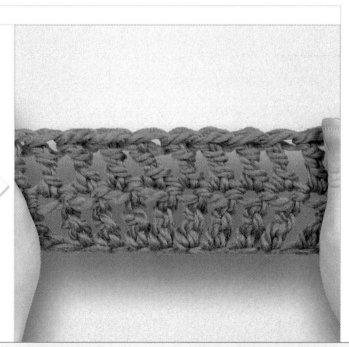

6 Complete the triple crochet stitch.

Note: To complete a triple crochet stitch, perform steps 5 to 11 starting on page 244, sliding the crochet hook through the first two loops in step 7.

7 To complete a row of triple crochet stitches, repeat steps 4 to 6 for each of the following triple crochet stitches in the row.

ROW 3 AND ALL REMAINING ROWS

1 To work additional rows of triple crochet stitches, repeat steps 1 to 7 for each row you want to complete.

- When you reach the end of each row, make sure you work a stitch into the top chain stitch of the turning chain in the previous row.

make a
slip stitch

The slip stitch is a versatile stitch that can be used for many purposes. The slip stitch is the shortest crochet stitch and is abbreviated as **sl st** in patterns.

When you have completed a crocheted piece, such as a baby blanket, you can use a row of slip stitches to create a firm edge for the piece. You can also use the slip stitch to carry yarn across the top of existing stitches without adding any noticeable height to your work.

The slip stitch is also used to join crocheted pieces together to assemble your work. When working in

rounds to create circular crocheted pieces, you use the slip stitch to join the ends of a round together. For more information on assembling your work and working in rounds, see pages 266 and 258.

You can also use the slip stitch to join a new ball of yarn to your crochet project when working in rounds. This is useful if your current ball runs out or you introduce a new color to your project. For information on joining new yarn, see page 262.

1 Make one or more rows of a crochet stitch.

Note: To make one or more rows of a crochet stitch, see pages 232 to 247.

2 Turn your work around so you can crochet back across the previous row.

3 Locate the first crochet stitch from the crochet hook. The top of each crochet stitch has two horizontal strands, shaped like a V.

4 Insert the crochet hook under the top two horizontal strands of the crochet stitch from front to back.

Can I create an entire crocheted piece using the slip stitch?

The slip stitch is not commonly used to create fabric. The slip stitch is a functional stitch that helps you complete tasks such as creating a firm edge, carrying yarn from one place to another and joining crocheted pieces together.

When starting a new row of slip stitches, do I need to make a turning chain?

No. Unlike other crochet stitches, when starting a new row of slip stitches, you do not have to make a turning chain to raise the yarn for the new row. Slip stitches are the shortest crochet stitch and do not require the height provided by a turning chain.

5 Bring the yarn over the crochet hook from back to front.

6 Catch the yarn with the hook of the crochet hook.

7 Slide the hook and the strand of yarn through the three loops on the crochet hook, allowing the three loops to fall off the crochet hook.

• You now have one loop on the crochet hook.

• You have created one slip stitch.

8 To create additional slip stitches, repeat steps 4 to 7 for each of the following crochet stitches in the row.

Note: We use a different color of yarn to crochet the slip stitches to more clearly show the example. You should use the same yarn you used to crochet the piece.

check your gauge

Gauge, or "tension," is the number of stitches and rows you produce per inch when crocheting. Gauge determines the size of your finished project.

Before you begin any project, you should always crochet a gauge swatch using the same yarn and crochet hook you will use for the project. A gauge swatch is a piece of crocheted fabric, usually at least a 4-inch square, which allows you to determine if you are producing the correct number of stitches and rows per inch.

Pattern instructions indicate both the number of stitches and the number of rows for the required gauge. For example, a pattern may specify "14 single crochet stitches = 4 inches" and "16 rows = 4 inches" for the gauge.

If you have too many stitches or rows for the required gauge, use a larger crochet hook and try crocheting another gauge swatch. If you have too few stitches or rows, try using a smaller crochet hook. You should not proceed with the project until you have attained the required gauge.

1 Make a foundation chain that measures more than 4 inches long. To make a foundation chain, see page 226.

2 Create rows of double crochet stitches until your crocheted piece measures more than 4 inches high. To create rows of double crochet stitches, see page 240.

Note: Your pattern may indicate a different type of stitch or pattern to use for the gauge swatch. In step 2, crochet that stitch or pattern instead.

3 Fasten off the last stitch in the last row. To fasten off, see page 264.

4 Smooth out the crocheted piece on a flat surface.

5 Place a ruler horizontally on the crocheted piece and mark 4 inches with pins.

6 Count the number of stitches between the pins.

What can affect the gauge ("tension") of my gauge swatch?

In addition to the size of the crochet hook, yarn thickness and type of stitch you are using, gauge can also be affected by how you hold the yarn. Beginners tend to hold the yarn tightly as they crochet and as a result, produce more stitches per inch than they should.

What size should I make my gauge swatch?

Some patterns may provide the gauge for a gauge swatch that is smaller than a 4-inch square. A smaller gauge swatch, however, is not an adequate sample to accurately measure the gauge. You should convert the gauge given in the pattern to determine the number of stitches and rows for a 4-inch square.

Do I have to make a gauge swatch?

Yes. If you do not make a gauge swatch and your project turns out too big or too small, you will be disappointed by the hours of work and cost of materials that have been wasted. Take the time to produce a gauge swatch so you can be confident your project will turn out the way you expect.

USING A STITCH GAUGE

7 Place a ruler on the crocheted piece vertically and mark 4 inches with pins.

8 Count the number of rows between the pins.

9 Compare the number of stitches and rows you counted to the numbers given in your pattern.

1 Create your gauge swatch by performing steps **1** to **3** on page 250.

2 Place a stitch gauge in the center of your crocheted piece.

3 Count the number of stitches and rows within the opening of the stitch gauge.

4 Compare the number of stitches and rows you counted to the numbers given in your pattern.

increase stitches

You can increase stitches to add stitches to your crochet project. Increasing stitches widens your fabric and allows you to shape items such as hats and sweaters.

To increase stitches, you can work two or more stitches into one stitch. You can also increase stitches by working two or more stitches into the space between stitches. Increasing stitches by working into a space is commonly done when making a granny square. For information on making a granny square, see page 272.

Increasing stitches adds stitches to the current row. For example, if you work two stitches into a stitch, you increase the number of stitches in the row by one. If you work three stitches into a stitch, you increase the number of stitches in the row by two. You can increase stitches at the beginning, middle or end of a row.

INCREASE STITCHES INTO A STITCH

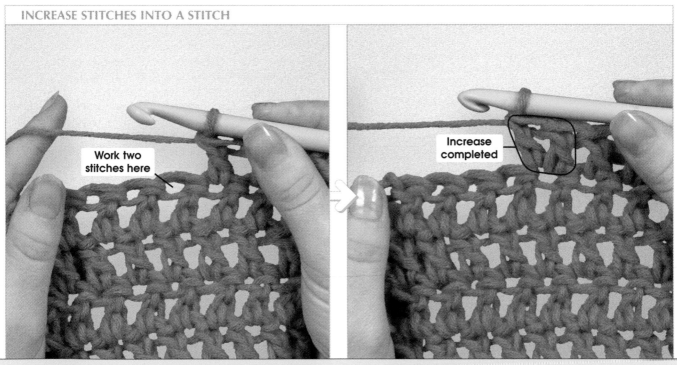

Work two stitches here

Increase completed

1 Crochet to where you want to make an increase.

2 Work a crochet stitch into the next stitch.

Note: You usually work the same type of crochet stitch that is currently in the row, such as a single crochet (page 232), half double crochet (page 236), double crochet (page 240) or triple crochet (page 244).

3 Work another crochet stitch of the same type into the same stitch.

• You have completed the increase.

How will I know where to increase stitches?

The pattern you are using to make your crochet project will specify where to make an increase and the type of stitch to use. For example, a pattern may specify "3 dc in next sp," which means you need to work three double crochet stitches into the next space.

What does "inc" mean?

A crochet pattern may indicate an increase using the abbreviation **inc**. For example, "inc 1 sc at each edge," which means you need to work two single crochet stitches into the first and the last stitch in the row.

INCREASE STITCHES INTO A SPACE

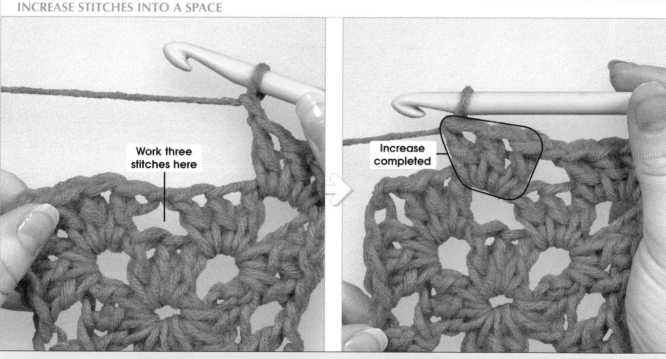

Work three stitches here

Increase completed

1 Crochet to where you want to make an increase.

2 Work a crochet stitch into the next space.

Note: You usually work the same type of crochet stitch that is currently in the row, such as a single crochet (page 232), half double crochet (page 236), double crochet (page 240) or triple crochet (page 244).

3 Work two more crochet stitches of the same type into the same space.

• You have completed the increase.

decrease stitches

You can decrease the number of stitches in your work to make your crochet project narrower. Decreasing stitches allows you to contour your work to create shaped items such as sweaters, socks and mittens.

To make a decrease, you begin with two partially completed crochet stitches and then combine them to create one stitch. For every decrease you make, you will have one less stitch to work into when you crochet the next row.

You will usually use the method described below to decrease crochet stitches in the second row or the following rows. When decreasing crochet stitches in a row, you can decrease stitches at the beginning, middle or end of a row.

You can also use the method described below to decrease stitches when working in rounds to create circular crocheted pieces. For information on working in rounds, see page 258.

SINGLE CROCHET DECREASE

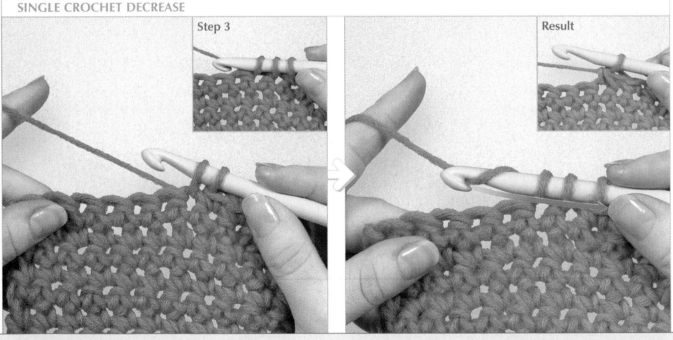

Step 3

Result

1 Crochet to where you want to make a decrease.

2 Work a single crochet stitch into the next stitch until the single crochet stitch is one step from completion. You will have two loops on the crochet hook. To make a single crochet stitch, see page 232.

3 Work a single crochet stitch into the next stitch until you have three loops on the crochet hook.

4 Bring the yarn over the crochet hook from back to front.

5 Catch the yarn with the hook of the crochet hook.

6 Slide the hook and the strand of yarn through the three loops on the crochet hook, allowing the three loops to fall off the crochet hook.

• You have decreased the number of single crochet stitches by one.

How is a single crochet decrease indicated in a pattern?

You will see two abbreviations commonly used in patterns to indicate that you should make a single crochet decrease—**sc2tog** and **1 sc dec**. The **sc2tog** abbreviation stands for "single crochet two together." The **1 sc dec** abbreviation stands for "one single crochet decrease."

How is a half double crochet decrease represented in a pattern?

In pattern instructions, a half double crochet decrease can be represented by the abbreviation **hdc2tog** or the abbreviation **1 hdc dec**. The **hdc2tog** abbreviation stands for "half double crochet two together." The abbreviation **1 hdc dec** stands for "one half double crochet decrease."

HALF DOUBLE CROCHET DECREASE

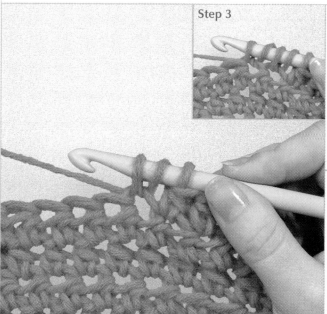

Step 3

Result

1 Crochet to where you want to make a decrease.

2 Work a half double crochet stitch into the next stitch until the half double crochet stitch is one step from completion. You will have three loops on the crochet hook. To make a half double crochet stitch, see page 236.

3 Work a half double crochet stitch into the next stitch until you have five loops on the crochet hook.

4 Bring the yarn over the crochet hook from back to front.

5 Catch the yarn with the hook of the crochet hook.

6 Slide the hook and the strand of yarn through the five loops on the crochet hook, allowing the five loops to fall off the crochet hook.

• You have decreased the number of half double crochet stitches by one.

CONTINUED...

decrease stitches *(continued)*

Removing stitches from your work, called decreasing, allows you to reduce the width of your crochet project. Removing stitches is useful if you are creating a project, such as a hat, that gradually gets narrower.

To decrease stitches in your work, you merge two partially completed crochet stitches together to form a single stitch. In the next row, you will have one stitch to work into at the location of the decrease, instead of two stitches.

You will usually use the method described below to decrease crochet stitches in the second row or the following rows. When decreasing crochet stitches in a row, you can decrease stitches at the beginning, middle or end of a row.

You can also use the method described below to decrease stitches when working in rounds to create circular crocheted pieces. For information on working in rounds, see page 258.

DOUBLE CROCHET DECREASE

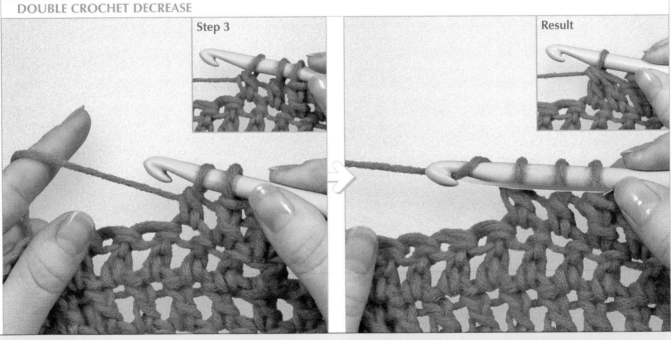

Step 3

Result

1 Crochet to where you want to make a decrease.

2 Work a double crochet stitch into the next stitch until the double crochet stitch is one step from completion. You will have two loops on the crochet hook. To make a double crochet stitch, see page 240.

3 Work a double crochet stitch into the next stitch until you have three loops on the crochet hook.

4 Bring the yarn over the crochet hook from back to front.

5 Catch the yarn with the hook of the crochet hook.

6 Slide the hook and the strand of yarn through the three loops on the crochet hook, allowing the three loops to fall off the crochet hook.

• You have decreased the number of double crochet stitches by one.

QUESTION & ANSWER ?

How is a double crochet or triple crochet decrease indicated in a pattern?

In pattern instructions, a double crochet decrease can be indicated by the abbreviation **dc2tog** (double crochet two together) or the abbreviation **1 dc dec** (one double crochet decrease). A triple crochet decrease can be indicated by the abbreviation **tr2tog** (triple crochet two together) or the abbreviation **1 tr dec** (one triple crochet decrease).

Are there other ways to decrease stitches?

Yes. For example, some patterns may tell you to simply skip over a stitch in a row or round of stitches to make a decrease. When working in rows, you may be instructed not to make a turning chain, which will also reduce the number of stitches in your work. You should always follow the pattern instructions to make your decreases.

TRIPLE CROCHET DECREASE

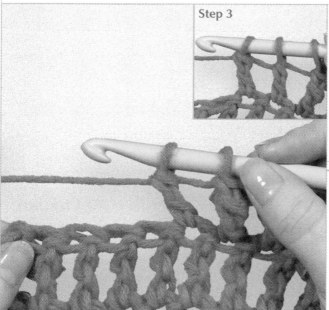

Step 3

Result

1 Crochet to where you want to make a decrease.

2 Work a triple crochet stitch into the next stitch until the triple crochet stitch is one step from completion. You will have two loops on the crochet hook. To make a triple crochet stitch, see page 244.

3 Work a triple crochet stitch into the next stitch until you have three loops on the crochet hook.

4 Bring the yarn over the crochet hook from back to front.

5 Catch the yarn with the hook of the crochet hook.

6 Slide the hook and the strand of yarn through the three loops on the crochet hook, allowing the three loops to fall off the crochet hook.

● You have decreased the number of triple crochet stitches by one.

work in rounds

You can work in rounds to create flat, circular crocheted pieces, often called motifs. When using the method shown below to work in rounds, the first step is to create a foundation chain and join the ends of the foundation chain to make a ring. The ring will form the center of your crocheted piece.

To start each round, you must make a starting chain to raise the yarn up to the proper height for the new round of stitches. The number of chain stitches required for the starting chain depends on the type of crochet stitch that you will work in the round. A round of single crochet requires one chain stitch.

A round of half double crochet requires two chain stitches. A round of double crochet requires three chain stitches. A round of triple crochet requires four chain stitches.

After you make the starting chain, you work the first round of crochet stitches by inserting the crochet hook into the center of the ring. You complete the crochet stitches as you would complete crochet stitches when working in rows. When working in rounds, you crochet with the right side of your work always facing you.

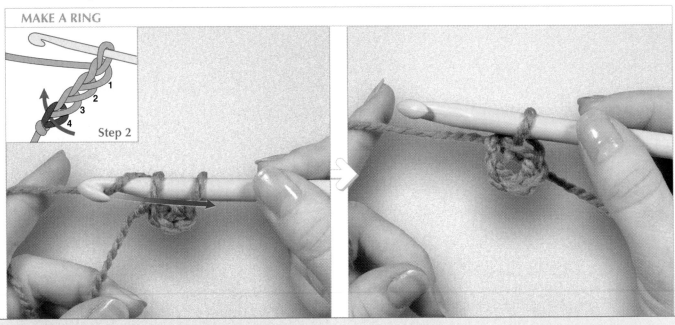

MAKE A RING

Step 2

1 Make a foundation chain to start your crochet project. To make a foundation chain, see page 226.

2 Insert the crochet hook under the top loop of the first chain stitch you made, from front to back.

3 Bring the yarn over the crochet hook from back to front.

4 Catch the yarn with the hook of the crochet hook.

5 Slide the hook and the strand of yarn through the two loops on the crochet hook, allowing the two loops to fall off the crochet hook.

• You now have one loop on the crochet hook.

• You have created a slip stitch and made a ring.

Does the starting chain count as the first stitch in the round?

When working in rounds of triple, double and half double crochet stitches, the starting chain counts as the first stitch in the round. When working in rounds of single crochet stitches, the starting chain does not count as the first stitch in the round.

Can I work in rounds to create shapes other than circles?

Yes. Depending on the pattern you are using, you can work in rounds to create shapes such as hexagons, ovals and squares. Creating squares, called granny squares, is a common task in crochet. For information on creating a granny square, see page 272.

ROUND 1

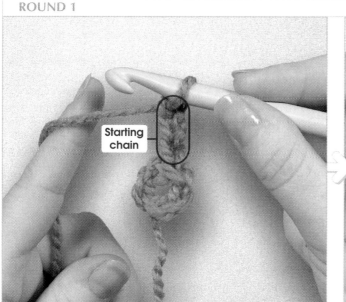

Starting chain

• To begin a round of crochet stitches, you must first make a starting chain to raise the yarn to the proper height for the new round.

1 To make a starting chain, make the required number of chain stitches. To make a chain stitch, see page 226.

Note: A round of single crochet requires one chain stitch. Half double crochet requires two chain stitches. Double crochet requires three chain stitches. Triple crochet requires four chain stitches.

2 Work a crochet stitch by inserting the crochet hook into the center of the ring from front to back.

Note: In this example, we complete a double crochet stitch.

3 Repeat step 2, rotating the ring clockwise until you have completed all the crochet stitches for the first round.

CONTINUED...

Once you have completed the first round of crochet stitches, you use a slip stitch to close the round. You can use a stitch marker or safety pin to mark the slip stitch at the end of each round. Marking the slip stitch will help you easily keep track of where each round ends and the number of rounds you have completed.

To start the second and all additional rounds of crochet stitches, you must first make a starting chain as you did for the first round. You work the second round of crochet stitches into the top of the stitches in the previous round. When working in rounds of

triple, double and half double crochet, you work into the second stitch in the previous round. When working in rounds of single crochet, you work into the first stitch in the previous round.

To create a flat piece when working in rounds, you must increase stitches in the second and all subsequent rounds. The example shown below increases stitches by working two stitches into every stitch in the previous round, but you should follow your pattern instructions to determine where to make your increases.

ROUND 1 (Continued)

4 To close the round, insert the crochet hook under the top two horizontal strands of the top chain stitch of the starting chain, from front to back.

5 Bring the yarn over the crochet hook from back to front.

6 Catch the yarn with the hook of the crochet hook.

7 Slide the hook and the strand of yarn through all the loops on the crochet hook, allowing the loops to fall off the crochet hook.

• You have created a slip stitch and closed the round.

8 To add a visual reminder of where the round ends and help you keep track of the number of rounds you have completed, you can mark the slip stitch with a stitch marker or safety pin.

When working in rounds, can I make a tube-shaped piece instead of a flat piece?

Yes. Creating a tube-shaped piece allows you to crochet items such as socks and toys. To make a tube-shaped piece, you do not need to increase stitches in the second and subsequent rounds. Instead, when you crochet the second and subsequent rounds, you can work one stitch into each of the stitches in the previous round. This will create rounds of stitches that stack up one on top of the other, forming a tube-shaped piece.

ROUND 2 AND ADDITIONAL ROUNDS

1 To make a starting chain for the new round of stitches, perform step **1** on page 259.

Note: In this example, we make three chain stitches for a round of double crochet stitches.

2 Work a crochet stitch under the top two horizontal strands of the second crochet stitch in the previous round.

Note: To work a single crochet stitch, work the stitch into the first crochet stitch in the previous round.

3 To increase the number of stitches in the round to create a flat piece, work another crochet stitch of the same type into the same crochet stitch.

4 Continue to work two stitches into each of the following crochet stitches in the previous round until you complete all the stitches in the round.

5 To close the round, perform steps **4** to **8** on page 260.

261

You can join a new ball of yarn to your project. Joining a new ball of yarn is useful if the ball you are currently using runs out or you want to introduce a new color of yarn to your project.

When working in rows, you join new yarn within a stitch. You can join yarn within any kind of stitch, including single crochet, half double crochet, double crochet and triple crochet.

You can join new yarn at the beginning, middle or end of a row. You should try to join new yarn at the end of a row when you find the ball you are currently using is running out. When you need to change colors, you can join new yarn anywhere in a row.

When working in rounds, you use a slip stitch at the end of a round to join new yarn. You usually join new yarn only at the end of a round. For information on working in rounds, see page 258.

WHEN WORKING IN ROWS

1 To join yarn at the end of a row, work the last crochet stitch in the row until the stitch is one step from completion.

Note: To join yarn within a row, work the stitch before the location where you want to join new yarn until the stitch is one step from completion.

• A single, double or triple crochet stitch will have 2 loops remaining on the crochet hook. A half double crochet stitch will have 3 loops remaining on the crochet hook.

2 Catch the new yarn with the hook of the crochet hook, leaving a tail of yarn approximately 6 inches long.

3 Slide the hook and the new strand of yarn through all the loops on the crochet hook, allowing all the loops to fall off the crochet hook.

4 Cut the old yarn, leaving a tail of yarn approximately 6 inches long.

5 Continue crocheting with the new yarn.

Note: When you finish your project, you can weave in the yarn ends. For information on weaving in yarn ends, see page 264.

When joining new yarn, can I weave in yarn ends as I work?

Yes. To weave in yarn ends as you work, lay the new yarn on top of the stitches in the previous row a few inches before you want to use the new yarn. Crochet across the row as you normally would. When you reach the location where you want to use the new yarn, perform steps **1** to **4** on page 262 to secure the new yarn. Lay the tail of the old yarn on top of the stitches in the previous row and crochet across the row with the new yarn for a few inches. Then cut the tail of the old yarn close to the surface of your work.

WHEN WORKING IN ROUNDS

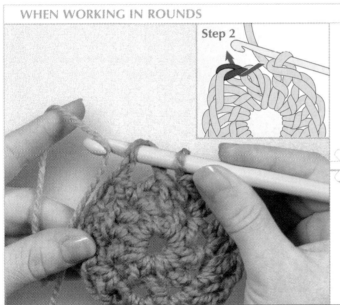

Step 2

1 Work the last crochet stitch in the round.

2 Insert the crochet hook under the top two horizontal strands of the top chain stitch in the starting chain, from front to back.

3 Catch the new yarn with the hook of the crochet hook, leaving a tail of yarn approximately 6 inches long.

4 Slide the hook and the new strand of yarn through all the loops on the crochet hook, allowing all the loops to fall off the crochet hook.

• You have created a slip stitch and joined the new yarn.

5 Cut the old yarn, leaving a tail of yarn approximately 6 inches long.

6 Continue crocheting with the new yarn.

Note: When you finish your project, you can weave in the yarn ends. For information on weaving in yarn ends, see page 264.

finishing your work

Proper finishing techniques can help you create a professional-looking crocheted piece.

After you complete the last crochet stitch in your work, one loop will remain on your crochet hook. You must fasten off this loop to prevent your work from unraveling when you remove the crochet hook. When fastening off, you can leave a 6-inch tail of yarn that will be woven into the crocheted piece.

Once you finish a project, you need to conceal all the dangling ends of yarn left over from creating the foundation chain, fastening off and from where you started new balls of yarn. Weaving in yarn ends allows you to incorporate the loose ends of yarn seamlessly into your crocheted fabric.

You weave in yarn ends on the wrong side of your work to keep the right side smooth and neat. To weave in a yarn end securely, you weave the yarn end 2 inches in one direction and then back an inch in the opposite direction.

FASTEN OFF

1 Complete the last crochet stitch in the last row. You should have one loop on the crochet hook.

2 Cut the strand of yarn connected to the ball, leaving a tail of yarn approximately 6 inches long.

Note: If you plan to use the tail of yarn to sew pieces of your work together, leave a longer tail. For information on sewing your work together, see page 266.

3 Bring the yarn over the crochet hook from back to front.

4 Catch the yarn with the hook of the crochet hook.

5 Slide the hook and the strand of yarn through the loop on the crochet hook, pulling the entire strand of yarn through the loop.

6 Pull the yarn gently to tighten.

Can I weave a yarn end vertically down the side edge of my work?

Yes. After threading a yarn end through a tapestry needle, you weave the yarn end into the crochet stitches down the side edge of your work for approximately 2 inches. You then reverse the direction of the tapestry needle, skip a crochet stitch and then weave the yarn end back through the same stitches for approximately 1 inch. To finish, cut the end of the yarn close to the surface of your work.

WEAVE IN YARN ENDS

1 Thread a yarn end through a tapestry needle.

2 With the wrong side of your work facing you, insert the tapestry needle into the stitches across your crocheted piece for approximately 2 inches.

Note: Make sure the yarn end you weave in will not show on the right side of your work.

3 Reverse the direction of the tapestry needle, skip a crochet stitch and then insert the needle back into the same stitches across your crocheted piece for approximately 1 inch.

4 Cut the end of the yarn close to the surface of your work.

5 Gently stretch your work in each direction to pull the yarn end into the work.

6 Repeat steps 1 to 5 for each yarn end you want to weave into your work.

assemble your crocheted pieces

Using the Invisible Seam

When all the pieces of your crochet project are complete, you can join, or seam, the pieces together. There are three commonly used seams for joining crocheted pieces—invisible seam, overcast seam and slip stitch seam. The invisible seam, also called the mattress stitch seam, produces a flat, smooth, flexible seam that is almost undetectable. This seam is ideal for assembling garments, particularly baby clothes.

In the example below, we use the invisible seam to join the side edges of crocheted pieces.

You can also use this seam to join the top edges of crocheted pieces.

To use the invisible seam to join side edges, your crocheted pieces should have the same number of rows and the rows should be aligned before you start. You can use straight pins to hold the crocheted pieces in place as you sew. When sewing the invisible seam, the right side of your work faces you, allowing you to see how the seam will look when finished.

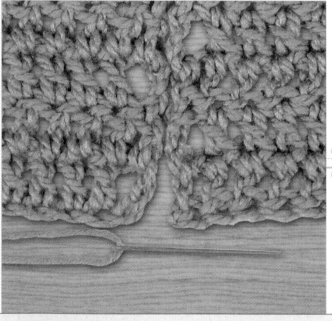

1 Place the two crocheted pieces you want to sew together side by side with the right sides facing you, the bottom edges at the bottom and the rows lined up.

2 Cut a strand of yarn long enough to sew the crocheted pieces together.

3 Thread the strand of yarn through a tapestry needle, leaving a tail approximately 6 inches long.

Note: We use a different color of yarn to sew the crocheted pieces together to more clearly show the example. You should use the same yarn you used to crochet the pieces.

4 On the bottom right corner of the left crocheted piece, from the back of the piece, insert the needle through the bottom of the first stitch. Then pull the yarn through.

5 On the bottom left corner of the right crocheted piece, from the front of the piece, insert the needle through the bottom of the first stitch. Then pull the yarn through.

Is there anything I need to do before assembling my crocheted pieces?

Some crochet patterns may instruct you to block your crocheted pieces before you assemble them. Blocking involves dampening the pieces so you can shape the pieces to their proper dimensions and flatten curling edges. In most cases, however, you will find that your pieces require little or no blocking, since crocheting usually produces a firm fabric that retains its shape. For more information on blocking, see page 196.

Is there another way I can sew pieces of a garment together?

You can also use the backstitch seam to sew pieces of a garment together. The backstitch seam is ideal when you are sewing curved edges together, such as attaching a sleeve to the body of a sweater. Compared to the invisible seam, the backstitch seam is stronger, less flexible and more noticeable. For more information on the backstitch seam, see page 202.

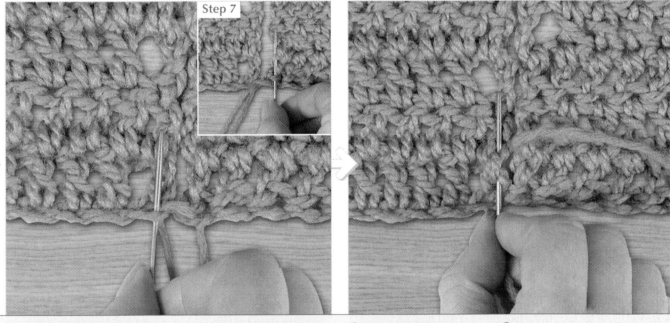

Step 7

6 On the bottom right corner of the left crocheted piece, from the back of the piece, insert the needle through the bottom of the first stitch again. Then pull the yarn through to secure the yarn.

7 On the first row of the right crocheted piece, insert the needle up through the first stitch, catching one or two loops of the stitch. Then pull the yarn through.

8 On the first row of the left crocheted piece, insert the needle up through the first stitch, catching one or two loops of the stitch. Then pull the yarn through.

9 Repeat steps 7 and 8, moving up one row at a time on each crocheted piece, until you have sewed the entire edge.

Note: To weave in the yarn ends left over from sewing the crocheted pieces together, see page 265.

CONTINUED...

assemble your crocheted pieces (continued)

Using the Overcast Seam

You can use the overcast seam, also called the whip stitch seam, to sew your crocheted pieces together. This seam can be used to assemble the pieces of a garment.

The overcast seam is usually worked with the right sides of your crocheted pieces facing each other and the edges lined up. You can pin the pieces together to make sure they do not move while you sew the seam. You sew the overcast seam from right to left,

using a strand of the same yarn you used to crochet the pieces. Be careful not to sew the overcast seam too tightly. After you complete the seam, there will be ends of yarn hanging from your project. You can later weave the yarn ends into your project.

In the example below, we use the overcast seam to join the top edges of crocheted pieces. You can also use the overcast seam to join the side edges of crocheted pieces.

1 Cut a strand of yarn long enough to sew the crocheted pieces together.

2 Thread the strand of yarn through a tapestry needle, leaving a tail approximately 6 inches long.

Note: We use a different color of yarn to sew the crocheted pieces together to more clearly show the example. You should use the same yarn you used to crochet the pieces.

3 Hold the two crocheted pieces you want to sew together with the right sides facing each other and the edges lined up. Make sure the edges you want to sew together are at the top.

4 At the top right corner of the crocheted pieces, insert the needle under the top two horizontal strands of the first stitch of both pieces, from back to front. Then pull the yarn through.

How can I create a flatter, smoother overcast seam?

To create a flatter, smoother overcast seam, perform the steps below, except insert the needle through only the outside horizontal strands of the stitches in step **4**, instead of all the horizontal strands. This technique is useful when you are using the overcast seam to join granny squares. For information on creating a granny square, see page 273.

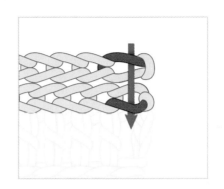

5 Bring the needle and yarn over the top edges of the crocheted pieces toward the back of your work.

6 Repeat steps **4** and **5**, moving one stitch to the left each time, until you have sewed the entire edge.

Note: To weave in the yarn ends left over from sewing the crocheted pieces together, see page 265.

CONTINUED...

Using the Slip Stitch Seam

You can use the slip stitch seam to join your crocheted pieces. The slip stitch creates a strong, inflexible seam that is best suited for joining straight edges, such as the edges of granny squares. For information on making a granny square, see page 273. The slip stitch seam is not suitable for assembling garments.

You use a crochet hook to make a slip stitch seam. Be careful not to work the slip stitch seam too tightly. To ensure your slip stitch seam is not too tight, you should use the same size hook you used for the crochet project or a hook one size larger. Instead of using a new strand of yarn, you will usually use a tail of yarn from one of the crocheted pieces to seam the pieces together.

In the example below, we crochet the slip stitch seam with the right sides of the pieces together and insert the crochet hook through only the inside horizontal strands of the stitches to make the seam less bulky and less visible.

1 Hold the two crocheted pieces you want to slip stitch together with the right sides facing each other and the edges lined up. Make sure the edges you want to slip stitch together are at the top.

2 At the top right corner of the crocheted pieces, insert the crochet hook under the inside horizontal strands of the first stitch of both pieces, from front to back.

3 Bring the tail of yarn you will use to slip stitch the seam over the crochet hook from back to front.

4 Catch the yarn with the hook of the crochet hook.

Note: We use a different color of yarn to slip stitch the crocheted pieces together to more clearly show the example. You should use a tail of yarn from one of the crocheted pieces.

QUESTION & ANSWER

Can I use the slip stitch seam as a decorative element in my project?

Yes. You can work the slip stitch on the right side of your project to create a more visible, raised seam, which can add a decorative element to your project. Perform the steps below, except hold the wrong sides of your crocheted pieces together in step **1**. In step **2**, insert the crochet hook under the top two horizontal strands of the first stitch of both pieces, instead of only the inside horizontal strands.

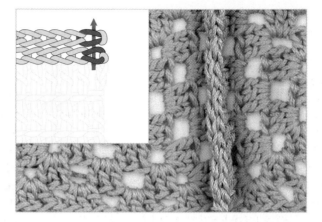

5 Slide the hook and the strand of yarn through all the loops on the crochet hook, allowing all the loops to fall off the crochet hook.

• You will have one loop on the crochet hook.

6 Repeat steps **2** to **5**, moving one stitch to the left each time, until you have slip stitched the entire edge.

7 When you have slip stitched the entire edge, fasten off the last loop on the crochet hook. For information on fastening off, see page 264.

Note: To weave in the yarn end left over from slip stitching the crocheted pieces together, see page 265.

crochet
designs

Abbreviation: tch = turning chain.

Ch 20 for the foundation chain.

Row 1: 1 sc into 2nd ch from hook, *skip 2 chs, 5 dc into next ch, skip 2 chs, 1 sc into next ch; rep from * to end of row, **turn.**

Row 2: Ch 3 (counts as 1 dc), 2 dc into first st, *skip 2 dc, 1 sc into next dc, skip 2 dc, 5 dc into next sc; rep from * to end of row, ending last rep with 3 dc into last sc, skip tch, **turn.**

Row 3: Ch 1, 1 sc into first st, *skip 2 dc, 5 dc into next sc, skip 2 dc, 1 sc into next dc; rep from * to end of row, ending last rep with 1 sc into top of tch, **turn.**

Rep Rows 2 and 3.

EASY

Abbreviation: tch = turning chain.

Ch 22 for the foundation chain.

Row 1: Skip first 3 chs (counts as 1 dc), *1 sc into next ch, 1 dc into next ch; rep from * to end of row, ending last rep with 1 sc into last ch, **turn.**

Row 2: Ch 3 (counts as 1 dc), skip 1 st, *1 sc into next dc, 1 dc into next sc; rep from * to end of row, ending last rep with 1 sc into top of tch, **turn.**

Rep Row 2.

EASY

Granny Square

INTERMEDIATE

Ch 5 for the foundation chain. Join with sl st in first ch made to form a ring.

Rnd 1: Ch 3 (counts as 1 dc), 2 dc into ring. (Ch 2, 3 dc into ring) 3 times. Ch 2. Join with sl st to top of beg ch 3.

Rnd 2: Sl st into each of next 2 dc and sl st into ch 2 sp of previous row. Ch 3. (2 dc, ch 2, 3 dc) into same space (corner made). *Ch 1, skip next 3 dc and into next ch 2 corner sp work (3 dc, ch 2, 3 dc) (corner made); rep from * twice. Ch 1, skip next 3 dc and join with sl st to top of ch 3.

Rnd 3: Sl st into each of next 2 dc and sl st into ch 2 sp of previous row. Ch 3. (2 dc, ch 2, 3 dc) into same space (corner made). *Ch 1, skip next 3 dc, 3 dc into next ch 1 sp. Ch 1, skip next 3 dc and into next ch 2 corner sp work (3 dc, ch 2, 3 dc) (corner made); rep from * twice. Ch 1, 3 dc into next ch 1 sp. Ch 1, skip next 3 dc and join with sl st to top of ch 3.

Rnd 4: Sl st into each of next 2 dc and sl st into ch 2 sp of previous row. Ch 3. (2 dc, ch 2, 3 dc) into same space (corner made). *(Ch 1, skip next 3 dc, 3 dc into next ch 1 sp) twice. Ch 1, skip next 3 dc and into next corner sp work (3 dc, ch 2, 3 dc); rep from * twice. (Ch 1, skip next 3 dc, 3 dc into next ch 1 sp) twice. Ch 1, skip next 3 dc and join with sl st to top of ch 3.

Chevron Stitch

INTERMEDIATE

Abbreviations: dc3tog=*yo, insert hook, yo and draw through loop, yo draw through 2 loops *; rep from * to * for next 2 sts to get 4 loops on hook, ending yo, draw through all loops on hook.
tch = turning chain.

Ch 23 for the foundation chain.

Row 1: Skip 2 chs (counts as 1 dc), 1 dc into next ch, *1 dc into each of the next 3 chs, work dc3tog over the next 3 chs, 1 dc into each of the next 3 chs, 3 dc into next ch; rep from * to end of row, ending last rep with 2 dc into last ch, **turn.**

Row 2: Ch 3 (counts as 1 dc), 1 dc into first st, *1 dc into each of the next 3 dc, work dc3tog over the next 3 chs, 1 dc into each of the next 3 dc, 3 dc into next dc; rep from * to end of row, ending last rep with 2 dc into top of tch, **turn.**

Rep Row 2.

shimmering striped scarf

· Easy Project ·

Shimmering Striped Scarf

Size

Approx. 60 x 6.75 ins (152 x 16.5cm).

Materials

Needful Yarns Filtes King Lamé (1.75oz/50g)
MC (Main Color) = #42 Charcoal, 2 balls
Contrast A = #41 Grey, 2 balls

Size G/6 US (4.25mm) crochet hook or size
needed to obtain gauge.

Gauge

18 double crochet and 11 rows = 4 ins (10cm).

Instructions

Abbreviations: ch = chain; dc = double crochet;
RS = right side; WS = wrong side.

When working in rows of dc, remember to ch 3 at
the end of each row for the turning chain and skip
the first dc in the next row. Also, remember to work
into the top ch of the previous row's turning chain
when you come to it.

Beginning at side edge, with MC, ch 270.
*Working in dc, work 2 rows in MC, 2 rows in A.
Rep from * 3 times. Work 2 more rows in MC.
Fasten off.

Fringe:
Cut 5 lengths of yarn 11 ins (28cm). Fold the lengths
in half.

Perform steps 4 to 10 on page 136 to make a section
of fringe at the corner of the scarf.

Add 1 section of fringe to each corresponding row
color.

moonlit sky
scarf

· Easy Project ·

Moonlit Sky Scarf

Size

Approx. 80 x 7 ins (203 x 18cm)

Materials

Needful Yarns Ker 1.75oz/50g, #712 Blue,
4 balls

Size K/10.5 US (6.5mm) crochet hook or size
needed to obtain gauge.

Gauge

11 single crochet (sc) and 12 rows = 4 ins (10cm).

Instructions

Abbreviations: ch = chain; RS = right side;
WS = wrong side; sc = single crochet.

Beginning at side edge, ch 27.

Row 1 (RS): 1 sc in 6th ch from hook *ch 5.
Skip 3 chs. 1 sc into next ch;
Rep from * to end of row, turn.

Row 2: *Ch 5. 1 sc into next 5 ch arch;
Rep from * to end of row, turn.

Rep Row 2 until work from beginning measures
80 ins (203cm).

Fasten off.

Fringe:
Cut 2 lengths of yarn 11 ins (28cm). Fold the
lengths in half.

Perform steps 4 to 10 on page 136 to make
a section of fringe at the corner of the scarf.

Add 1 section of fringe to each arch.

Chapter 11

This chapter is a great resource for accessing information quickly. You can refer to the comprehensive glossary in this chapter when you need to look up a knitting or crocheting term. There is also an extensive list of abbreviations commonly used in knitting and crocheting patterns and instructions.

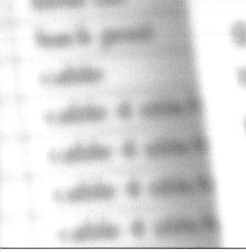

Quick Reference

In this Chapter...

Glossary

Common Abbreviations

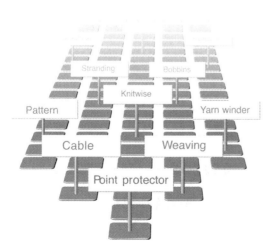

glossary

B

Back loop Of the two horizontal loops of a crochet stitch, the one that is farthest away from you when you are working on a piece.

Backstitch A strong seaming stitch that is used to sew pieces together.

Binding off A method of securing the stitches on a completed knitted piece to keep them from unraveling. Also known as casting off.

Blocking A procedure involving dampening and then shaping a piece to help even out stitches, flatten curling edges and ensure the piece has the correct dimensions.

Bobbins Plastic devices that you can use to hold short lengths of yarn when working with multiple yarn colors. Using bobbins helps to prevent tangles.

Bobble A ball-shaped decoration that you create by adding several stitches to your project and then working those stitches back into a single stitch.

Button band A strip of knitted or crocheted fabric onto which you sew buttons.

Buttonhole band A strip of knitted or crocheted fabric into which you work buttonholes.

C

Cable A group of stitches that cross in front or behind another group of stitches to form appealing designs in your fabric.

Cable needle A small, double-pointed needle that is often curved. You use a cable needle to temporarily hold stitches when creating a cable pattern.

Casting off *See* Binding off

Casting on Adding the first row of stitches to your knitting needle.

Chain A sequence of chain stitches.

Chain stitch The most basic crochet stitch.

Circular needle A knitting needle that consists of a pair of short, straight needles attached by a flexible cord. Circular needles allow you to knit in a circle, which is referred to as knitting in the round or circular knitting.

Continental knitting A style of knitting in which you hold the yarn in your left hand.

Crochet To join loops of yarn with a crochet hook to create fabric.

D

Decrease Performing a decrease reduces the number of stitches in your piece, making your work narrower.

Double crochet stitch A commonly used crochet stitch that creates an open fabric.

Double-pointed needle Straight needles that have a point at each end. These needles are useful for knitting small tubular items, such as socks.

Dropped stitch A stitch that has slipped off the end of your needle and has not been knitted or purled.

Dye lot number Yarn is dyed in specific lots and each lot is assigned a dye lot number. Balls of yarn that have the same dye lot number will be the identical shade.

E

English knitting A style of knitting in which you hold the yarn in your right hand.

Eyelet A small, decorative hole. Also a type of lace fabric that features decorative holes.

F

Fair Isle knitting A color knitting technique in which you frequently change between two or more colors of yarn in the same row to create a pattern.

Fasten off A method of securing the last loop on your crochet hook to prevent your work from unraveling.

Flat knitting A common knitting method involving working on the right side of the knitted fabric, then turning the piece over and working on the wrong side.

Foundation chain The first row of chain stitches you complete, which forms the base on which you will crochet all the other rows in your piece.

Front loop Of the two horizontal loops of a crochet stitch, the one that is closest to you when you are working on a piece.

Fully fashioned shaping To shape a knitted piece by placing decreases or increases in a visible location, such as one or two stitches from an edge.

G

Garter stitch A ridged fabric formed when all the stitches are either knit on every row or purled on every row of flat knitting. A knitted fabric created in garter stitch looks exactly the same on the front and back.

Gauge The number of stitches and rows you should have in a square of knitted or crocheted fabric to ensure your finished project will be the correct size. Also called tension.

Gauge swatch A piece of knitted or crocheted fabric that allows you to determine if you are producing the correct number of stitches and rows per inch for a project.

Grafting An invisible seaming method used to join the edges of two knitted pieces that contain stitches that are not yet bound off. Also called the Kitchener stitch.

H

Half double crochet stitch A basic crochet stitch that creates a moderately dense fabric.

Hank A loosely twisted coil of yarn. You must wind hanks into balls before working with the yarn.

I

Increase Performing an increase adds to the number of stitches in your piece, making your work wider.

Intarsia knitting A knitting technique that involves using different colored yarns to create attractive designs and pictures in your fabric.

K

Kitchener stitch *See* Grafting

Knitting Performing the basic knit stitch. Also generally refers to creating a knitted piece.

Knitting in the round Refers to knitting tubular items, such as socks or sweater bodies.

Knitwise Inserting the right needle into the front of a stitch from left to right. This is the same way you insert the needle when you perform the knit stitch.

L

Live stitches Stitches that are not yet bound off on a piece of knitted fabric.

M

Mattress stitch A seaming method that produces a flexible, almost undetectable seam. Also called the invisible seam.

N

Needle gauge A device you can use to determine the size of needles that are not labeled.

glossary

Pattern A set of instructions for creating a knitted or crocheted project.

Point protector A small rubber cap you put on the pointed end of a needle to help keep the stitches from falling off when you put away or transport your work.

Post The vertical part of a crochet stitch. Also called the leg or bar.

Purling Performing the basic purl stitch.

Purlwise Inserting the right needle into the front of a stitch from right to left. This is the same way you insert the needle when you perform the purl stitch.

Reverse stockinette stitch A fabric formed by alternating between a row of purl stitches and a row of knit stitches. The fabric is bumpy (purl stitches) on the right side and smooth (knit stitches) on the wrong side.

Ribbing A stretchy fabric that is made by combining knit and purl stitches in the same row to create vertical ridges.

Right side The side of your fabric that will show outside when your project is complete.

Ripping out stitches Refers to unraveling your stitches to return to a location in your knitting where you made a mistake. You can then fix the mistake and continue knitting.

Row counter A device you can place on the end of your needles to keep track of how many rows you have completed.

Seaming Sewing your finished knitted or crocheted pieces together to complete your project. Also called sewing seams.

Selvedge stitch A stitch used to form a border around a knitted piece.

Short rows A shaping technique that allows you to curve or taper areas of your project without increasing or decreasing stitches. Also called partial knitting.

Single crochet stitch One of the most basic crochet stitches. It is a short stitch that creates a dense fabric.

Single-pointed needle A straight needle with a point at one end for knitting and a knob at the other end to keep the stitches from falling off the needle. Single-pointed needles are ideal for flat knitting.

Skein An oblong-shaped ball of yarn.

Slip knot A knot that makes a loop you can use as the starting point for your crochet or knitting project. In knitting, the slip knot serves as your first stitch. In crochet, the slip knot is not counted as a stitch.

Slip stitch In knitting, a stitch that is moved from one needle to the other needle without knitting or purling the stitch. In crochet, the shortest stitch that can be used to join seams, create firm edges or carry yarn across stitches.

Stash An assortment of yarns a knitter stores with the intention of using them at some future time.

Stitch One of a series of loops that hold together to form a piece of fabric. One horizontal line of stitches is called a row of stitches.

Stitch holder An accessory used to temporarily hold stitches you are not working with to prevent them from unraveling.

Stitch marker A small circular item used to leave a visual reminder of where pattern changes occur and to maintain your place in knitting.

Stockinette stitch A fabric formed by alternating between a row of knit stitches and a row of purl stitches. The fabric is smooth (knit stitches) on the right side and bumpy (purl stitches) on the wrong side. Also called stocking stitch.

Stranding A method used to carry yarn across stitches so you can make a color change. You usually use this method when carrying yarn across four or fewer stitches.

T

Tail A strand of yarn that is left over when you begin a piece, finish a piece or start a new ball of yarn.

Tapestry needle Similar to a large sewing needle that has a dull tip. A tapestry needle is often used to sew seams and weave in yarn ends. Also known as sewing, darning and yarn needle.

Triple crochet stitch One of the tallest crochet stitches. The triple crochet stitch creates an airy, delicate fabric. Also known as the treble crochet stitch.

Turning chain One or more chain stitches that you make at the beginning of each row of crochet stitches to bring the yarn up to the proper height for the new row.

Twisting stitches A method of overlapping one or more stitches in your work to create a cable effect, without requiring the use of a cable needle.

W

Weaving A method of securing yarn that is being carried across four or more stitches so you can make a color change. Also refers to working in a strand of yarn that is left over when you add stitches, finish stitches or start a new ball of yarn.

Whip stitch A seaming stitch that produces a strong, but somewhat bulky seam. Also called overcasting.

Work even Work in the established pattern without increasing or decreasing stitches. Also called work straight.

Wrong side The part of a fabric that will face inside when your project is complete.

Y

Yarn end *See* tail

Yarn over In knitting, a method of increasing stitches that results in a small, decorative hole being formed in your work. In crochet, the basic movement used to create stitches.

Yarn winder A device you can use to wind yarn into balls or skeins.

common abbreviations

alt	alternate *or* alternating
approx	approximately
beg	beginning
bet	between
bk lp	back loop
blo	back loop only
BO	bind off
bp	back post
C	cable
C4B	cable 4 stitches to the back
C4F	cable 4 stitches to the front
C4L	cable 4 stitches to the left
C4R	cable 4 stitches to the right
CC	contrast color
ch(s)	chain stitch(es)
cl	cluster
CL	cross stitches to the left
cm	centimeter
cn	cable needle
CO	cast on
col	color
cont	continue
CR	cross stitches to the right
dc	double crochet
dc dec	double crochet decrease
dc2tog	double crochet two stitches together
dec	decrease
dpn	double-pointed needles
dtr	double triple crochet
ea	each
est	established
flo	front loop only

foll	follow *or* following
fp	front post
ft lp	front loop
g	gram
hdc	half double crochet
hdc dec	half double crochet decrease
hdc2tog	half double crochet two stitches together
hk	hook
in(s)	inch(es)
inc	increase
incl	including
K	knit
k1b	knit one stitch in the row below *or* knit one stitch through the back loop
K1tbl	knit one stitch through the back loop
K2tog	knit two stitches together
K2tog tbl	knit two stitches together through back loop
keep cont	keeping continuity
kfb	knit into front and back of next stitch
kwise	knitwise
LH	left hand
lp	loop
LT	left twist
m	meter
m1	make one increase
MB	make a bobble
MC	main color
mm	millimeter
oz	ounce

P	purl
P1b	purl one stitch through back loop
p2sso	pass 2 slipped stitches over
P2tog	purl two stitches together
P2tog tbl	purl two stitches together through back loop
pat	pattern
pm	place marker
psso	pass slipped stitch over
pu	pick up
pwise	purlwise
rem	remaining
rep	repeat
rev St st	reverse Stockinette stitch
RH	right hand
rib	work in ribbing
rnd	work in rounds
RS	right side
RT	right twist
sc	single crochet
sc dec	single crochet decrease
sc2tog	single crochet two stitches together
sk	skip
skp	slip one stitch, knit one stitch, pass slipped stitch over
skpo	slip one stitch, knit one stitch, pass slipped stitch over
sl	slip
sl st	slip stitch
Sl1	slip one stitch
sl1 k1 psso	slip one stitch, knit one stitch, pass slipped stitch over

sl1 k2tog psso	slip one stitch, knit two stitches together, pass slipped stitch over
Sl1K	slip one stitch knitwise
Sl1P	slip one stitch purlwise
Sl1PB	slip slipped stitch purlwise back to left hand needle
sl2tog k1 p2sso	slip two stitches together, knit one stitch, pass the two slipped stitches over
sp(s)	space(s)
ssk	slip slip knit
st(s)	stitch(es)
St st	Stockinette stitch
tch	turning chain
T2L	twist two stitches to the left
T2R	twist two stitches to the right
tbl	through back loop
tog	together
tr	triple crochet or treble crochet
tr dec	triple crochet decrease
tr2tog	triple crochet two stitches together
WS	wrong side
wyib	with yarn in back
wyif	with yarn in front
yb	yarn back or yarn behind
yf	yarn forward
yfrn	yarn forward round needle
yfwd	yarn forward
yo	yarn over
yon	yarn over needle
yrn	yarn round needle

index

Numbers and Symbols

A

B

C

index

index

index

index

index

Teach Yourself VISUALLY
GUITAR

Teach Yourself VISUALLY Guitar is an excellent resource for people who want to learn to play the guitar, as well as for current musicians who want to fine tune their technique. This full-color guide includes over 500 photographs, accompanied by step-by-step instructions that teach you the basics of playing the guitar and reading music, as well as advanced guitar techniques. You will also learn what to look for when purchasing a guitar or accessories, how to maintain and repair your guitar and much more.

Whether you want to learn to strum your favorite tunes or play professionally, Teach Yourself VISUALLY Guitar provides all the information you need to become a proficient guitarist.

BOOK BONUS!

Visit www.maran.com/guitar to download MP3 files you can listen to and play along with for all the chords, scales, exercises and practice pieces in the book.

ISBN: 0-7645-2581-6

Price: $24.99 US; $36.99 CDN;   £14.99 UK

Page count: 320

Teach Yourself VISUALLY
PIANO

Teach Yourself VISUALLY Piano is an information-packed resource for people who want to learn to play the piano, as well as current musicians looking to hone their skills. Combining full-color photographs and easy-to-follow instructions, this guide covers everything from the basics of piano playing to more advanced techniques. Not only does Teach Yourself VISUALLY Piano show you how to read music, play scales and chords and improvise while playing with other musicians, it also provides you with helpful information for purchasing and caring for your piano. You will also learn what to look for when you buy a piano or piano accessories, how to find the best location for your piano and how to clean your piano.

ISBN: 0-7645-6915-5
Price: $24.99 US; $36.99 CDN; £14.99 UK
Page count: 304

Teach Yourself VISUALLY Dog Training is an excellent guide for both current dog owners and people considering making a dog part of their family. Using clear, step-by-step instructions accompanied by over 400 full-color photographs, Teach Yourself VISUALLY Dog Training is perfect for any visual learner who prefers seeing what to do rather than reading lengthy explanations.

Beginning with insights into popular dog breeds and puppy development, this book emphasizes positive training methods to guide you through socializing, housetraining and teaching your dog many commands. You will also learn how to work with problem behaviors, such as destructive chewing, excessive barking and separation anxiety.

ISBN: 0-7645-6913-9
Price: $19.99 US; $29.99 CDN; £13.95 UK
Page count: 256

Teach Yourself VISUALLY
KNITTING & CROCHETING

Teach Yourself VISUALLY Knitting & Crocheting contains a wealth of information about these two increasingly popular crafts. Whether you are just starting out or you are an experienced knitter or crocheter interested in picking up new tips and techniques, this information-packed resource will take you from the basics, such as how to hold the knitting needles or crochet hook and create different types of stitches, to more advanced skills, such as how to add decorative touches to your projects and fix mistakes. The easy-to-follow information is communicated through clear, step-by-step instructions and accompanied by over 600 full-color photographs—perfect for any visual learner.

This book also includes numerous easy-to-follow patterns for all kinds of items, from simple crocheted scarves to cozy knitted baby outfits.

ISBN: 0-7645-6914-7

Price: $24.99 US; $36.99 CDN; £14.99 UK

Page count: 304

Teach Yourself VISUALLY
WEIGHT TRAINING

Teach Yourself VISUALLY Weight Training is an information-packed guide that covers all the basics of weight training, as well as more advanced techniques and exercises.

Teach Yourself VISUALLY Weight Training contains more than 500 full-color photographs of exercises for every major muscle group, along with clear, step-by-step instructions for performing the exercises. Useful tips provide additional information and advice to help enhance your weight training experience.

Teach Yourself VISUALLY Weight Training provides all the information you need to start weight training or to refresh your technique if you have been weight training for some time.

ISBN: 0-7645-2582-4
Price: $24.99 US; $36.99 CDN; £14.99 UK
Page count: 320

Teach Yourself VISUALLY
YOGA

Teach Yourself VISUALLY Yoga provides a wealth of simplified, easy-to-follow information about the increasingly popular practice of Yoga. This easy-to-use visual guide is a must for visual learners who prefer to see and do without having to read lengthy explanations.

Using clear, step-by-step instructions accompanied by over 500 full-color photographs, this book includes all the information you need to get started with yoga or to enhance your technique if you have already made yoga a part of your life. Teach Yourself VISUALLY Yoga shows you how to safely and effectively perform a variety of yoga poses at various skill levels, how to breathe more efficiently, how to customize your yoga practice to meet your needs and much more.

ISBN: 0-7645-2580-8

Price: $24.99 US; $36.99 CDN; £14.99 UK

Page count: 320